Human Resources Administration

A School-Based Perspective

Third Edition

Richard E. Smith

EYE ON EDUCATION
6 DEPOT WAY WEST, SUITE 106
LARCHMONT, NY 10538
(914) 833–0551
(914) 833–0761 fax
www.eyeoneducation.com

Library of Congress Cataloging-in-Publication Data

Smith, Richard E., 1941-
     Human resources administration : a school-based perspective / Richard E.
Smith.--3rd ed.
          p. cm.
     Includes bibliographical references and index.
     ISBN 1-930556-84-5
     1. School personnel management--United States. 2. School-based manage-
ment--United States. I. Title.
     LB2831.58.S57 2004
     371.2'01--dc22

                                                            2004047215

     10 9 8 7 6 5 4 3 2 1

Editorial and production services provided by
Richard H. Adin Freelance Editorial Services
52 Oakwood Blvd., Poughkeepsie, NY 12603-4112
(845-471-3566)

Also Available from EYE ON EDUCATION

**Introduction to Educational Administration:
Standards, Theories, and Practice**
Douglas J. Fiore

School Community Relations
Douglas J. Fiore

**School Leader Internship: Developing, Monitoring,
and Evaluating Your Leadership Experience**
Gary E. Martin, William F. Wright, and Arnold B. Danzig

The ISLLC Standards in Action: A Principal's Handbook
Carol Engler

Exemplars of Curriculum Theory
Arthur K. Ellis

Instructional Supervision: Applying Tools and Concepts
Sally J. Zepeda

**Introduction to Educational Leadership
and Organizational Behavior**
Patti L. Chance and Edward W. Chance

Money and Schools, Second Edition
David C. Thompson and R. Craig Wood

**Handbook on Teacher Evaluation:
Assessing and Improving Performance**
James H. Stronge and Pamela D. Tucker

**Handbook on Teacher Portfolios
for Evaluation and Professional Development**
Pamela Tucker, James Stronge, and Christopher Gareis

The Principal As Instructional Leader
Sally J. Zepeda

What Great Principals Do Differently:
15 Things That Matter Most
Todd Whitaker

Dealing with Difficult Teachers, Second Edition
Todd Whitaker

Motivating and Inspiring Teachers
Todd Whitaker, Beth Whitaker, and Dale Lumpa

Staff Development:
Practices that Promote Leadership In Learning Communities
Sally J. Zepeda

Data Analysis for Continuous School Improvement,
Second Edition
Victoria L. Bernhardt

Beyond Measure:
Neglected Elements of Accountability
Edited by Patricia E. Holland

Harnessing the Power of Resistance:
A Guide for Educators
Jared Scherz

BRAVO Principal!
Building Relationships with Actions that Value Others
Sandra Harris

Acknowledgments

The author gratefully acknowledges the competent and diligent work of several graduate students who share the author's interest in human resources issues. These students have visited numerous schools and districts, making this text tightly connected to the best practices of some of the most effective schools. The examples listed as figures and incorporated in the text represent potential solutions to both recurring and new human resources problems. The author appreciates the willingness to share materials by school districts and their best principals.

Ankeny School District, IA
Bainbridge Island School District, WA
Council Bluffs School District, IA
Edmonds School District, WA
Educational Service District No. 113, WA
Elk Grove School District, CA
Everett School District, WA
Highline School District, WA
Issaquah School District, WA
Key West School District, FL
Lake Stevens School District, WA
Lake Washington School District, WA
Marysville School District, WA
Mukilteo School District, WA
North Slope Borough School District, AK
Oak Harbor School District, WA
Port Angeles School District, WA
Renton School District, WA
Shelton School District, WA
South Kitsap School District, WA
Sumner School District, WA
Wenatchee School District, WA
Westborough School District, WA
West Valley School District, WA

In addition, Dr. Randy Dunn of Southern Illinois University at Carbondale and Dr. Thomas Williams of California State University, Sacramento provided comments and advice on early drafts of this manuscript. Their advice was very helpful and appreciated. Prof. Frances Kayona, St. Cloud University, Minnesota; Prof. Douglas Magann, University of Central Florida; Prof. Phyllis Hensley, University of the Pacific, Stockton, CA; Professor A. Reynaldo Contreras, San Francisco State University; and Prof. Margaret Harrington, DePaul University, Chicago reviewed the manuscript for the third edition. They made significant contributions which were appreciated. Further, Dr. Larry Nyland, my former colleague at Seattle Pacific University and presently, Superintendent of the Marysville (WA) School District, made significant contributions to the chapter on Continuity and Legal Issues, while Dr. Sharon Hartnett, also from Seattle Pacific University, contributed to the chapter on the Marginal Teacher. My graduate students also aided in the research for the third edition and were always liberal with their advice to improve the text from a students' point of view.

Special thanks to Leo Blodgett, a career educator now retired, who hired me as a beginning teacher and later encouraged me to become a principal and superintendent. He set my course for which I am especially grateful. Mr. Jaye Compton of Sue's Secretarial Center in Lacey, Washington, prepared the manuscript and was always professional and timely in his assistance. Thanks also to Tina Barland, an outstanding copyeditor, and to Richard Adin whose attention to detail is deeply appreciated. Special thanks to my wife, Malisent, for her support of me and my career including the work on this book. Finally, I was able to learn from both my son, Mark, and daughter, Angela, who both are teachers. I thank them for entering this profession which creates all the others.

Table of Contents

Preface

Many human resource functions that had previously belonged to the central office are now the responsibility of principals. The principal's role is changing, but how that role is orchestrated within the context of site-based management is also changing. This text is a guide to the understanding of those changes and provides both the principal-in-training and the experienced principal with a resource to some of the best practices to use in this ever-changing and increasingly demanding role.

A few examples will give some perspective: Principals are taking on more of an active and decision-making role in interviewing and the selection of prospective teachers. Previously, the staff at the central office was the major player in recruiting, announcing the vacancy, and developing the selection criteria, with the principal getting involved at the end of the process to interview the final three to five candidates and make his or her selection/recommendation. A more common current practice is to involve the principal from the very beginning of the hiring process.

Induction of staff is another area which was previously the responsibility of the central office and now is the responsibility of the principal and staff. Selecting quality staff members is a major task, but assisting them to become effective teachers is now a major duty of today's principal.

The field of personnel and human resources administration is changing rapidly. Consider the major Supreme Court rulings on affirmative action and you soon come to the conclusion that the principal needs to be cognizant of the changing legal landscape. This text is aimed at assisting both the principal-in-training and the experienced principal in these areas. It is meant to be used as a guide to some exemplary practices and as a future reference.

1

Introducing Human Resources Administration

Reasons for Studying Human Resources Administration

♦ In any school approximately 80% of the budget is spent on the human resources function. This includes the salary, benefits, and training costs of the certificated, classified, and administrative personnel in the school. As such, it is clear that principals must have a comprehensive understanding of the human resources function if they are to be accountable for their school.

♦ When people fail at their job it is not always because of their lack of technical expertise, but more often because of their poor interpersonal relations.

♦ You cannot use yesterday's skills for today's job and expect to be in business tomorrow. The principal's knowledge, skills, and abilities must be current for the school to be effective.

♦ The whole is greater than the sum of its parts. It is critical that the principal have an understanding of the interrelated parts of the human resources system.

> *Schools are, after all, a people business.*

Introduction

This chapter provides an overview for the book. It briefly discusses the major topics and provides an overall framework for the more detailed chapters that follow. The principal should think of the spiral curriculum in which the topics are first introduced, then explained in detail. This book discusses these topics from the perspective of the school principal and the school. Central office human resources specialists and superintendents will also benefit from this book because it will give them an understanding of the emerging

♦ 1

role of principals in human resources administration so they can provide guidance to them.

Preceding each chapter are the Interstate School Leaders Licensure Consortium (ISLLC), Standards for school principals that are covered within that chapter. These standards give a national frame of reference and assist the professor and the student in meeting the standards. Each chapter concludes with comprehension questions, expanded learning experiences, and a case study. In addition, technology and its practical application to the chapter's topic is integrated within each chapter.

The chapter topics are:

- Planning
- Recruitment
- Selection
- Orientation and Induction
- Supervision and Evaluation
- Assisting the Marginal Teacher
- Staff Development
- Collective Bargaining
- Continuity and Legal Issues
- Technology and Human Resources
- A Glance into the Future of Human Resources

Figure 1.1 graphically gives the reader a template for this chapter as well as for the remainder of the book. But first some sample definitions of Human Resources Administration.

Figure 1.1 An Effective Educational Human Resources Management System

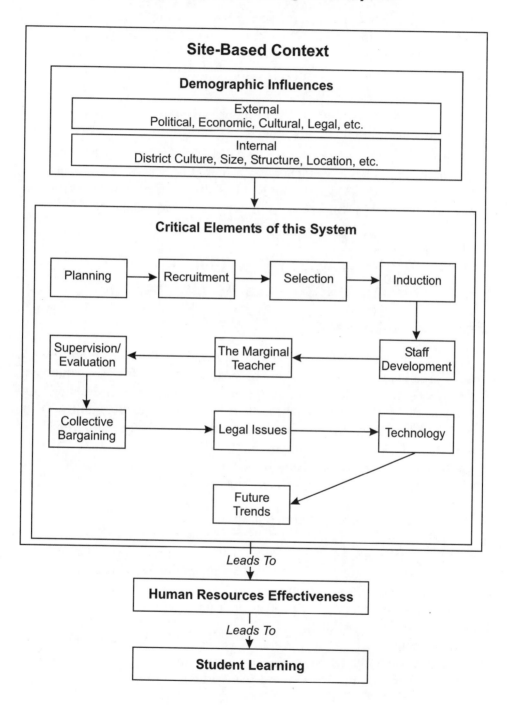

Site-Based Context

Demographic Influences

External
Political, Economic, Cultural, Legal, etc.

Internal
District Culture, Size, Structure, Location, etc.

Critical Elements of this System

Planning → Recruitment → Selection → Induction

Supervision/Evaluation ← The Marginal Teacher ← Staff Development

Collective Bargaining → Legal Issues → Technology

Future Trends

Leads To

Human Resources Effectiveness

Leads To

Student Learning

Definitions of
Human Resources Administration

♦ It is the balance between the school's need to accomplish its mission and the individual's need to achieve and to perform useful, satisfying work.

♦ It is an attitude that people are paramountly important in any organization, especially schools.

♦ It focuses on everything that influences the effectiveness or ineffectiveness of school personnel.

♦ It is doing *what is best for teachers*. Principals should adopt this definition much like teachers believe that they should do *what's best for students*. Most, if not all of the time, doing what's best for students is, for principals, doing what's best for teachers.

♦ It is concern for people—all staff members and their needs.

The Major Critical Elements of
Human Resources Administration

School-Based Leadership

One of the recent major changes in education is the movement toward school-based leadership (SBL). Many of the management functions that were previously centralized for control and standardization are now being decentralized to the building level where they become the responsibility of the principal and/or the school-based council made up of the principal, teachers, parents, and students. It is in this context that this section is included in a text on human resources administration. School-based leadership is the framework in which the human resources function is, and increasingly will be, implemented.

Given this context, it is incumbent upon the principal to develop knowledge, skills, attitudes, and the ability to be effective in this redefined role. The staff at the district office in small school districts is almost nonexistent (other than the superintendent who already wears too many hats). In larger districts the pressure to cut the administration and overhead has resulted in the cutback and/or elimination of the professional staff and thus, the services of the human resources department.

The principal's ability to provide effective leadership to the human resources function of the school will, in large measure, determine the effectiveness of the teachers, the school, and the students. Whereas in the past, the principal was often called upon to be the instructional leader of the school, now the principal will be called upon to be the leader—of instruction, of human resources, of the plant, and of public relations. The ability to set up the framework for school-based leadership and to provide leadership within that framework is critical. Teachers, parents, students, superintendents, and communities are expecting that the "new" principal will be able to accomplish all this and more. School-based leadership is not a normal topic for a textbook on human resources leadership, but things are changing. Principals must be proactive in developing new abilities within this new context.

Planning

This is both a short- and long-term focus on the future. Most schools have long-term planning for the curriculum and textbook adoptions but rarely focus on the needs of the teachers and others who will implement those plans. The failure to plan is to "plan to fail," especially when there is a crisis.

Almost all principals who are providing leadership in their school will fight any movement to reduce the planning time for teachers. Teachers need it and principals safeguard it at almost all costs. Further, principals will also agree that planning is one of their key responsibilities, along with organizing, directing, and supervising. However, few if any principals have a designated time for planning during the school day and almost feel guilty if they are in their office planning for their school and the people in it.

Principals are excellent at daily planning as witnessed by their calendars. However, most of the items on the calendar are activities and few are related to the goals and mission of their school or district. Chapter 2 helps principals to focus on monthly and yearly planning by giving examples and a format to accomplish the goals and mission of the organization. Being busy is not important to the role of the principal—accomplishing goals is.

Recruitment

The recruitment of teachers is a critical element of the human resources function, because no matter how sophisticated your selection process is, if you don't have the right people in the applicant pool, it is impossible to select them. Many school districts and schools boast about the number of applicants for a position. However, the emphasis should not be on quantity, but rather on the quality of applicants who meet the preestablished criteria.

Often recruitment is done through college and university placement offices, professional associations, or regional school districts that notify teachers of the vacancy in a school district. Increasingly, districts and schools are taking advantage of the vast possibilities the Internet and World Wide Web can offer their human resources departments and the principal. Brochures are also an asset to the recruiting process. One of the major, usually untapped, sources for the recruiting of teachers is the current staff. These individuals often may know of teachers who possess characteristics that would match the community, district, and school culture. There should be a systematic effort to seek referrals from the staff.

Additionally, districts that are attempting to diversify the teaching force will have to use special efforts to reach special groups of applicants. College or job fairs are also sources of potential applicants. Most often the recruitment element is neglected while selection gets most of the attention. Good recruiting increases the possibility of good selection, whereas poor recruiting methods almost always lead to poor selection.

Selection

The selection process generally has three main components: paper screening, personal interviewing, and reference checking.

It is helpful to draw the parallel between the requisitioning of a capital purchase and teacher selection: for example, a $100 student desk and the selection of a $1 million-plus teacher (over a 30-year career). The principal will very tightly specify what is wanted: seven-ply top with medium brown plastic laminate, chrome legs, book rack under the seat, solid thermo-set plastic back ¾" thick, all metal joints welded by 1" welds, 17" high seat, etc. This process is usual for the requisition and purchase order process. Now, contrast that with the usual personnel requirements: we need a high school mathematics teacher, or a fourth grade teacher. Clearly it is incumbent on principals to be much more specific about the qualities of the teachers they wish to hire. As they review the completed files of teachers they need to make accurate judgments about applicants and make a match between the applicant and the opening.

Key Idea

Do not use teachers, students, parents, or community members on the selection team unless you train them in the selection/confidentiality process.

The *completed files* need to be reviewed according to the criteria of the certificated personnel requisition by either the principal or the principal and selection team. A strong word of caution here: The files that are being reviewed are confidential, and when there are many people reviewing them there is a chance that the confidentiality might be violated. Therefore, do not use teachers, students, parents, or community members on the selection team *unless* they are trained in the selection/confidentiality process. Not doing so violates the writer of the letters of reference—usually other principals.

One usual part of the complete file is an *application*. This usually consists of three or four pages to be completed by the applicant. Applicants who want to put their "best foot forward" will type their application responses. However, the skill of using a typewriter in the age of the computer is weak; the application form blanks are never long enough for long-charactered school districts (Steilacoom Historical School District No. 1) or names (Dr. Marilyn R. Johnson-Bender) and there are no two application forms alike. These factors can be very discouraging to the applicant who is applying for many positions in different districts. Some suggestions:

♦ Complete the district application over the Internet and send it electronically.

♦ Develop a region-wide application to be used by many districts.

♦ Use only the applicant's letter of application, professional résumé, copy of license to teach, and placement file/letter of reference to select interviewees. All other information (disclosure forms, transcripts, application forms) is needed only for the candidate who has been selected for recommendation to the superintendent and the school board.

The *interview* is the most time-consuming part of the process. The interview consists of getting more information from the candidate for responses to preestablished questions. The major error in this segment of the selection process is that there is no agreement on what constitutes a good response to the questions. The parallel here is that after a teacher makes out a test for students, an answer key must be developed. The same must be done for the interview questions. The "look-fors" must be identified in advance or major discrepancies may surface later in the process.

It is most helpful to the principal if the selection committee does not rank-order the candidates but instead lists strengths and weaknesses and questions that should be investigated during the reference checks. If the committee must rank-order the candidates, then have each member do that individually. What may happen is one dominating selection committee member can unfairly influence the decision. Consider this case: The selection committee ranks the candidates first, second, and third. During the reference checks, the first candidate does not check out clearly and the second candidate decides to take another position. The principal then is left with the third candidate or reopening the position and repeating the process. Suppose the third candidate gets the position. The selection committee now feels that it was not listened to and the principal feels that the decision must be explained to the committee—a possible relationship problem.

The *reference check* is another phase of the process to which care must be given. A key point here is to contact people who are *not* on the list of references. Find professionals who would know the candidate's ability but are not listed on the résumé or the application and call them. If the principal and representatives of the selection committee can visit the school of the applicant, do it. A major decision is about to be made and the decision makers need all the information they can get.

Induction/Orientation

Induction can be considered assistance to your newly hired employees and consists of two main segments for two different types of employees. Figure 1.2 illustrates the emphasis to be considered here.

Figure 1.2 Induction/Orientation of New and Experienced Teachers

Teachers	Orientation	Year-Long Induction
New	Emphasis	Emphasis
Experienced	Emphasis	Secondary Emphasis

Most districts have a short orientation process of one to three days for all teachers new to the district. However, the wise principal would also develop a comprehensive program to assist teachers new to the profession throughout the entire school year. The experienced teacher could also be invited, encouraged, and in some cases directed to attend all induction activities. It is not surprising that many teachers new to the profession do not return after one or two years. In many cases this decision can be traced to the lack of proper induction to the school, district, and community.

Further, attention should be given to transfers to new assignments within the building. Department chairs, grade level coordinators, and cocurricular advisors are also key employees that deserve attention during the induction process. Finally, the employees involved in the induction process should be given an opportunity to evaluate the process and make suggestions for future induction activities, or even leading some of them.

Supervision and Evaluation

The process of supervision and evaluation is critically important for both the teacher and principal. It is important for the teachers to receive support or redirection. They deserve support if they are doing well, and redirection if improvements are needed. In both cases this is the task of the principal and it relates directly to teacher effectiveness and student learning.

The principal must develop a trusting relationship with the teachers and have the skills to furnish them with objective data about their teaching. It is helpful for principals to think of an instructional model when they are in the role of teacher/coach to the employee. They should prepare to teach, teach, and reflect on the teaching. That is, they must be *well-planned* to conduct the preobservation conference, the observation, and the postobservation conference. Prior to the postobservation conference, the principal should consider the information gathered during the observation, as well as the curriculum and the learner (teacher), and then determine the *most effective method of sharing* the data with the learner. The principal also will want to *reflect on the effectiveness of the entire supervision cycle* and continue to refine his or her skills as a supervisor and evaluator.

Key Idea

If the teacher won't do the job, then you have a motivational problem. If the teacher can't do it, then you have a training problem.

This supervision and evaluation process is important to the principal because failure to evaluate can become very serious, even leading to dismissal of the principal. A teacher would never think of not grading the students, likewise, a principal should also never think of not evaluating the teaching staff.

Supervision is much like formative evaluation while evaluation is similar to summative evaluation. In both cases, teacher growth and student learning are the goals.

Assisting the Marginal Teacher

The marginal teacher represents a special case of supervision and evaluation. Fortunately, there are few of these teachers in the system, but there are some, and thus, the principal needs to identify and provide assistance to them. In most cases, these teachers will take more of the principal's time, planning, and energy than all the others combined. This is an example of the *Pareto Principle*: Twenty percent of the teachers will take 80% of the time.

In many cases, the principal can assist the teacher significantly. In other cases, extra resources and professionals will be needed to assist both the teacher and the principal. It is key that the principal work diligently with the marginal teacher because students' learning is affected. This takes courage on the part of the principal, as well as support from the district.

The marginal teacher may be one who needs the services of an Employee Assistance Program (EAP). The principal must be skilled in recognizing these problems and in making appropriate referrals and furnishing support as needed.

Key Idea

You may feel that you do not have a *marginal* teacher; however, you always will have a *weakest* teacher who needs your assistance to improve.

Staff Development

The old adage "hire the best, train the rest" is no longer appropriate, if it ever was. The growth and development of staff is directly related to the growth and development of students. Teachers are generally well trained at the initial level when they receive their license to teach. However, the principal must continue that growth and training to assure that the school's and teachers' goals be realized.

This development process starts with the induction program and continues throughout the teacher's career. The principal is the coach in the development of the teacher as a person and as a professional. If done correctly, the principal will feel a sense of accomplishment, much like a teacher does who sees the students growing, developing, and succeeding.

The development of staff is dynamic and comprehensive. Its objective is to increase student achievement through ongoing staff development. A comprehensive staff development program includes:

- Training in curriculum development and implementation
- Training in instructional strategies
- Employee Assistance and Wellness Programs
- Climate improvement
- Incentives
- Supervision

Collective Bargaining

The role of the principal in collective bargaining is often a secondary but important one. However, the basic techniques of collaborative bargaining are ones that will serve the principal well during the daily tasks of leadership and management. Communication, listening, working together, and understanding others are all basic skills which the principal needs to develop to be effective.

Further, the principal, who is part of the district's leadership team as well as the leader of the school, is in a vital position to assist both the district and the education association with the collaborative process.

The salary schedule and benefits program are subjects of bargaining and are addressed superficially since those activities are almost entirely the responsibility of the district staff and school board.

Continuity and Legal Issues

The principal plays a minor role in this area at the present time. However, with the downsizing of the central office staff, many of these responsibilities could become part of the principal's responsibility. Nevertheless, the exposure to an understanding of basic principles, as well as potential problems, will alert the principal of dangers and when to seek outside assistance. It is recognized that most universities offer complete courses in school law. The advantage here is that this chapter focuses on the human resources aspect of school law. As with evaluation, if it precedes the course, consider it an introduction; if it follows the law course, consider it reinforcement.

Technology and Human Resources Leadership

This topic is no longer a stand-alone chapter. Just as technology is integral in our professional lives, it is integrated within each chapter to give the principal a comprehensive understanding of the practical elements of technology. In most chapters there are internet sites that are worth visiting to gain expanded and enriched understanding and practical application of human resources. The wise principal will continue to develop technological skills to provide effective and efficient service, as well as modeling, to the staff.

A Glance into the Future

Some trends are discussed briefly regarding the future of human resources administration. These trends could provide a base for understanding and anticipating the future. They could also provide discussion topics and growth areas for principals.

The previously outlined information provides an introduction and template for the principal to anticipate the areas that will be covered in detail in the forthcoming chapters. Figure 1.3 is an example of the human resources responsibilities of the principal in a school-based leadership district.

Figure 1.3 Human Resources Administration Responsibilities for the Principal Working in a School-Based District

The principal shall, within district policies, the superintendent's guidelines, and the management team's decisions and agreements, administer and direct all activities of the personnel assigned to his/her school.

Duties and Responsibilities

- Direct and supervise all personnel assigned to the school.
- Maintain only a working personnel file for all employees of the school except for the principal.
- Determine staffing needs in cooperation with the various department chairs and direct the staff selection process.
- Cooperate with others to develop a program of recruitment of classified, professional, and paraprofessional personnel large enough to provide an uninterrupted flow of qualified new employees and replacements.
- Be actively involved in recruiting activies.
- Participate in state and national recruitment fairs.
- Supervise job descriptions and writing of job postings, obtain job applications, and screen applicant files and conduct interviews.
- Conduct all reference checking of new employees.
- Recommend employment of classified, professional, and para-professional personnel to the superintendent.
- Develop a professional growth program for all staff assigned to your school.
- Develop both long- and short-range plans for the personnel needs of your school.
- Work cooperatively with others to maintain a pool of substitutes to provide for the needs of the school and district. Evaluate the work of substitutes.

- Act as compliance office for employment and assignment of all personnel.
- Evaluate and supervise all employees of the school according to the district-approved forms and procedures.
- Conduct a comprehensive induction program at your school and grade level.
- Actively participate in a training program for evaluators.
- Monitor and support the student teaching programs in your school.
- Monitor and support the administrative internship programs in your school.
- Be actively involved in the preparation of staffing reports and other personnel-related information for district and state records.
- Support the district goals regarding diversity.
- Support the district Employee Assistance Program.
- Support the district Wellness Program.
- Perform such other related duties assigned by the superintendent.

These functions and responsibilities have been discussed and agreed to this _____ day of _____, 200___.

Signed (Principal): _____

Signed (Superintendent): _____

Case Study—You Will Have to Do More

Beth Porter had completed a successful first year as high school principal of Hazel Valley High School. After serving as an assistant principal for three years in a neighboring district, Beth was excited to be selected as the principal. She had a vision of providing instructional leadership to the district's only high school. The faculty and staff as well as the community had captured her vision and Hazel Valley was poised to experience the needed instructional and organizational reforms. Beth's second year was going to be a great one for Beth as well as the students and staff of Hazel Valley. Everyone had given Beth the credit for the leadership of the new school vision. The staff appreciated her positive attitude, her skills, and the long hours that she put in to improve the climate at the high school. With such a successful first year behind her Beth also felt that she was still improving as a leader and needed to work hard and smart to continue the gains made in the first year. She developed her performance portfolio and self-evaluation and was eager to share them with the superintendent at her summative evaluation conference. But Beth was not ready to hear all that was going to be shared with her by the superintendent.

Beth knew the district was experiencing a slight decrease in enrollment, including at the high school. At the end of the evaluation conference, which was very positive, the superintendent concluded by saying that the board had reduced the central office staff by one certificated staff member and thus, the superintendent was reassigning those duties to the principals, including Beth. For the following year besides being the high school principal, Beth would also be the Director of Staff Development for the district. Her mouth and heart dropped. She could hardly believe it. There seemed to be no other alternative. The superintendent said that while he was very appreciative of the first year that during her second year she would simply have to do more. The district needed her.

Questions to think about:

♦ What should Beth do?

♦ How could Beth lead the high school and also provide district leadership as Director of Staff Development?

Technology in Human Resources

Here are some general web sites that are of a general interest in the field of human resources:

♦ http://humanresources.about.com

Complete human resources website. Gives tips on performance management, recruit/retention, policies/handbooks, and other human resources strategies.

♦ http://www.shrm.org

Society for Human Resources Management website is a professional website offering advice and services in the human resources field.

♦ http://www.insightlink.com

This site provides custom surveys, self-serve employee surveys, and exit interview surveys.

Conclusion

This chapter provided an introduction to the human resources administration topics to be covered in detail in the remaining chapters of this book.

Comprehension Questions

1. Consider the critical elements from Figure 1.1. What elements do you know the most about and what elements do you need to emphasize?

2. What examples of duties in your district were the responsibility of the district office that are now the responsibility of the principal?

Extended Activities

1. Interview your **principal** to get his/her perception of the importance of human resources administration and the changes that may be anticipated.

2. Interview the **human resources director** or **superintendent** to get his/her perception the importance of human resources administration and the changes that may be anticipated.

3. Compare and contrast the two views. Which do you is the most accurate view of human resources for the principal? Why?

2

Strategic Human Resources Planning

Reasons for Studying Human Resources Planning

- ◆ Planning is one of the most critical management functions.
- ◆ Planning leads to organization and the development of effective work plans.
- ◆ Planning is a prerequisite to the achievement of goals and accountability.
- ◆ Planning is an important part of effective time management.

ISLLC Standards Covered in this Chapter

Standard 1:

- ◆ A school administrator is an educational leader who promotes the success of all students by facilitating the development, articulation, implementation, and stewardship of a vision of learning that is shared and supported by the school community.

Standard 6:

- ◆ A school administrator is an educational leader who promotes the success of all students by understanding, responding to, and influencing the larger political, social, legal, and cultural context.

We need to be concerned about the future, for that is where we will spend the rest of our lives.

Introduction

The purpose of this chapter is to provide for school administrators, *particularly building principals*, an overview of what *strategic human resources planning* is at the building level. This is followed by strategic human resources planning within the context of districtwide comprehensive strategic planning, and then by the process of collaborative planning at the building level. Schematics are presented depicting the role and duties of a building level human resources administrator (principal) both within the context of the school district and at the building level.

What Is Strategic Planning and Why Do We Do It?

> *Planning is...attending to the goals we ought to be thinking about and never do, the facts we do not like to face, and the questions we lack the courage to ask.*
>
> Bruce Perryman

What is strategic planning? Strategic planning arose within the business community in the 1970s as a technique for helping managers make decisions which maximize organizational objectives. Pfeiffer, Goodstein, and Nolan (1986) defined strategic planning as

> the process by which an organization *envisions its future* and develops the necessary procedures and operations to achieve that future. This vision of the future state of the organization provides both the direction in which the organization should move and the energy to begin that move.

When an organization has *"envisioned its future"* it has begun the process of strategic planning. Strategic plans are about "seeing" the future and finding a *vision* of what an organization might become in this future.

Why do we do strategic planning? L.E. Scarr, former superintendent of the Lake Washington School District (WA), introduced a planning document by writing about *why* it is that we plan:

> It is a rare individual, a rare organization, which is capable of altering its behavior or managing itself successfully without a well-defined plan.

Educators today understand how Daniel felt among the lions. Armed with tattered spears of an antiquated authority, we field questions from parents about the value of education programs and even the idea of public education itself. We try to answer concerns about rising costs and decreasing test scores. We scramble to meet the needs of children from single-parent families, from families of non-English speaking refugees, of handicapped children, and parents with diverse interests and needs. We strive to fulfill the requirements of No Child left Behind (NCLB) and the demands for Adequate Yearly Progress (AYP).

New pressures and demands require new skills. New roles must be carved for school staff. New processes to include the community and business in educational planning must be developed. New attitudes about ideas like involvement, authority, and expertise must be developed among the entire educational community.

Key Idea

You can not use yesterday's skills for today's school challenges and expect to be in business tomorrow.

Change seldom happens by accident. It must be carefully planned, orchestrated, measured, and revised. It must be nurtured, encouraged, and watched closely to make sure the results benefit children. It must be tailored to fit individual school districts, communities, and students.

The model for district master planning is a practical process for bringing staff, parents, students and community along a path of *planned* change and improvement.

What Is Strategic Human Resources Planning?

Strategic human resources planning is a subset of district-wide strategic planning. Specifically, it is an organized process of enabling an organization to achieve its mission by the effective anticipation of human resources needs. The plans developed by this process must be directly related to, and congruent with, the organization-wide strategic plan.

The Strategic Planning Model (Figure 2.1) illustrates the process of human resources planning. It is important to scan both the external (society) and internal (district and school) environment as an initial part of the planning activity. There are several reasons for this:

 ◆ Schools are a subset of society and as such are reflective and dependent upon it.

 ◆ An examination of past trends allows us to understand the present and anticipate the future.

Figure 2.1 Strategic Planning Model

Environmental Scanning

External Scanning   Internal Scanning

Strategic & Operational Planning

Strategic Plan

| Develop Mission | Develop Strategic Objectives | Conduct Gap Analysis | Develop Strategies |

Operational Plans

School Operational Plans

School 1
- Budgeting
- **Personnel**
- Pupil Services

School 2
- Budgeting
- Personnel
- Pupil Services

School (n)

System Operational Plans

| Pupil Personnel Services | Human Resources | Finance & Business Affairs | Area (n) |

Feedback

Feedback

Implementation

- Schools have been called upon by society to solve many of its problems. A thorough understanding of such problems provides an opportunity for taking appropriate action with regard to program and personnel development.

- Schools and the school staff are part of this culture. An understanding of the culture helps us understand and meet staff needs.

If schools are to be ready to meet the challenges of the twenty-first century with appropriate programs and personnel, then the principals must be aware of the national and local demographic trends as the first step in environmental scanning of strategic human resources planning process.

Key Idea

Demographics, whether national, state-wide, and local, need to be studied in order to effectively plan for the future.

External Scanning

National Demographic Trends

Environmental scanning is a process of analyzing local, state and national data, and trends for influence and impact on schools, students, programs, and educational personnel. The detail presented here is offered as a template for the principal to understand and use the environmental scanning step in the total planning process.

Students in the twenty-first century will be much different than the students of the past. Because of the demographic changes in contemporary society, today's student will be much more likely to:

♦ have more handicaps

♦ have more special needs

♦ represent more cultures

♦ have English language deficiencies, yet have efficiencies in another language

♦ have more choices for education, for example, home school, private education, charter schools.

Population Projections

The Census Bureau predicts that the states of California, Texas, and Florida will account for more than one-half of the U.S. population growth that will occur before the turn of the century. California will remain the most populous state, Texas will move into second place, and New York will descend to third. Arizona will be the fastest growing state. There will be general movement to the south and west. Many people will leave large cities to reside in the suburbs. Between 1991–1993 enrollment increased most dramatically in these states: New Jersey, New York, Pennsylvania, Florida, Georgia, Louisiana, North Carolina, Tennessee, and Texas (increased 104,000 students).

Further, Robert A. Rosenblatt, a writer for the Los Angeles Times states, that "[T]he 2000 census is painting a statistical portrait of a nation that is still majority white, but increasingly diverse. The nation's total populations are 70 percent non-Hispanic white down form 76 percent in 1990." He further states, "diversity is no longer restricted to the coasts or the large cities. "… the results are showing rapid increases in the Hispanic and Asian populations in virtually all sections of the country." Blacks are the largest minority group with a population ranging from 34.6 million to 36.4 million, up from 30 million in the 1990 census.

These population projections need to be understood to anticipate student enrollment increases or decreases and the related impact of the number of teaching and non-teaching staff members. It is important for the principal to reflect on these trends and accept, reject, or modify them based on his/her community and attendance area.

Special Education/Handicapped Enrollment

During the 1998–1999 school year, 11.46% of all children in public school received special education services (ages 3–21). Most of those special education students (46.17%) needed help for specific learning disabilities, while 18.13% had speech or language impairments, and 10.25% were mentally retarded. The remainder had serious emotional disturbances, hearing or orthopedic impairments, or multiple disabilities. Massachusetts serves the largest percentage of children with disabilities (15.7). Of the other states, 25 had special education populations of 10% or more. In 1999–2000 the state of Washington spent approximately $247 million a year to meet a federal requirement to completely pay for services to the disabled. The number of disabled grew from 107,434 in 1995 to 116,233 in 1999. Money is distributed according to the average needs of a disabled child and does not address the children with high degrees of need.

Violence

Communities across the United States—large and small—are struggling under the dramatic increases of violence. The impact of the heightened crime rate has been felt in the schools. District staffs are forced to handle deaths, fights, deal with gang activity, and confiscate weapons in schools as never before. Many districts have implemented strong safety measures to ensure the safety and security of their students. A poll funded by the Joyce Foundation and conducted by Louis Harris of LH Research for the Harvard School of Public Health reported these results about children 10–19 years of age:

- 15% said they had carried a handgun within 30 days of the survey
- 4% said they had taken a handgun to school at least once during the past year
- 9% said they had shot a gun at someone else
- 11% said they had been shot at by someone else in the past year
- 22% said they would feel "safer" having a handgun if they were going to be in a physical fight
- 39% said they know someone who has either been injured or killed by gunfire
- 59% said they could get a handgun if they wanted one

Parents are looking to the schools to guarantee the safety of their children. The schools have an increasingly tough responsibility. Funding that might have gone toward school programs now must be used to keep the students safe.

At-Risk (At-Hope) Students

Students at-risk of school failure are becoming more clearly identified. With school failure comes the inevitable economic and social failure, posing a major concern to educators. Having one or more of the at-risk indicators (Figure 2.2) becomes nearly universal by eleventh grade (86%). Educators have been identifying the problems and have developed programs aimed at prevention and/or early intervention in the lives of our youth. It would be wise to intensify the efforts not only for the health of our children and schools, but also for the prosperity of our country's economic health. At-hope student is a rather new term that is sometimes used to identify these students but projects a more positive tone.

Figure 2.2 Indicators of High Risk of Dropping Out of School

School

- Lack of basic skills
- Performance consistently below potential
- Poor grades or failure in subjects
- Record of non-promotions
- Low standard test scores
- Irregular attendance and frequent tardiness
- Pattern of disruptive or aggressive behavior
- Poor study and work habits
- Lack of academic motivation
- Little or no participation in extra-curricular activities

Personal/Family

- Alcohol or drug abuse
- Physical health problems
- Mental health problems
- Poor self-concept
- Married or pregnant
- Poor social skills
- Friends not school-oriented
- Lack of realistic goals
- Lack of supervision
- Low educational level of parents
- Family pattern of dropping out
- Negative parental attitudes
- Broken/unstable home environment
- Frequent family moves
- Parent unable to find employment
- Low economic status

Ethnic Diversity

It is important for those involved in education to know that the ethnic make-up of the United States is changing. Migration, fertility patterns, and immigration are changing the ethnic makeup of our country's youth today. "Geographical, racial, economic, and cultural diversity in the student body means a diversity of parent attitudes toward children, child rearing, and school responsibility" (Moore, 1994). In the next decade, 90% of the immigrants will settle in U.S. metropolitan areas—specifically, cities such as New York, Los Angeles, and Chicago.

White students are already in the minority in the state of California. Nonwhites comprise 51.3% of California's school-age population—31.4% Hispanic, 8.9% black, and 11% Asian and other nonwhite groups. Even when people of all ages are included, whites only make up 58% of California's population. Previously thought of as minorities, these students are already in the majority in the District of Columbia, Hawaii, Mississippi, New Mexico, and Texas.

Public schools, especially, will have to meet the needs of increasing culturally diverse students. Once, America was a microcosm of European nationalities. Today, America is a microcosm of the world. People of color are comprising a larger proportion of the student population in many districts across the nation. In 2000, 21% of American children were ethnic minorities—primarily black or Asian-American. If the white Hispanic population under age 18 was added to black and Asian populations, the minority youth population reached 34% in 2000. By the year 2010, as many as 38% of Americans under the age of 18 will belong to minority groups. In seven states and the District of Columbia, more than half of the children will be nonwhite. In the overall population, the rate of growth among whites is not keeping pace with that of other ethnic groups.

Figure 2.3 Diversity of Teachers and Students by Race/Ethnicity

Teacher Race/Ethnicity	1987–1988	1999–2000	Students Race/Ethnicity	Fall 1986	Fall 2000
White, non-Hispanics	86.9%	84.3%	White, non-Hispanics	70.4%	61.2%
Black, non-Hispanics	8.2%	7.6%	Black, non-Hispanics	16.1%	17.2%
Hispanics	2.9%	5.6%	Hispanics	9.9%	16.3%
Asia or Pacific Islander	0.9%	1.6%	Asia or Pacific Islander	2.8%	4.1%
American Indian or Alaskan Native	1.0%	0.9%	American Indian or Alaskan Native	0.9%	1.2%

Source: U.S. Department of Education (may not add up to 100% because of rounding)

Diversity Among Teachers

In 2003 article, Greg Toppo reported in the *USA Today (July 3, 2003)*

that fifteen years ago, nearly nine out of ten public school teaches were white and more than seven in 10 were women. Now in 2003 there is still a white woman at the head of the class. She's better qualified but, otherwise, the typical teacher hasn't changed much. While public school students have grown much more diverse, school still rely overwhelmingly on white women to teach them. And despite decades of efforts to attract more minorities and men, they simply aren't stepping into the frame. While race and gender don't mean everything—and they certainly don't make up for poor training—experts say the lack of male and minority role models may be exacerbating a nagging achievement gap.

Cities like Denver, Jacksonville, and Columbus, Ohio, have tried unique approaches to attracting minorities by working with universities to establish "professional development" schools. Teach for America, which sends new college graduates into inner-city schools and Troops to Teachers which trains former military personnel for careers in teaching seem to hold promise.

Gary Marx, president of the Center for Public Outreach, a research group based in Vienna, Virginia, states that educators will be under pressure to ensure equal opportunity, to work hard to close the achievement gap between the races, and yo strive to diversify their work force.

School Choice

Student enrollment in the public schools of this country is primarily influenced by changes in birth rate, migration patterns, and social/economic conditions. This population can also be affected by the presence of local private schools and, to a lesser degree, by the number of families choosing to home school their children. A good rule of thumb is that approximately 10% of the student population in most areas or communities will attend private schools or participate in home-based schooling. The Department of Education's National Center for Educational Statistics predicts there will be about 6 million additional students enrolled in private schools by 2003.

The number of students attending private schools is increasing due to several factors:

- the removal of traditional religious influence from the public schools
- the parents' desire for a "family-like" atmosphere
- private schools being responsive to parents and students
- the ability of private schools to control the type of student populations
- parents perceive them as "safer" schools
- baby boomers are turning to religion
- students can attend specialized schools
- communities are experiencing a growth in fundamentalism and localism

The home school movement continues to grow across the country as parents exercise their right to accept the responsibility to teach their own children. Parents choose to home school for a variety of reasons, but at the core is their desire to control what their children are learning. National support for the movement has increased. Home school families often work in cooperation with their local public schools to supplement areas of their child's curriculum and to also provide for them an opportunity to be involved in sports and other extracurricular activities. The home school movement will no doubt continue to grow, and greater cooperation between home and school will be necessary.

School choice (vouchers) also continues to gain popularity nationally, although it has suffered some setbacks. With the number of people dissatisfied with the effectiveness of the public schools, school choice may become inevitable. The concept of charter schools has also gained attention and will provide a growing option for the education of students.

Locating Local Demographic Data

Many principals are unaware of the vast amount of demographic data available to them. Often those who propose changes for the educational systems of the future only take into account the implication of the total number of students without looking at the compositions of the total. For example, when we consider that in the year 2000 the majority of the population in some states consisted of minorities, it becomes clear that it is not to everyone's best interest to ignore the ethnic changes in the population. Failing to consider the specific changes that are occurring can result in educational programs that are not pertinent to the students; many students may underachieve, become disruptive, or drop out of school. No matter what the curriculum content, if students have difficulty understanding the material because of cultural and language barriers, content becomes irrelevant. And the teacher who can meet their needs, more significant.

Computerized statistical packages have a place in assisting in short-range projections of five years or less. Other sources of demographic data include census data, county planning departments, building permits, district surveys, health departments, commercial surveys and projections, utility companies, and a community's Chamber of Commerce.

Implications for
Human Resources Planning

The previously mentioned concerns have many implications for schools and school districts. To meet the needs of this new student profile, school staffs must offer services that correspond to student needs. Schools must plan to develop:

- ◆ early childhood education programs
- ◆ daycare centers in schools
- ◆ parenting education
- ◆ health clinics in schools
- ◆ dropout prevention programs

- improved preparation of students for the transition to the work world
- a broader base of offerings instead of a more limited curriculum

Changing demographics will have implications for school staffing. Teachers in the future will have to be prepared to face:

- more special-needs children in the mainstream
- larger classes
- the need to be more of a social worker than a subject matter specialist
- more home/school responsibilities
- greater skills as career and guidance counselors
- students with a wider range of needs and problems, and must be capable of instructing, motivating, and controlling a group with more diverse needs

Figure 2.2 (page 24) lists factors influential in students' choosing to drop out of school.

Following is a brief checklist for a principal's external and internal environment check:

Strategic Personnel Planning Checklist

*Clarify the **External** Context (Opportunities and Threats)*

- community input on what students need to know and be able to do
- culture, demographics
- racial/ethnic community composition
  - age distribution
  - socioeconomic status
  - politics
  - poverty rates
- legal arena
- technology
- relationships with teacher training institutions
- competition with private schools, other districts, and programs, e.g., Running Start
- **scan and communicate the trend in terms of threats and opportunities**

*Clarify the **Internal** Context (Strengths and Weaknesses)*

- history
- board policies
- capacity to implement anything
- organizational culture and climate
- financial human, facility resources
- employee dress, greetings, body language, ceremonies, gossip, jokes
- how decisions are made
- real versus formal leadership
- how individuals and organization controls information; how system communicates; how people communicate
- **scan and communicate the trends in terms of strengths and weaknesses**

Strategic Planning

Diligent environmental scanning efforts lay the groundwork for the general strategic plan, from which the strategic human resources plan will arise. Strategic plans follow organizational *mission statements*, but before discussing mission statements, consider how mission statements come to be. Mission statements often arise out of *dreams and visions*. Dreams and visions are hard to describe; they are often based on demographic and environmental scanning work, but take place in the heart of educators who begin to get a mental picture of what they want their school to look like.

Mission statements apply more precise and more measurable language to dreams and visions. Many, many hours of collaborative planning by administrators, staff, and community members are required to produce a mission statement. But they are hours well spent because mission statements are an essential part of strategic planning.

Ground rules for the development of mission statements:

- A mission statement must be stated in specific and definitive terms. It must be the motivational focus that encourages all points of view and still maintains a coherent organization moving toward common aims.

- Any mission statement should include the following three primary elements

  - "Schools are for kids"

- "Schools belong to the people"
- "Schools are people developers"
- ◆ To receive commitment to a mission, people in an organization need to go through four steps:
  - awareness that the mission exists
  - written communication to all in the organization of what the mission is
  - planned and intermittent reinforcement of the intended mission
  - power to perpetuate that mission
- ◆ The mission statement must be developed by a team effort if there is going to be commitment to that statement. A sample mission statement follows:

Sample Mission Statement A

Our mission is to develop the intellectual, vocational, physical, creative, cultural, and social capabilities of students. Our plenary commitment is to develop young people and to build positive relationships with them. We recognize that a quality staff is the key to providing quality education. We are dedicated to the development of professional skills and the full human potential of all staff members.

Sample Mission Statement B

The mission of every school is the growth and development of students through the growth and development of staff.

Sample Mission Statement C

All students: learning, growing, succeeding.

Out of the mission statement should come strategic objectives that are clear and measurable. Webb et al. recommend a "gap analysis," which is another way of saying that we should understand the difference between where we are today and where we want to be concerning each strategic objective. From these objectives and a sense of where we are *now*, strategies are developed that lead to a reasonable realization of the mission statement. Following is a principal's checklist regarding things to think about during the strategic planning process:

Strategic and Operational Planning

*Commit to quality service, continuous development;
seek optimum professional staff mix.*

Strategic Plan

♦ Develop **Mission**

- accommodate environmental dynamics
- clarify function of school system
- clarify who it will serve
- clarify how it will go about its business

♦ Develop **Strategic Objectives**

- establish critical success indicators that clients understand and value
- connect indicators and objectives to resources (time, energy, $)

♦ Conduct **Gap Analysis**

- compare desired outcomes to current status

♦ Develop **Strategies**

- clarify how strategic objectives will be achieved

Building-Level Operational Planning

The critical aspects of operational planning are depicted in the darkly shaded section of the strategic planning model *(Figure 2.1). This is planning at the building level, where the principal is most involved. The operational plans at the school level are to be consistent with the strategic plan developed at the district level, as the graphic demonstrates, but also each school should do its own strategic planning process, its own environmental scanning, and its own strategic planning, with mission statement, strategic objectives and strategies to realize these objectives. Note the two-way arrow between the school operational planning box and the environmental scanning box at the top of the chart. It denotes that the process is interactive.* Personnel planning, highlighted in bold in Figure 2.1, is to be done with general district and building strategic plans in mind and in cooperation with the human resources department at the district office. Following are some suggestions concerning building level operational planning that principals should keep in mind:

Strategic Personnel Planning Checklist
Operational Plans

Integrate School Operational Plans and human resources operational plan.

- Create professional staff mix to accommodate needs of school.
- Make data-based decisions; involve people or sources of relevant information in decision making.
- Create short-term plan (12-month calendar).
- Create long-term plan (60-month calendar).
- Plan personnel staffing needs and goals before budget; budget can reflect needs.
- Attach specific assignments and responsibilities to all activities.

Strategic Human Resources Planning Checklist

Surge *and* Flow or Surge *Versus* Flow

In nonsystematic and nonstrategic personnel planning the calendar and actions duplicate a volunteer fire department fighting a fire: no prevention, all time and activities are spent fighting fires. In this model of personnel *un*management, vacancies occur, the most convenient applicant is quickly interviewed and hired to fill the spot, handed a grade book and chalk, wished well and not seen again until the law mandates an evaluation, or the applicant drops off the grade book and unused chalk at the office with a notice of resignation. The vacancy occurs, the most convenient applicant is quickly interviewed and hired to fill the spot, handed a grade book…and the process repeats itself like fires occur in the community.

In systematic and strategic personnel planning, there is room for the surge times of the year and there is room forcibly made for an ongoing flow of planning, implementing, and evaluating with feedback as shown in Figure 2.4. Proactive planning means that before the first moment of recruitment, all the prerequisite steps of environmental scanning and strategic planning must be in place. Feedback from previous exit interviews should be incorporated into both recruiting and selection plans and strategies. Then operational plans for recruitment can occur. Part of the recruitment effort is to package the strategic plan and environment in a brochure or other handout that can be sent to prospective applicants so that they can self-appraise their compatibility with the school and the district. Also, the recruiting administrator should have a very clear sense of what kind of person she or he is seeking. Proactive clarification will avoid the waste of energies and resources on applicants out of synchronization with what the administrator is seeking. Since travel and advertising logistics are involved in the recruiting efforts, planning in advance will assure travel and purchased advertising in a most cost-productive manner. But one should not conclude that recruitment should be relegated to a particular time of the year; it can and should occur all the time. Conferences, college homecomings, weekend ski trips, summer vacations, any time there is a gathering of people, who might be interested, is a recruiting opportunity. To be sure, the best thing for recruiting is to have a very good school that sells itself.

Figure 2.4 Personnel System Overview

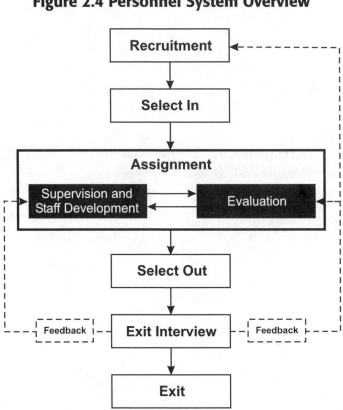

During the recruitment phase, the selection criteria and process, the nature of supervision, staff development opportunities, and evaluation procedures and criteria should be thought out and available as information to the prospective candidate. More thoughtful candidates are going to inquire about such matters and the principal had better have the answers.

Thus, planning should be seen as a constant necessary *flow* of energy—the *important* aspect of personnel systems. Recruitment, selection, staff development, evaluation, and exiting processes should be seen as *surge* activities and are appropriately *urgent*. Flow *and* surge are both critical to human resources. Presented below is a broad checklist of things to remember when implementing a strategic human resources plan.

Strategic Personnel Planning Checklist
Implementation

♦ Capture product and process data that become feedback for the entire plan

♦ Forecast personnel needs and student enrollments

♦ Recruit

♦ Select in

♦ Assign

  • Supervise and develop staff

  • Evaluate staff

  • Compensate staff

  • Induct staff

♦ For staff selecting out, conduct exit interview and provide feedback to the selection and assignment process.

Figure 2.5 is a sample planning document that a principal can use to accomplish the school and district goals. This document is used by the principal in coordination with the daily and weekly planning calendar.

Figure 2.5 Strategic and Operational Planning: Monthly Calendar

PERSONNEL Strategic and Operational Planning: Monthly Calendar

Month: **August** My Objectives/Activities: _____

	Objective/Activity	Accomplished	Carry to Next Month
✓	New teacher/mentor selection with Education Association		
✓	Orientation of new Certificated/Classified staff		
✓	Orientation of experienced staff		
✓	Present list of substitutes to Superintendent/School Board for approval		
✓	Welcome letter to continuing and new subs		
✓	Present list of volunteer coaches to Superintendent/School Board for approval		
✓	Plan teachers' aides schedules.		
✓	Schedule preobservation conferences for teachers.		
✓	Welcome letter to staff.		
✓	Finalize staffing needs.		
✓	Conduct last round of interviews, selection of staff for last-minute vacancies.		
✓	Introduce and Celebrate new employees.		
✓			
✓			
✓			

Notes/Feedback for next year planning:

Comments about the Big Picture:

PERSONNEL Strategic and Operational Planning: Monthly Calendar

Month: **September**   My Objectives/Activities: _____

	Objective/Activity	Accomplished	Carry to Next MonthT
✓	Check first aid certification of staff.		
✓	Collect and compare enrollment data.		
✓	Reminder: set time line for "at-risk" teachers' evaluations.		
✓	Coordinate mentor participants.		
✓	Plan committees.		
✓	Finalize teachers' aides schedules.		
✓	Finalize schedule of preobservation conferences for teachers.		
✓	Promote staff attendance of October Professional organization conferences.		
✓	Introduce and Celebrate new employees.		
✓	Welcome letter to new and continuing substitute teachers.		
✓	Visit all new teachers' classrooms (informal).		
✓	Visit all new employees at work site (informal).		
✓			
✓			
✓			

Notes/Feedback for next year planning:

Comments about the Big Picture:

PERSONNEL Strategic and Operational Planning: Monthly Calendar

Month: **October**   My Objectives/Activities: _____

	Objective/Activity	Accomplished	Carry to Next Month
✓	Conduct enrollment and class size counts.		
✓	Develop staff profile.		
✓	Introduce and Celebrate new employees.		
✓	Attend October Professional Conferences.		
✓	Have staff members report on Professional Conferences.		
✓	Report on Summer Staff Development Activities.		
✓			
✓			
✓			
✓			
✓			
✓			
✓			

Notes/Feedback for next year planning:

Comments about the Big Picture:

PERSONNEL Strategic and Operational Planning: Monthly Calendar

Month: **November**   My Objectives/Activities: _____

	Objective/Activity	Accomplished	Carry to Next Month
✓	Notify local media of staff highlights or news.		
✓	Provisional employees evaluated by 90th calendar day.		
✓	Schedule spring staffing conference with Personnel Department.		
✓	Introduce and celebrate new employees.		
✓			
✓			
✓			
✓			

Notes/Feedback for next year planning:

Comments about the Big Picture:

PERSONNEL Strategic and Operational Planning: Monthly Calendar

Month: **December**   My Objectives/Activities: _____

	Objective/Activity	Accomplished	Carry to Next Month
✓	First observations completed for all provisional employees.		
✓	Plan for evaluation of classified staff.		
✓	Orientation of experienced staff.		
✓	Possible probation? Need 3 observations and evaluation.		
✓	Present list of volunteer coaches to Superintendent/School Board for approval.		
✓	Introduce and celebrate new employees.		
✓			
✓			
✓			

Notes/Feedback for next year planning:

Comments about the Big Picture:

PERSONNEL Strategic and Operational Planning: Monthly Calendar

Month: **January** My Objectives/Activities: _____

	Objective/Activity	Accomplished	Carry to Next Month
✓	Begin staff projections.		
✓	January 15—Probation Conference Deadline; make recommendations to Superintendent.		
✓	January 25—notify probationary teachers.		
✓	Work with site council on March Inservice and general staff development options for next year.		
✓	Introduce and celebrate new employees.		
✓			
✓			
✓			
✓			

Notes/Feedback for next year planning:

Comments about the Big Picture:

PERSONNEL Strategic and Operational Planning: Monthly Calendar

Month: **February**   My Objectives/Activities: _____

	Objective/Activity	Accomplished	Carry to Next Month
✓	Review nature of probationary period and procedures with staff on probation.		
✓	Gather staffing information, including leaves being taken and duration.		
✓	Update staffing projections with Personnel Services.		
✓	Start building master schedule with class size and staffing expectations.		
✓	Introduce and celebrate new employees.		
✓			
✓			
✓			
✓			

Notes/Feedback for next year planning:

Comments about the Big Picture:

PERSONNEL Strategic and Operational Planning: Monthly Calendar

Month: **March**   My Objectives/Activities: _____

	Objective/Activity	Accomplished	Carry to Next Month
✓	Attend recruiting fairs off campus.		
✓	March 15: Applications for leaves and sabbaticals due.		
✓	Internal transfers requested and assignments settled.		
✓	Administrative intern applications due.		
✓	Introduce and Celebrate new employees.		
✓			
✓			
✓			
✓			

Notes/Feedback for next year planning:

Comments about the Big Picture:

PERSONNEL Strategic and Operational Planning: Monthly Calendar

Month: **April**   My Objectives/Activities: _____

	Objective/Activity	Accomplished	Carry to Next Month
✓	April 1: Contracts issued.		
✓	April 15: All resignations, retirements, terminations shall be in writing and submitted to Personnel Office.		
✓	April 15: All department head positions and job openings for the next school year posted.		
✓	April 24: Contracts returned.		
✓	District meetings to determine staffing needs and priorities among buildings.		
✓	Recruiting continues at college career fairs.		
✓	Meeting with teachers to establish career goals.		
✓	Administrative observation due.		
✓	PTSA gives annual awards for Teaching Excellence.		
✓	Introduce and celebrate new employees.		
✓			
✓			
✓			
✓			

Notes/Feedback for next year planning:

Comments about the Big Picture:

PERSONNEL Strategic and Operational Planning: Monthly Calendar

Month: **May**   My Objectives/Activities: _____

	Objective/Activity	Accomplished	Carry to Next Month
✓	May 1: Probationary period ends for teachers on probation. Consult with Personnel, Superintendent, and lawyer regarding recommendations/findings.		
✓	Department chairpersons chosen. Names forwarded to Personnel.		
✓	By May 15: Notify teachers on probation of the results of probation.		
✓	By May 15: Complete teacher evaluations and teacher conferences.		
✓	Continue working with Personnel Department on staffing for next year.		
✓	Known vacancies posted for voluntary transfers (curricular and extra-curricular).		
✓	Celebrate retiring employees.		
✓	Introduce and celebrate new employees.		
✓			
✓			
✓			
✓			
✓			

Notes/Feedback for next year planning:

Comments about the Big Picture:

PERSONNEL Strategic and Operational Planning: Monthly Calendar

Month: **June**   My Objectives/Activities: _____

	Objective/Activity	Accomplished	Carry to Next Month
✓	By June 5: Provide all Certificated staff with written documentation of final evaluation.		
✓	By June 12: Deliver completed evaluation documentation for continuing and provisional employees to Personnel.		
✓	Coordinate exit conference and interview for employees with Personnel Department.		
✓	Continue working with personnel regarding staffing.		
✓	Finalize contract for next year.		
✓			
✓			
✓			

Notes/Feedback for next year planning:

Comments about the Big Picture:

PERSONNEL Strategic and Operational Planning: Monthly Calendar

Month: **July**   My Objectives/Activities: _____

	Objective/Activity	Accomplished	Carry to Next Month
✓	Continue interviewing and hiring teachers as needed.		
✓			
✓			
✓			
✓			

Notes/Feedback for next year planning:

Comments about the Big Picture:

Conclusion

The effective principal with increased responsibilities in the same amount of time needs to plan well. The human resources responsibilities of the principal in a site-based leadership school are enormous in both number and significance. The principal needs to understand and anticipate the internal and external demographic changes, understand the strategic planning model, and be able to implement the plans effectively to realize the mission and goals of the school and district. One of the main planning responsibilities of the principal is the recruitment of staff, which is the focus of the next chapter.

Planning—Case Study

Chet was an excellent elementary principal. His school of 450 students was in a growing section of the city while the rest of the district was not decreasing but was very stable. During Chet's tenure of four years his school mirrored the rest of the district—very stable. As Chet drove around his attendance area he noticed three new apartment complexes in the process of being completed.

It was the spring of the year and the district business manager told the administrative team including Chet that they would be staffed on last year's enrollment since the district had a very stable enrollment pattern. This strategy was generally a sound one but for the coming school year Chet felt he needed to talk with the business manager and seek to convince him to increase the enrollment so that he could staff his building this spring instead of waiting until fall when many of the teachers would already be hired elsewhere.

1. What should Chet do as he plans his meeting with the business manager?
2. What risks would Chet be taking if he went with the business manager's enrollment and staffing?
3. If the business manager did not change his staffing, what should Chet do?

Comprehensive Questions

1. Why is the study of demographics so vital to strategic human resources planning?
2. America is a microcosm of the world. What are some ways principals can meet the needs of the upcoming diverse population?
3. Why must the development of a mission statement be labor and time intensive?

Extended Activities

1. Develop a format to be well-planned by the day, month, year, and five years.
2. Obtain critical dates for the human resources function and place them on a calendar.
3. Find out what information is available via the web for use in planning.

Technology in the Planning Process

Check out these sites for more information on planning:

- www.hrps.org
- www.ascd.org/publications
- www.edreform.net
- www.ael.org

    This is a clearinghouse of school reform that can provide information for strategic planning purposes.

- www.temple.edu/lss/highschoolmeeting.htm

    This is a discussion of the types of strategic planning process that work well.

- www.plainsvilleschools.org/boe/stategicplan.shtml
  This is a model for a district's strategic plan.
- Google Search for Educational Demographics
- Google Search census data

References

Duckworth, A., and R. Kranyik (1984, August). What business are we in? *The School Administrator.*

Harrison, R. (1983). Strategies for a new age. *Human Resources Management, 22,* 217–223.

Hart, T. E., and L. S. Lumsden (1990). Demographic analysis. *OSSC Bulletin, 34*(4), December.

Moore, A. J. (1994). Meeting the challenges of the principalship in a complex society. *NASSP Bulletin, 78*(558).

Nkomo, S. M. (1980). Stage three in personnel administration: Strategic human resources management. *Personnel, 57*(4).

Pfeiffer, J. W., L. D. Goodstein, and T. M. Nolan (1986). *Applied strategic planning: A how to do it guide.* San Diego, CA: University Associates.

Scarr, L. E. (1984). *Rx for effective schools.* Lake Washington School District, WA.

Webb, L. D., et al. (1987). *Personnel administration in education.* Columbus, OH: Merrill Publishing Company.

3

Recruitment

Reasons for Studying Recruitment

♦ Many personnel systems focus on the selection process; however, if you do not have the right people in the applicant pool it is difficult to select them.

♦ Visiting colleges and universities increases district visibility and personal relationships with the faculty and placement officials.

♦ Recruiting at Career Fairs also increases district visibility and you can gain ideas from other districts.

♦ Your current teachers are often an excellent source for leads on prospective applicants. You need to tap that source in an organized fashion.

♦ Recruiting is a good reason for the district to develop a brochure clarifying the district mission and its selection criteria for new teachers.

ISLLC Standards Covered in this Chapter

Standard 2:

♦ A school administrator is an educational leader who promotes the success of all students by advocating, nurturing, and sustaining a school culture and instructional program conducive to student learning and staff professional growth.

Standard 3:

♦ A school administrator is an educational leader who promotes the success of all students by ensuring management of the organization, operations, and resources for a safe, efficient, and effective learning environment.

> *Recruitment is not so much about the numbers of applicants as it is about the number of quality applicants who match the criteria.*

Introduction

There is no question that the number one influence on the quality of schools and the instruction they provide is the quality of excellence found within their instructional staff: *Teachers*! It is the caliber of the personnel in a district that makes it mediocre or effective. It is not the rules, policies, procedures, or curriculum programs that bear the burden, but rather those who teach the students. Thus, it follows that significant effort should be spent in seeking the very best match for each and every position opening in the schools, from Kindergarten to Honors English, from Music to Science, and from elementary to middle to high school. Anyone can fill a position, for where there is an opening, there will be many candidates to fill it. The focus of this chapter is not on "filling" an open position, but rather on the recruiting phase, which, if done well, will lead to the selection of an outstanding staff member.

Figure 3.1 denotes the elements of key personnel functions. It is helpful to refer to this figure to develop an understanding of the role recruitment plays in the total system.

Why Recruit?

The question isn't whether you can fill a teaching position or how to fill it, but rather can you do it well. There are three compelling rules for effective recruitment of school personnel:

1. *Recruit Widely*—Good instructional programs rely on having high quality staff members.

   Schools should seek out only highly qualified personnel to fill positions in order to maintain quality organizations. This is often not the case. Rather, schools and administrators seek only to fill positions, holding the notion that "a good teacher can teach anywhere" and thus, look for generic qualities like "a fourth grade, or social studies" teacher. These approaches are generic and mediocre at best. Administrators must change their frame of reference and processes to seek out the perfect match for each and every individual job opening. Whether it be to balance out a program, bring in "new blood" and ideas, bring on a veteran to provide stability, or whatever the criteria, it must be done to improve the quality of the instructional programs. Teaching will only be as good as the person doing the teaching! The current emphasis on test score improvement and demands for academic accountability are reason enough to recruit widely and with a purpose. The provisions of the No Child Left Behind Act also require teachers of high quality.

Figure 3.1. Personnel System

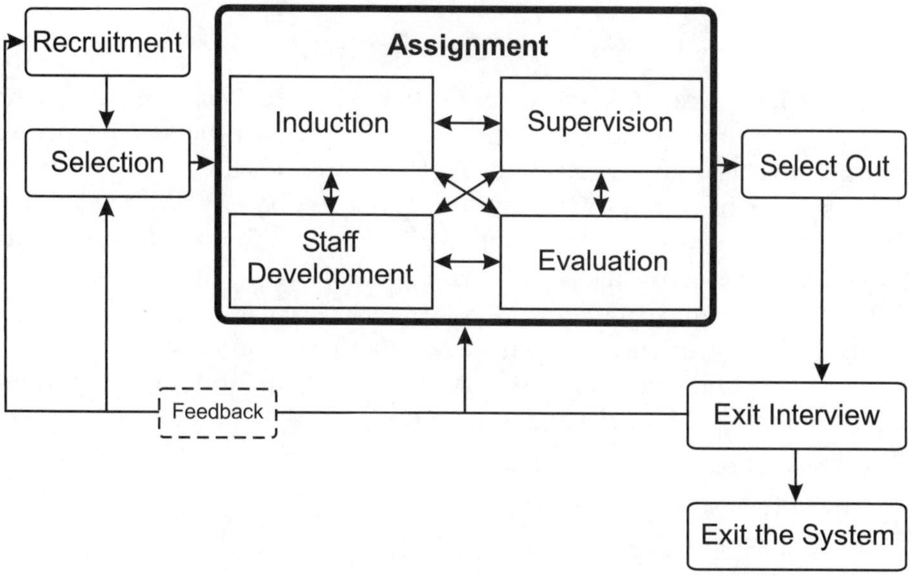

2. *Recruit Efficiently*—Filling positions costs money and failing to do it well costs even more.

   Every time a position is filled it costs a district substantial money. Funds are allocated on time invested in arriving at desired needs and writing of job description, posting, advertising, form processing, and on interviewing, induction, and training. The average cost for this process can be in the range of five figures. Keeping this in mind, schools and districts would be wise to do it well the first time. A wrong selection not only costs monetarily, but also costs in lost effectiveness for staff and students.

3. *Recruit Legally*—Fairness is the right thing to do.

   It is important that applicants are treated equally, honestly, fairly, and with caring. A system and procedure should be developed and followed in order to stay out of trouble legally and ethically. Further, administrators should be careful to consider district-adopted affirmative action guidelines as well as the Americans with Disabilities Act when recruiting. In addition, state and private colleges, professional associations, and current employees are often excellent sources for applicants.

The principal and others must be careful not to allow personal biases to adversely affect the recruitment process.

Before You Recruit

Prior to recruiting, time should be taken to seek feedback from the departing teacher or staff member through the *exit interview* process. This process generally reveals both positive and negative comments. Both are helpful as feedback to the human resources system. If the feedback is positive, then administrators can use that information to plan future activities. If it is negative, now is the time to make modifications, if possible.

In either case, the exit interview is a necessary tool to help in planning for recruiting. The experienced employee has an idea of the system's strong and weak points. Saville and Hill (1989) suggest a formal, oral interview scheduled within the last 4 weeks of employment should include:

- reason for separation
- positive aspects of the job
- employees' feelings about their supervision
- adequacy of salary, benefits, and working conditions
- employee complaints or suggestions
- possible existence of unresolved problems
- separation formalities/information/benefits

Of course, there are some problems with administering such interviews, such as persuading the employee to tell the truth about reasons for leaving or changing positions. In a paper submitted to a regional conference of businessmen, these research suggestions were compiled as considerations to minimize problems for the interviewer:

- prepare carefully for the interview
- put the employee at ease
- seek information
- use tact
- be honest
- conclude the interview
- complete the exit interview report (Schmidt, 1984)

During the exit interview, administrators need to express "thank you and best wishes" if that is suitable, especially to an employee retiring or moving to another district. The employee also can benefit, by being viewed as an expert who can contribute to effective management, and whose contribution will be significant in helping the school or district further its goals.

In most cases, it is best if the human resources department conducts the exit interview and develops a report of all such interviews to the superintendent, board of directors, and principals. If trust between the principal and the departing teacher is high, then the teacher could request that the principal also be involved in the interview to aid the communication process. The goals of the exit interview are to:

- assist the employee with the transition
- provide feedback for the school and district
- turn the departing teacher into an ambassador for the school district

Figure 3.2 is an example of an exit interview survey.

Figure 3.2 Sample Employee Exit Interview

The purpose of this survey is to give you an opportunity to provide feedback regarding your employment experience here. In your specific area of expertise, please make suggestions about what the district can do to make improvements and to make the _____ School District a better place to work.

Please Note: If you have been covered by a district medical/dental plan, you may be eligible for COBRA benefits. If you have not received a notice about COBRA, please contact the Payroll Department (555-XXXX) immediately.

Name: _____

Employment Location: _____

Job Title: _____

Date Last Worked: _____
(month, day, year)

Reason for Leaving (please circle):

1. Other position/new business
2. Retirement
3. Moving from area
4. Dissatisfaction with job

5. Going back to school
6. Medical
7. Cost of living
8. Other _____
(specify)

Please indicate a rating for the areas listed below by circling a number on the scale of **4 (highest) to 1 (lowest)**:

A. Were you satisfied with your job location?

    4 3 2 1

B. Were you satisfied with your work environment?

    4 3 2 1

C. Were you satisfied with your opportunity for growth?

    4 3 2 1

D. Were you satisfied with consistency of supervision when performing job duties?

    4 3 2 1

E. Were performance expectations clearly defined?

    4 3 2 1

F. What suggestions do you have for improving your teaching position?

G. What suggestions do you have for improving the school?

H. What suggestions do you have for improving the district?

I. What suggestions do you have for improving the recruitment and selection process?

J. How can the school or district help you?

Certificated Personnel Requisition

Having identified needs and acquired recommendations from the exit interview process, that information can be used by the principal to complete the Personnel Requisition (see Figure 3.3). The principal would be well-advised to seek input regarding the completion of this form from staff members who would be the most affected by the new staff member. Its purpose is to let staff and other administrators know what type of employee is being sought. Further, such a format better assures getting the right person into the "pool" to select a candidate. It is from this requisition that the Position Description (Figure 3.4) will be developed. The requisition also provides the characteristics and criteria to select the top four or five candidates for interviews. With the idea that the right people can "make a difference," a district's planning to recruit the best personnel will fit with its mission and purpose.

In the "Special Requirements" section of the requisition form (Figure 3.3), certain considerations must be included:

- ◆ conditions which might have immediate impact on the position such as pending state or local funding
- ◆ inclusion of curriculum requirements
- ◆ special teamwork expectations
- ◆ staff development as chosen by district/building in previous planning year, and so on.

It is important and commonplace for a school principal to complete purchase requisitions for desks, chairs, and other capital outlay in detail to make certain it gets what it wants. The same is true for human resources, only more so since they cannot be sent back as easily and any mistake in hiring is very costly.

Figure 3.3 Sample Certificated Personnel Requisition

1. Position Title:

   Elementary _____

   Secondary _____

2. Experience Requirements:

   Teaching _____

   Other related experience _____

3. Educational Requirements:

   Degree _____

   Major _____

   Minor _____

   Specialities _____

   Rank in class (Academics):

   Average _____;   Superior _____

   Special Courses: _____

4. Personal Requirements: (i.e., self-confidence, stability, adaptability, empathy, humor, organization, creativity, firm discipline, etc.) Rank in order of importance:

   a. _____   d. _____

   b. _____   e. _____

   c. _____   f. _____

5. Position Requirements:

   Is this position likely to change? _____

   If so, how?

   a._____

   b._____

   What special things is this person expected to do?

   Classroom expectation: _____

   _____

   Extra duty assignments: _____

   _____

   Daily Schedule and class load:

   a. _____ _____   e. _____ _____

   b. _____ _____   f. _____ _____

   c. _____ _____   g. _____ _____

d. _____ _____   h. _____ _____

What special programs will this person have to teach?

_____

6. Special Requirements: _____

Figure 3.4 Position Description—English Department

Position Title: Ninth Grade Language Arts Teacher

Division Title: Instruction

School: Junior High

Title of Immediate Supervisor: Principal

General Duties:

♦ Develop and maintain a classroom learning environment that places students' needs in a primary position.

♦ Develop and maintain a classroom management policy that is friendly, fair, firm, and consistent.

♦ Present a role model that sets the example for the development of good citizenship by the students.

♦ Perform your "fair share" of co-curricular and other duties beyond regular classroom activities as determined by the principal. Fair share equates to approximately four evenings/nights per year.

♦ Provide for the care of school property and see that pupils use equipment and utilities properly.

♦ Maintain cordial and cooperative working relationships with colleagues and participate in the business and activities of the faculty.

♦ Recommend to the department head suitable programs, courses of study and materials that meet the needs of ninth grade Language Arts students.

♦ Perform other duties as may be assigned.

Specific Duties:

♦ Follow policies and procedures as set forth in the Teachers' Handbook.

♦ Develop short-term instructional objectives consistent with the district's and school's long-range educational goals. These objectives should identify the end results or standards of performance expected.

- ◆ Plan and implement an instructional program to assist all students to progress toward the accomplishment of established goals and objectives.
- ◆ Cooperate with and participate in the planning and evaluation of the school program.
- ◆ Direct and evaluate the learning experiences of the pupils and maintain adequate and careful records as required by the principal, superintendent, and state.
- ◆ Participate in such staff meetings and in-service training programs as are scheduled for teachers in our building and/or district.
- ◆ Make adequate and regular reports to parents as required by district policy.
- ◆ Participate in the formulation of the annual budget by submitting budget requests for supplies and equipment *on schedule*.
- ◆ Maintain close and continued communications with parents when dealing with student problems.

Qualifications:

Required:

- ◆ B/A in Education—major in English/Language Arts
- ◆ Appropriate state professional education certification.
- ◆ If not current regular employee—an I-9 form to provide proof of employment eligibility.
- ◆ Persuant to state law, as amended, a disclosure form, criminal conviction history record, and submit to be fingerprinted.
- ◆ Candidate must have the ability to maintain and continue a tradition of excellence in English educational techniques.
- ◆ Candidate must be able to work positively with diverse students and staff.

Desired:

- ◆ Skills, competencies, and knowledge of the English language as it relates to junior high/adolescent learning styles.
- ◆ Candidate should enjoy adolescent students, be a positive and active role model as well as have a good sense of humor.
- ◆ Should be flexible.

- Should have ability to organize ideas, time, and materials to accomplish goals.
- Should be enthusiastic.
- Should possess ability to express ideas clearly.
- Should have ability to learn new ideas and skills.
- Should have ability and willingness to develop favorable relationships with students. Should possess current knowledge of approaches to teaching.
- Should have willingness to model behavior deemed appropriate by the district and community.

This position description has been discussed in full and agreed to this _____ day of _____ 200__ by (administrator) _____ and (new hire) _____.

Position Announcement

If an exit interview has been conducted of the teacher exiting the position, the information should be used as part of the new job description and vacancy announcement. Likewise, the basic needs of the district, its demographic makeup, the particular school and its students will all be factors in designing the unique match of candidate to the position.

Within the framework of the Personnel Requisition, the additional specifics would be listed by the principal. It seems obvious then that the district mission statement or outcomes of it should be part of the Position Announcement format, as well as an analysis of the position based on the previous exit interview. The Sumner School District of Sumner, WA, announces its position vacancies with the introductory question, "Is this the position for you?" It then states four specific descriptors necessary for teachers who become a part of their instructional team. They are: "We're looking for teachers who—"

- believe in setting high expectations for themselves and their students
- possess a core of professional knowledge and skills that enable them to be effective with all students
- have knowledge and skills specific to the developmental stages and social and emotional needs of students
- can demonstrate depth and breadth of knowledge in the content areas, as well as skill to facilitate students becoming active learners.

Figure 3.5 is an example of a Position Announcement for an elementary teacher with a mathematics emphasis. Such a descriptions would be sent as an announcement to regional placement or personnel offices as well as posted in the district's central office and other personnel areas. Remember, this is but one step in the recruitment process.

Figure 3.5 Position Announcement— Elementary Teacher with a Math Emphasis, Pacific School District No. 204

Mission Statement: The mission of our district is the growth and development of students through the growth and development of staff.

Position Announcement

The Pacific School District is seeking the best teachers to assure that the pursuit of excellence and academic success for every student is attained. Teachers who are dedicated to collaborative team work, creative new ideas in teaching, the belief that every student can be successful, and act the lead in the partnership of parents, faculty, and students are highly sought.

Major Responsibilities:

- ◆ Provide an enthusiastic and positive learning climate, which promotes appropriate behavior and successful learning.
- ◆ Create a positive learning environment in which students are engaged, challenged, and safe.
- ◆ Promote high expectations, demonstrate caring attitude, and establish an appropriate environment to enhance learning.
- ◆ Administer a fair and consistent classroom management system.
- ◆ Utilize appropriate teaching strategies based on individual needs, interests, abilities, and learning styles.
- ◆ Maintain a professional attitude when interacting with students, parents, colleagues, and supervisors.
- ◆ Establish and maintain partnerships when interacting with students, parents, colleagues, and supervisors.
- ◆ Establish and maintain collaborative and cooperative relationships with colleagues.

Contribute to the development of a positive school climate and team-building atmosphere.

- • **Work Year** 183 days (New District employees will have 188 days).

- **Salary** Determined by placement on teachers' salary schedule.
- **Benefits** Benefits package includes health insurance coverage, retirement plan, and other benefits to be discussed upon hiring.

Qualifications Required:

- ◆ Valid State Teaching Certificate with appropriate endorsement(s) in Math and Elementary Education (K–8).
- ◆ Knowledge of district and state learning requirements and education reform.
- ◆ Skills to communicate clearly and directly, both orally and in written form.
- ◆ Minimum of two years of successful experience in teaching middle or junior high school.
- ◆ Knowledge and ability to implement assessment of student learning.
- ◆ Willingness to learn new and different skills and techniques to better student learning.
- ◆ Skills in developing and implementing instructional lessons based on strengths and deficiencies of individual students.
- ◆ Ability to create and maintain a positive classroom atmosphere that encourages student learning, "risk-taking," and overall growth and development.

Application Information:

- ◆ Submit a completed *District Application* (application packets available from the Personnel Department).
- ◆ In-district applicants applying for this position must submit a letter of application.
- ◆ Please include authorization for the hiring committee to review your personnel file.
- ◆ Applications and/or letters of application must be submitted by closing date.
- ◆ All other questions are to be directed to the Human Resources Department at 555-555-1212.

Upon Hire:

If you are hired, you will need to complete an Employment Eligibility Form and present documentation to Human Resources for review and verification to comply with the Federal Immigration Reform and Control Act.

It is the policy of the District not to discriminate in employment on the basis of race, creed, color, national origin, sex, marital status, age, or disability, as required by state and federal laws.

Key Idea

If you don't know what you are looking for, you won't know when you've found it.

Advertising the Position

When advertising a teaching position, information on the school district, the school, and the position are all essential. All three must be supplied to ensure a match. The position to be filled is not the only item being advertised, but rather all three. As the principal, you are looking for a person to fulfill not only your criteria, but also you want to be sure that your position is a match for the candidate. This means that you want the candidate to be well-informed, rather than "in the dark" about key elements of the position. You want to present potential employees with factual (all sides, not just the "glowing") information on which they can base their decision. You want to avoid the scenario of you having found the perfect person for the job, but come to find out that he or she was misled and is unhappy about every other aspect of working for you (i.e., not liking the community, district, staff, school location, weather, and so on). This can be educationally detrimental and expensive for all parties involved.

It is important for a school and district to put some thought (and, yes, money) into an attractive portrayal of what the schools and surrounding community have to offer a candidate. Through this process, the administrator will find not just outstanding teachers for the positions, but also community members who are happy in all areas of their lives.

Sources of Recruitment

As stated previously, recruiting potential employees is definitely a sound human resources practice. There are many places to consider when seeking candidates:

◆ Lateral transfers or internal recruiting of current staff members

This is a very viable avenue for finding a match for your opening. You may well have someone *within the building* who not only has the right qualifications, but also is looking for a move. This person may be stuck in an inappropriate match, or may just be looking for a change. Schools need to look to promoting from within, like many businesses do. It sends the message that "you are important and valuable" and you aren't "stuck" in the same spot forever. Lateral transfers should only be done once you have made an appraisal of current staffing and the certified personnel requisition. It may be that even though someone is qualified, you may need to go outside for reasons like equity, diversity, balance, and so on. Lateral moves *within the district* are also a good option. This works in cases where the person is not in a conducive environment, but you can offer it, or where personality conflicts may need to be defused, or just a change is needed, and the person meets your predetermined criteria. Be cautious here in that students from poverty school areas have a disproportionate share of beginning instructors.

Key Idea

The spring rite of internal transfers of incompetent teachers, or as some call it "the dance of the lemons," must be avoided.

- ◆ External recruiting
  - • Referrals from current staff members

    Don't overlook the rich resource you have in your current people. They may know of an outstanding candidate that you wouldn't otherwise reach. Caution is warranted to avoid hiring within a "friendship" circle. If you have carefully followed all previous steps, then this is avoided.

  - • Placement offices of colleges and universities

    This can often be done through reputable acquaintances who can steer you in the direction of their "brightest." It is advisable to actually set up interviewing times at or near the colleges in order to narrow down the selection field. This is often done by the district office personnel as well as by principals.

  - • Placement services of professional organizations

    Probably not a conventional avenue to follow in school districts, but an opportunity may arise in which you can utilize organizations outside the school sector to fill a vacancy.

- Recruiting letters

  These can be written to professional colleagues. They may well know of a candidate they would hire in a minute, but can't because there is no available position. Or, they may know of someone who would be perfect for your position, but not for their own. Use the people you know, they are valuable resources!

- Newspaper advertising—locally and statewide

  Don't feel you have to limit your search within your city or to your neighboring college. Expand your search to reach out and find the quality people you are seeking. Remember that you are not looking to fill a position, but rather to find the best person available.

- Advertising in professional education journals and newsletters

  This type of search will take you to a national audience. You may find the perfect teacher who is looking to relocate, but be very careful in your reference checks.

- Services of "search" consultants

  Most districts cannot afford such a service for teaching positions, but in certain instances, to fill a particularly specialized and hard-to-fill position such as high school principal, this may be a good option.

Successful Recruiting Plan

Inclusive of the above elements, but not exclusive to them, is the following plan which is designed to enhance the recruitment process:

- ◆ The district administration and school board need to make a public statement through written policies, district goals, and budget about the commitment of the district to recruiting. If your district will not do so, this doesn't mean that you as principal cannot do so on your level.

- ◆ The recruiting program must be a year-round program. It should also be ongoing in that you can have your connections in continuous touch, and your "feelers" out, so that when your opening comes you have an action plan. The time to begin the search is not when the opening is posted. Administrators need to be alert to coming changes, know the staff and their plans, and look early to ensure the best candidates are available.

- Recruiters need to be carefully selected and trained (especially if you go outside the administrative staff).

- Recruiters must accurately portray the community as well as the school and the district.

- The district's intent to hire the best needs to be publicized with staff, community, and potential candidates. This alone may attract the quality personnel you are seeking.

Recruiting

The success or failure of a recruiting program rests primarily with the individuals who do the recruiting. Personnel decisions will be influenced by the evaluations of the applicants submitted by the recruiter. Candidates see the school system through the presentation of the recruiters. Should the impression be unfavorable, the chances of the candidate accepting employment are slim. Therefore, the selection and training of recruiters is extremely important.

- Selecting recruiters:
  - Recruiters need to be very knowledgeable about the district and the community
  - Recruiters must be from the various grade levels and areas: for example, K–3, 4–8, 9–12, special education
  - Principals who go through personnel training should be selected to recruit
  - District teachers, after training, may also be part of the recruiting team
  - When an administrator is attending a conference, seminar, and so on, the administrator should contact a college and/or university in that area for possible arrangements for interviewing potential applicants
- Recruiting sources:
  - Other school districts, in state and out of state
  - Colleges and universities in state and out of state
  - Publications such as *Reading Teacher Journal*, and so on
  - Job Fairs

♦ Recruiters need to:

- Know what questions are legal; generally the law requires that information requested from an applicant focus on job-related considerations
- Be familiar with and be prepared to explain postinterview procedures and hiring timelines during the interview
- When possible, hold campus group interview seminars in order to influence a large group of teachers-in-training
- Feel comfortable interviewing for all levels of positions
- Be able to discuss salary schedules, extracurricular, insurance plans, tax-sheltered annuities, leave regulations, and so on
- Be aware of type of positions currently available within the district
- Be aware of the special endorsement requirements
- Be aware of qualifications requirements
- Be able to tell the applicants what they should do next

♦ Aggressive recruiting strategies:

- There is a difference between interviewing and recruiting. Interviewing is what takes place after applicants sign up to be considered for the position. Recruiting is what a school district does to ensure that quality applicants sign up to interview. Special effort usually generates special results. Some special efforts include:
  - inviting career/placement center personnel to visit your district
  - inviting major educational professors to visit the district to learn about curriculum and facilities
  - sending district representatives to college campuses to meet and talk to career/placement staff about district goals, accomplishments, needs, and benefits
  - sending preorientational material to individuals and colleges
  - making a request to present programs to student educational groups on college campuses
  - developing a videotape about the school district so that it may be shown when recruiting
  - hosting a reception for applicants and faculty the night before a job fair or scheduled interview day

- If an applicant is found who is too good to pass up and needs immediate consideration, the Human Resources Office should have special procedures to follow.

Technology in the Recruitment Process Listing Systems

A computerized job listing service available on the World Wide Web, *Project Connect*, is basically a paperless employment agency. After registering for the service, districts can enter vacancies by processing them directly into an online form. The vacancies are then sent to colleges and universities throughout the United States.

Teachers who are seeking positions can use the service at the Project Gopher site. They are able to search for vacancies nationally as well as internationally. To find vacancies, the teacher candidate would enter the grade level, subject area, and the geographical preference.

The teacher could also use the service's online candidate form to send a personal information sheet to school districts. This service is available 24 hours a day.

The features of *Project Connect* are:

- Online search of participating colleges and districts.
- School and college profiles online.
- Online Listserv management. Participants are be able to make and change their Listserv connection online.

One of the most comprehensive sites can be found on the Internet at www.resumix.com. Principals should learn the potential of this and similar sites as they perform their responsibilities in human resources.

Applications

With few exceptions when applications are provided by districts "online," they are provided in either PDF (Adobe Acrobat) format or as a Word file. Both formats allow the applicant to edit the document and fill out the application on their computer. In most cases, completed applications can simply be e-mailed back to the personnel department.

Résumé Scanning

Screening résumés is a major human resources activity that can benefit from the latest technological innovations including scanners, sorting systems, and online data pools. George Carlson, a recruiter for Motorola's Land Mobile Products Division in Ft. Lauderdale, FL, designed a desktop document management system using a Hewlett Packard ScanJet IIcx scanner and

PageKeeper document management software from Caere Corp. With this new system, résumés received in hard copy format can be scanned into the system. Those received electronically can be easily imported directly into PageKeeper.

IntelliMatch, Inc., of San Jose, CA, has an online system that converts résumés from a summary of experiences to a summary of skills. The system searches according to skill level, recency, years of experience, geographic preferences, education level, and other specifications set by the employer. Weighted values can also be assigned to the various criteria.

Job seekers can also benefit from another product available on the World Wide Web called Résumé Builder from Resumix Inc. Résumé Builder formats résumés so they can be more easily read by scanners and processing systems.

Some internet sites that would be helpful in recruiting:

♦ www.human-resources.org

   This is an excellent comprehensive site for human resources management and development from the business perspective.

♦ www.toolkit.cch.com

♦ www.cepm.uoregon.org

   This is the site of the former ERIC Center for Educational Management. Beginning in January, 2004 it was no longer to be operated as an ERIC Center.

♦ www.rnt.org

   This is the site of the National Recruiting Teachers Clearinghouse. It is an excellent source of information regarding recruiting.

♦ www.sdhc.k12.fl.us

   This is the site of the School District of Hillsborough County, Florida. It is fairly typical of a local school district site regarding recruiting and employment.

♦ www.ebrschool.org/recruiting

   This site provides a recruiting plan for the East Baton Rouge Parish Schools that is very extensive and thorough.

♦ www.k12jobs.com

   A general site for job searching and listing.

Conclusion

This chapter on recruitment emphasized these points:

♦ Recruitment is essential to the selection of teachers and, as such, should be well-planned.

- The exit interview is at the end of the employment cycle but is the place to start when considering recruitment.

- The certificated staff requisition is a very useful tool and should be used. The old adage, "if you don't know what you are looking for, you won't know it when you find it," applies here.

- All certificated teachers come initially from the colleges and universities, thus it will pay dividends to visit the campus and maintain a professional relationship with the placement officials.

- The district's current teachers are a source of leads for new teachers.

- A position description should be developed, discussed, and signed by the teacher and the principal. Teachers need to know what they are responsible for.

- The principal must learn from the human resources department personnel and principals from other districts, new and creative approaches to the recruiting process.

The next chapter, "Selection," continues the process started in recruiting.

Recruitment—Case Study

Megan Ware was by all accounts the best secondary teacher in science and the best science teacher to come out of the science department in the eight years Mark Pitts has been the Dean at this regional university.

David Steele was the high school principal and was on a recruiting trip to the university to find candidates for some hard-to-find positions, in this case, science. He had high standards and was unable to find a top candidate until Megan entered the recruiting office. As the interview progressed, David could tell that Megan was indeed a top candidate and exceeded the criteria on the personnel requisition. He told her that he wanted to invite her for an in-district interview. She said that she was excited about the in-district interview and the potential of teaching in Fred's school. However, Megan told David that she was going to be married during the summer and that her fiancé was an accounting major and would be looking for his job first and then she would hopefully find a job within commuting distance.

David thought about this and decided to call a friend of his who was in the accounting field to ascertain if he had any openings. David was determined to go the second mile to attempt to hire Megan for his staff and that seemed to mean finding a job for Megan's fiancee.

1. Should David become involved in the job search for Megan's fiancee?

2. Should schools and districts actively seek to employ married couples as a package deal?

3. What are some of the problems associated with this recruiting effort?

Comprehensive Questions

1. Why should a principal utilize the information from an exit interview prior to recruiting?

2. What process should a principal follow to know what kind of employee he's looking for?

3. How should a principal engage his current staff in the recruitment of staff?

4. How would you retain teachers in a high-poverty school, when the union contract gives teacher with seniority preferences when it comes to hiring within a district?

Extended Activities

1. Develop a visibility plan for your district's recruitment process.

2. Talk with your business manager to get a financial profile of hiring costs.

3. Plan position descriptions with each grade level in the spring to be implemented in the fall.

4. Talk with teachers of color and other protected classes to gain insight from them on the recruiting process.

5. Develop a "black book" or computer directory of potential candidates even though you may not have an opening.

6. Interview your substitutes (guest teachers). Find out their interests, concerns, and possible availability to teach on a regular basis.

7. What are some of the potential problems with recruiting on the internet?

References

Anfusa, D. (1993). Recruitment by the numbers. *Personnel Journal*. December, 71–74.

Fielder, D. J. (1993). Wanted: Minority teachers. *The Executive Educator*, 15(5), 33–34.

Jensen, M. C. (1986). *Recruiting and selecting the most capable teachers*. Eugene: Oregon School Study Council, University of Oregon.

Osborne, J. E. (1992). Job descriptions do more than describe duties. *Supervisory Management*, February, 8.

Saville, A., and J. Hill (1989). *The exit interview: A generic model*. Non-classroom Material. ERIC Document Reproduction Service No. Ed. 310–523.

Schmidt, W. V. (1984). The exit interview as monitor for change: A review of the literature. Paper presented at the annual conference of the American Business Communication Association. San Antonio, TX.

Witty, E. P. (1990). *Teacher recruitment and retention*. West Haven, CT: NEA Professional Library.

4

Selection

Reasons for Studying Personnel Selection

- The single most important decision you make for students is to hire a teacher.
- The selection process has legal implications that must be understood and followed.
- It is important to have a process that is fair to all—candidates, students, staff, and principal.
- If you don't think the teachers in your school are more important than the curriculum, think of this: What would you rather have: the 10 best basketball plays or the 10 best basketball players?

> *What is needed in schools are persons who are tender of heart and extraordinarily sensitive to the needs of students. Such persons are not ordinary in society. Perhaps it is time we consider extraordinary means of selecting them.*
>
> Phillip Schlechty

ISLLC Standards Covered in this Chapter

Standard 2:

- A school administrator is an educational leader who promotes the success of all students by advocating, nurturing, and sustaining a school culture and instructional program conducive to student learning and staff professional growth.

Standard 3:

- A school administrator is an educational leader who promotes the success of all students by ensuring management of the organization, operations, and resources for a safe, efficient, and effective learning environment.

Introduction

As demographic and curriculum changes influence the direction of the education system, selection of the best teacher candidates becomes more and more specific, and in turn, more critical, since it is the teacher who is responding to the demographic needs of children and the curricular changes of the school and district. The match of candidate to position must be decided by individuals who understand both the specific needs of the position as well as the characteristics, education, and experience of the chosen applicant.

The instructional need of the individual classroom is necessarily bound by the district goals, curriculum choices, and individual building administrators and their current staff. Responding to a district population's social, physical, and educational needs is a continuous evaluation process—not a final decision. So, then, recruiting and selecting the best teachers possible will have great impact on the effectiveness of the education system. It is clear that selection is both a marvelous opportunity and a time of great risk, if done without care in the decision-making process.

As shown in Figure 4.1, the selection process might best start with a statement of a district's central focus, such as Wenatchee (WA) School District's "most important component of any organization is its people." It further noted that the specific goal of the Staff Selection Service is to "search out, select, and maintain outstanding employees to lead, educate, and provide supportive services to the students of the district." Through such statements, presented in a brochure for distribution to interested applicants during the recruitment and selection process, applicants would have a heightened awareness of Wenatchee's vision of employing an excellent staff.

Figure 4.1 Wenatchee School District No. 246
Staff Selection Process

Goals of the Wenatchee School District

We believe that the most important component of any organization is its people. With this in mind, we recognize the importance of selecting excellent employees. All people in the district, regardless of role, are part of the future of the young people they seek to serve.

Goals of Staff Selection/Staff Development Services

It is the purpose of the Personnel Office in the Wenatchee School District to search out, select, and maintain outstanding employees to lead, educate, and provide supportive services to the students of the district. All of the efforts of personnel services are ultimately directed toward this task.

The Selection Process

This handbook describes the selection process used in the Wenatchee School District. The selection process for hiring personnel will have several ingredients in common for each employee, but there are three separate and distinct processes. One process focuses upon the selection of teachers and other nonadministrative certificated staff members. A second category focuses upon certificated administrators at the school site and the administrative services center level. The third category focuses upon the noncertificated/classified staff selection...

Additionally, some school districts involve the staff members with the development of generic characteristics of effective staff members. The list of characteristics enables the school and district to be clear about what they are seeking in a teacher and conversely, for the teacher to know the high standards and expectations. Such a list is the Bellevue (WA) School District's Characteristics of Effective Certificated Staff (Figure 4.2).

Figure 4.2 Bellevue School District— Characteristics of Effective Certificated Staff

1. Flexibility
   - is willing to learn new concepts or ways of doing things
   - adapts to changing conditions in the learning environment
   - adapts to professional changes
   - cooperates with students and adults
   - uses democratic approach to teaching and decision making
   - incorporates new technology into job performance
   - deals effectively with ambiguity
2. Commitment to Accomplishment
   - possesses sense of mission
   - desires and exerts efforts to attain particular goals
   - organizes ideas, time, materials, and space to accomplish goals
   - demonstrates regular attendance and punctuality
   - demonstrates ability to prioritize and be thorough on important tasks

- has evidence of past and current success
- is self-motivated

3. Enthusiasm
   - has overall optimism and zeal for what he/she is doing
   - encourages and promotes willingness of others to be involved in task
   - fosters interpersonal relations with others

4. Communication Skills
   - demonstrates clarity of expression
   - listens with understanding
   - uses nondefensive communication skills
   - comprehends and follows oral and written directions
   - is sensitive to nuances of language
   - maintains confidentiality when appropriate

5. Conceptual and Technical Skills
   - demonstrates commitment to lifelong learning
   - adapts to function effectively in the local setting
   - learns new concepts and skills as the job changes
   - uses new ideas and skills to solve job-related problems
   - is willing to develop curriculum
   - applies knowledge of effective classroom management and behavior management skills

6. Professional Orientation
   - has high interest in students
   - is willing to work out problems so that all involved are satisfied
   - has working knowledge of current approaches to teaching
   - has working knowledge of learning and child development
   - possesses breadth of background and applies it for the benefit of the school district
   - has ability and willingness to work with others in a team
   - is constructive in relationships with others
   - demonstrates awareness of community need
   - is willing to share concerns and raise questions openly

7. Modeling Appropriate Behavior
   - models appropriate behavior
   - demonstrates global perspective
   - maintains a sense of humor
   - demonstrates confidence in own abilities
   - has positive models/mentors
   - demonstrates higher level thinking skills
   - uses a variety of problem-solving techniques
8. Relating to Students/Staff
   - has ability and willingness to develop favorable relationships with students and staff
   - likes students and staff
   - exhibits listening, patience, caring, empathy
   - responds to students/staff needs
   - is open and desires to have a positive relationship with students/staff
   - has high expectations of students/staff
   - believes every student can learn
   - accepts responsibility to motivate students/staff
   - instills confidence in the abilities of student/staff
9. Relating to Parents and Community
   - exhibits listening, patience, caring, and empathy
   - involves parents in classroom; recognizes parents as valuable contributors to the learning process
   - is willing to work in a partnership with community, parents, and business
   - values and is willing to use parents in the decision-making process when appropriate
   - is willing to involve self and students in community when appropriate

The Application Process

In reality, teacher selection is a rather complex process rather than an event, and selection decisions are made at several stages within the process. The two main stages are: (1) the screening of the applicants' papers to select applicants to be interviewed; and (2) the interview, reference checks and subsequent selection of the candidate who best matches the criteria set forth in the personnel requisition. This section deals with the application and initial screening stages.

When developing your application forms, ask only for information that you need and will use in your screening process. Most information falls into one of the following categories: personal data, education and/or professional preparation, experience, and references. In addition to factual information, application forms can also devise methods of extracting applicant's attitudes, opinions, and values. Many districts do this through a writing sample, or the answering of predetermined questions. This format can help provide additional information to help you decide who should be interviewed.

Key Idea

The application form should ask only for information which will assist in the screening of applicants.

Items typically requested from candidates as part of the screening process include:

- a placement file usually requested by the applicant from the college career planning and placement office or letters of recommendation and references
- a letter of interest in the position
- a professional résumé

In addition, most school districts require:

- a completed application form
- copies of transcripts

The key point here is to request only those items that pertain to this position and will be used in the screening process. The preference of a few districts is not to use an application form for professional positions like teaching but to use the letter of application, placement file, and professional résumé to provide a completed file. This provides ample information on which to screen for an interview and does not duplicate information. Transcripts generally are only required of the successful candidate. This is a very "user friendly" approach. A compromise to no application is the Professional Employment Application from the Lake Washington School District (Figure 4.3). Prior to paper screening of applicants, each packet should be received by a designated central-office staff member who checks for completeness, dates each, and files them appropriately for the screening team. This step provides integrity to the process and will establish a method of monitoring the progress of filling positions. Figure 4.4 is a more traditional sample application form.

Figure 4.3 Professional Employment Application Lake Washington School District

Professional Employment Application

Name: _____

Home Address: _____

City: _____ State: _____ Zip: _____

Home Phone: _____ Email: _____

To which educational position do you aspire?

☐ Administrator	☐ Counselor	☐ Librarian
☐ Nurse	☐ Occupational Therapist	☐ Physical Therapist
☐ Shool Psychologist	☐ Social Worker	☐ Special Education
☐ Speech Language Pathologist	☐ Substitute Teacher	☐ Teacher

Please list in order your choices by subject or grade. Secondary, please check middle or high school or no preference.

☐ Middle School	☐ High School	☐ No Preference

Please submit the following along with this application or you may visit our web site at lkwash.wednet.edu *and apply online:*

- a professional résumé
- copy of transcripts
- two confidential professional recommendations
- two confidential professors/personal recommendations

Thank you for your interest in the Lake Washington School District.

The Lake Washington School District is an equal opportunity employer.

Figure 4.4 Educational Employment Experience

(List experience beginning with most recent)

Student Teaching Experience

Dates	District	City	State	Grade	Subject

Guest (Substitute) Teaching Experience

Dates	District	City	State	Grade	Subject

Contracted Experience

Dates	District	City	State	Grade	Subject

Related Experience (List experience beginning with most recent)

Dates	District	City	State	Grade	Subject

References

Name:	Title:	Employer:	
Address:	City:	State:	Zip:
Day Phone:		Evening Phone:	
Name:	Title:	Employer:	
Address:	City:	State:	Zip:
Day Phone:		Evening Phone:	
Name:	Title:	Employer:	
Address:	City:	State:	Zip:
Day Phone:		Evening Phone:	

Some school districts also require that an applicant give professional reference forms directly to supervisors, which are then returned to the district.

Other districts also request Affirmative Action information, which is collected, summarized, and reported to the Board of Directors as part of an Affirmative Action Plan.

Figure 4.5 Public Schools Personnel Cooperative—
Certificated Employment Data Form

Name _____

Please mark the positions for which you are *ENDORSED* or *CERTIFICATED* to teach. You may list non-endorsed/certificated experience on your resume.

Locations

☐ Centralia	☐ Griffin	☐ Olympia	☐ Tenino	☐ Yelm
☐ Chehalis	☐ Napavine	☐ Onalaska	☐ Toledo	
☐ ESD 113	☐ Oakville	☐ Southside	☐ Tumwater	

Administrator   ☐ Elementary   ☐ Middle School

☐ High School   ☐ Alternative

☐ Assistant Principal   ☐ Principal

☐ Assistant Superintendent   ☐ Program Coordinator

☐ Athletic Director   ☐ Special Education Director

☐ Curriculum Director   ☐ Other

Teacher   ☐ Preschool   ☐ Elementary   ☐ Middle School

☐ High School   ☐ Alternative   ☐ Remedial

☐ Primary—Grades K–3	☐ English	☐ Mathematics
☐ Intermediate— Grades 4–6	☐ English as a Second Language	☐ Physical Education
☐ Agriculture Education	☐ English/Language Arts	☐ Reading Specialist
☐ Art/Visual Arts	☐ Family & Consumer Sciences	☐ Social Studies
☐ Business Education	☐ Health/Fitness	☐ Technology Education
☐ Computer Education	☐ History	☐ **Traffic Safety**
☐ Designated Arts (Dance)	☐ Library Media	☐ Classroom Instruction
☐ Drama	☐ Marketing Education	☐ Behind the Wheel Inst.

Designated World Languages

☐ French	☐ German	☐ Russian	☐ Other
☐ Spanish	☐ Japanese	☐ Latin	

Music

☐ Band	☐ Choral
☐ General Music	☐ Orchestra

Science

☐ Biology ☐ Physics ☐ Earth Science

☐ Chemistry ☐ Science

Special ED

☐ Infant/Toddler ☐ Preschool ☐ Elementary

☐ Middle School ☐ High School ☐ Remedial

Positions	Areas of Disability	Instructional Mode*:
☐ Teacher	☐ Autism	☐ Home/Hospital
☐ Audiologist	☐ Communication Disability	☐ Inclusion
☐ Intervention Specialist	☐ Deaf/Blind	☐ Resource Room
☐ Occupational Therapist	☐ Developmental Delay	☐ Self Contained
☐ Physical Therapist	☐ Emotional/Behavior Disability	☐ *Have Experience/Preference*
☐ School Psychologist	☐ Health Impaired	**Work Setting*:**
☐ Social Worker	☐ Hearing Impaired	
☐ Speech Language Pathologist	☐ Learning Disability	☐ Military Base School
☐ Vision Specialist	☐ Mental Retardation	☐ Private School
	☐ Multiple Disabilities	☐ Public School
	☐ Orthopedic Disability	☐ State School
	☐ Traumatic Brain Injury	☐ *Have Experience*
	☐ Vision Impaired	

Name: _____

Counselor

☐ Elementary Counselor ☐ Middle School Counselor ☐ High School Counselor

Vocational ED ☐ Middle School ☐ High School

☐ Agriculture Education ☐ Family & Consumer Sciences Ed ☐ Technology Education

☐ Business Education ☐ Health Occupations ☐ Trade & Industrial Education

☐ Diversified Occupations ☐ Marketing Education ☐ Other _____

Coach/Extra Curricular ☐ Middle School ☐ High School ☐ Head Assistant

☐ Activities Coordinator ☐ Drill/Dance Team ☐ Skiing

☐ Annual/Year Book	☐ Football	☐ Swimming
☐ Athletic Trainer	☐ Golf	☐ Tennis
☐ Baseball	☐ Gymnastics	☐ Track and Field
☐ Basketball	☐ Hockey	☐ Volleyball
☐ Bowling	☐ Intramural	☐ Weight Lifting
☐ Cheer Leading	☐ Newspaper	☐ Wrestling
☐ Debate/Speech	☐ Soccer	☐ Other _____
☐ Drama	☐ Softball	☐ Other _____

Further, many districts are encouraging applicants to visit the web site and apply electronically. This approach is gaining popularity with both districts and applicants.

Screening

After the closing date or opened-until-filled (OUF), three weeks minimum, the completed applications need to be reviewed and screened according to predetermined criteria. During this stage of the process it is important to make fine distinctions between excellent and good candidates, and between that which you are searching for, and that which you are not!

Paper screening of applicants is the reviewing of all required forms and materials submitted by the applicant. The criteria used in examining the application file needs to match the need assessment and personnel requisition done earlier in the process. Below are suggested general criteria for narrowing the field for interview purposes:

♦ **Incomplete or late applications and files** are good indicators of a candidate's competency, organization, and effectiveness and should send up a "red flag." In most cases, this means an automatic rejection. In other cases, it may clearly be a clerical mistake, and a highly qualified educator may be overlooked. This is something that will have to be determined at the individual site.

♦ **Written statements of philosophy or a portfolio** should contain ideas, beliefs, and values related to education and the applicant. They should be supported with evidence, not just the applicant's self-serving statements. These materials provide information about the applicant's ability to organize thoughts, think, communicate, and use correct English.

♦ **Questions specific to the position, district, or philosophy** can also assist in the screening process. These do essentially the same as a statement of philosophy but can make even finer distinctions because questions can be narrowed and directed to address a specific position or target of interest.

- **Review transcripts if requested** that give attention to the overall GPA and to grades in the academic major. Look in depth at the areas or courses that relate to the personnel requisition.

- **Check for academic awards** given at the university level. Those with honors have demonstrated exceptional ability, and when considered with other factors, these applicants can serve as models for students, and will tend to be adaptive to the many shifts in teaching.

- **Make direct contact with the candidate's personal and professional references.** You should not only contact those people listed, but also make an effort to contact at least one reputable person not listed who will give you an honest evaluation of that individual. This is a key point. You must inquire from professionals other than those listed on the reference forms or applications. Having a conversation with such persons enables you to probe areas of strength and areas of needed growth. Remember to ask open-ended questions, and always ask this question near the end of reference checking, "You know this applicant better than I do, what should I ask about this applicant that I haven't?" Reference checking can be done at this stage, or it can be used after the applicant field has been narrowed and interviewed. It will be looked at in depth in a subsequent section. Pay attention to who is listed as a reference and who wrote letters. Ministers, friends, and coworkers should carry less weight than supervisors and principals.

Practitioners generally put less value on the recommendations of college supervisors but they can provide valuable information. While the college supervisor may not know the person's work in great detail, he or she has watched the applicant in the college class as well as during student teaching and can also rate one candidate against many others at the same stage of development. The supervisor usually has responsibility for 10–15 teachers per year. This perspective should be important to the principal.

- **Look at whether the file is "open" or "closed."** If open (nonconfidential), most writers will tend not to be as candid, and a closed (confidential) file can prove to be more accurate. This is not always true, as there is really no such thing as a "closed" file since access often can be obtained through devious ways.

♦ **Look for gaps in credentials, employment, references, time, or paper.** You need to have specific criteria by which you will evaluate each application. You can do this by using a screening or application checklist and rating system. This will allow you to keep a record of why a candidate met or did not meet the criteria. One caution is to be sure that all of your criteria in your search are legal and nondiscriminatory. Legalities related to screening are discussed in more detail in the legal chapter.

The following are instructions and a scale for rating the applicant's file:

Application Rating Instructions

♦ Rate applicants one at a time.

♦ Read the application form or résumé to get a clear understanding of the applicant's work history, training, and education. Consider the organizational setting, the length of time employed, and role in the organization.

♦ Consider all of the evidence provided in the letter of application to substantiate that the applicant can do the job. Focus as much as possible on the content; the format, presentation, and so on, should carry less value unless the rating criteria specifically calls for it. Differentiate between the "steak" and the "sizzle."

♦ Do not give credit for claims to have done the work ("I have done this for 10 years") unless there is other information in the applicant's materials to substantiate the claims.

♦ Avoid giving too much consideration to credentials for credentials' sake; rather, consider how the credentials relate to the applicant's ability to perform the work.

♦ Avoid giving consideration to other things you may personally know about the applicant. Rate the information and evidence provided by the applicant.

♦ Using the rating scale and the specific criteria listed under each element, rate the applicant in each of the major elements based on work experience and training, and the specific examples provided.

- Add up the major element ratings, and put the total at the bottom of the rating sheet. The total of the major element ratings will be the applicant's rating.

- Typically, applicants who receive below a marginal rating (see Application Scale immediately following) on major elements would be considered "below passing." Applicants who receive an average of acceptable or better rating could be considered for an interview, since they have been identified as being acceptable or better applicants. However, you may want to interview only "good" or "superior" applicants, depending on the total number of applications received.

Application Rating Scale

- **Unacceptable.** The applicant presents *no* evidence that he or she has done this aspect of the work in the past, or would not be able to perform this aspect of the work if hired.

- **Marginal.** The applicant has some understanding or familiarity with this aspect of the work, but would require *significant* guidance, training, or help to perform at an acceptable level.

- **Acceptable.** The applicant provides evidence from prior employment and/or training that he or she could perform this aspect of the work at an acceptable level, given normal orientation and training for the position.

- **Good.** The applicant provides evidence from prior employment and/or training that he or she could perform this aspect of the work at a proficient level and would require little or no guidance.

- **Superior.** The applicant provides evidence from prior employment and/or training that he or she could perform this aspect of the work at a *highly proficient* level. The applicant could train or instruct others in this aspect of the work.

Figure 4.5A is an example of the form used to rate and summarize the information from the applicant's file.

Figure 4.5A Electronic Reference Form

File Review Screening—Certificated Applicants

Score _____

Applicant Name: _____

Position: _____

Screener: _____ Date: _____

Credential File: _____ Open _____ Closed

Instructions from screener:	**Summary File Screening Rating:**
_____ Request additional information or references (see comments)	_____ 1 Superior (5%)
_____ Arrange a screening interview	_____ 2 Good (10%)
_____ Other: _____	_____ 3 Acceptable (25%)
Comment: _____	_____ 4 Marginal (50%)
_____	_____ 5 Unacceptable (below 50%)

		High				Low
A.	Letter of Application or Essay/Transcripts (Neatness, organization, completeness/G.P.A. in Major, Overall G.P.A.)	1	2	3	4	5
B.	References of Professional Characteristics (Key words—outstanding, enthusiastic, bright, caring, cooperative, success oriented)	1	2	3	4	5
C.	References of Personal Characteristics (Key words: friendly, team player, pleasant, dedicated, patient, good personality)	1	2	3	4	5
D.	Knowledge of Subject Matter/Coursework (Depth, breadth of training and background, flexibility)	1	2	3	4	5
E.	Related Experiences and Skills/Teaching Experience (Travel, co-curricular, hobbies, other work experiences, community activities/years of experience)	1	2	3	4	5

Other:_____

_____

Total Points (Add A–E)
Transfer average score to upper right hand corner of this form _____

When the files have been evaluated, the principal completes the Certificated Hiring Checklist (Figure 4.6). Completing this form can assist the administrator in organizing this stage and the interviewing stage of the selection process.

Figure 4.6 Certificated Hiring Checklist

Please complete this form, sign, and return with the applicant's file.

Position: _____ Location: _____

Position Closing Date: _____ Administrator: _____

Check Completed	Activity

_____ Screen applications, using District File Review Screening Sheets. Review supporting papers in personnel files of any in-district applicants. Indicate applicants selected for interview. If any in-district applicant is not to be interviewed, note the specific requirements he/she fails to meet.

_____ Appoint interview team. Notify Personnel of team members. Orient team to hiring procedures/process.

Members: _____ _____

_____ _____

_____ _____

_____ Schedule interviews or contact Human Resources to do so. If scheduling from the building, please inform Personnel of the schedule in order to assist in answering public inquiries.

Date: _____ Time: _____ Location: _____

Candidates _____ _____

_____ _____

_____ _____

Use sample provided by Human Resources or design interview questions/rating sheet related to criteria listed on the job announcement and from other factors determined to be related to predicted job performance. Use Interview Rating Sheet to accurately document responses and objectively rate each candidate.

_____ Conduct interviews, asking each candidate the same questions. Each interview team member completes a rating sheet for each candidate. Complete Candidate Rating Form for each candidate.

_____ Rate and identify top candidate(s) from interviews using the Candidate Rating Form.

_____ Conduct employment reference checks (2 minimum, 3 recommended, contact at least one reference who is not listed by the applicant) and include notations as part of formal documentation. Use the Telephone Reference Form.

_____ Contact Human Resources regarding the following:

Recommended Candidate: _____

Reasons: _____

Requested Start Date: _____

Recommended Contract: _____ or Long-Term Substitute _____

_____ Deliver interview/recommendation materials to the Human Resources Department:

_____ Applications

_____ Interview questions/rating sheets with notes

_____ Reference check notations

_____ Certified Hiring Checklist

Principal's Signature: _____

Return to Human Resources

Human Resources Department:

_____ Confirm receipt of required materials.

_____ Confirm candidate recommended; review related issues. (Certification, Affirmative Action, district employee, overlap time, etc.)

_____ Authorize contact with successful candidate.

_____ Notify candidates who were interviewed but not selected for the position.

_____ Process paperwork for payroll.

Screening Team

If done well, the recruiting and application screening stages should provide excellent candidates who match school and district needs. It is also critical to have qualified, trained people to do the screening. If you do not have competent personnel doing the screening, you may miss out on excellent candidates who would have been a match for the position. Typically, paper screenings are done by the personnel department and selected district administrators based on predetermined characteristics as defined by your team. However, as a principal you should be on the screening team so that you have a hands-on look and can use your best judgment rather than relying solely on others to compare applicants against the criteria. The compilation of a screening summary report for each candidate to be considered, including specific reasons for elimination, is recommended.

Principals should consider use of either of these two methods of selecting those to be interviewed and subsequent steps to be followed.

Method 1

♦ Completed Application

♦ Reviewed by the Principal

- Applicants Selected by the Principal for Interview
- Train the Interviewers
- Selection Team Interview
- Recommendation to Principal
- Principal Interviews
- Principal Does Reference Checks/Site Visits
- Principal Recommends to Superintendent/Human Resources to Hire
- School Board Offers Contract

Method 2

- Completed Application
- Review by the Principal and Selection Team
- Applicants Selected Cooperatively by the Principal and the Selection Team
- Train the Interviewers
- Selection Team and the Principal Interview
- Recommendation to the Principal
- Principal/Selection Committee Does Reference Checks/Site Visits
- Principal Recommends to Superintendent/Human Resources to Hire
- School Board Confirms Contract

Selection of Interviewees and Notification of Nonselected Applicants

The applicant pool now is in two groups: those who have been selected for interviews and those who have not. The principal typically notifies the district human resources department to notify both groups. As school-based management becomes more of a reality, it will increasingly become the principal's role to notify the applicants. Typically, the nonselected applicants are notified by letter at this stage since there is usually such a large quantity. Candidates to be interviewed are notified by phone and scheduled for an interview.

Preparing for the Interview

The importance of the interview is paramount. The administrator should be well prepared for this stage of selection since it involves a commitment of time and resources. Several aspects will be looked at:

Interview Team

It is not enough to simply select the best people to conduct the interview; they also need to be trained in interviewing. Let's look first at the format and selection of the team:

Selection

It is recommended to select five to nine people on the interview team. How you choose to format the interview is of personal choice. You may choose to:

- Do team interviews (including the Principal)
- Interview with Principal alone followed by the team interview
- Group interview the candidates and then individual interview: This is a concept where candidates come together and are given a task to perform while the team watches them interact and their roles and behaviors observed. Then, each candidate is interviewed individually by the team.

When choosing those to be on the interview team, they must, above all else, agree to use whatever criteria and guidelines are chosen. You should also strive to get as heterogeneous a group as possible in terms of age, gender, status, and attitudes. If you get a group that is simply made up of clones of you, then there is no way to reach the best possible hiring decision. Beyond that, the suggested makeup of your team might include any of the following:

- One administrator of the building Principal's choice
- The team leader/department or grade level chair in the area of the vacancy
- Two members of the department or grade
- One other teacher (other grade level or subject area) and maybe one specialist
- One or two parents
- One or two students
- Secretary, or classified staff where applicable
- Alternates for each category in case of absences

Figure 4.7 Sample Confidential and Ethical Statement for the Interview Team

Coupeville School District, Hiring Process Confidentiality and Ethics

The issues of confidentiality and ethics are extremely important when taking part in selection of new staff. Each member of the selection team must make the commitment to have the process remain strictly confidential. The following issues are not for public discussion:

◆ Documents developed

◆ Statements made by the team or applicant

◆ Deliberations

◆ Impressions

◆ Opinions

Confidentiality is our obligation—to protect the rights and preserve the self-respect of the candidates. Confidentiality is the obligation of the team, not the candidate. All selection process materials will be collected and filed in the district office.

The only people authorized to give information are the administrator and team member(s) chosen to give feedback during the post interview conference upon the request of the candidate. The data goes only to the specific candidate.

At the foundation of our work is trust, which we develop through respect, cooperation, communication, and developing safety for everyone in the group. Trust and confidentiality are essential elements of a successful team hire process. As a team, we each agree:

◆ to observe the confidentiality and ethic statement above.

◆ to communicate openly and directly, sharing any concerns with my fellow team members.

◆ to honor and respect points of view that may be different than mine.

◆ to equally share the decision-making process with my fellow team members.

◆ to express my feelings and thoughts in a constructive way to facilitate and validate the selection process.

◆ to work to make this a positive, warm, welcoming, and professional experience.

I accept my obligation to support the selection process in a totally confidential and ethical manner.

Signed: _____ Dated: _____

Training of Team

Once you have selected your interview team, they must be trained for the interview. Keep in mind that you will need to adapt these suggestions to whatever interview model you choose to use. Following are elements of training:

♦ **Understanding the purpose of interviewing.** Each interviewer needs to have a clear understanding of the objectives: the selection of the best qualified candidate for the position, determining appropriate experience, training and personality for the given position, narrowing down to who is most able to perform effectively within the job description and environment, and to choosing a match for the demographics, culture, and needs of your students, staff, and community. The group should refer regularly to the Personnel Requisition Form used to initiate the selection process.

♦ **Applicant information file.** Interviewers should have knowledge about the individual's background in terms of information from the district application form, the résumé, and other pertinent data. Most often, the practice is to give the confidential placement file to the team. However, it is recommended that the letters of reference, placement file, and phone references should be seen and handled only by the building administrator in the interest of confidentiality for all involved. The ultimate responsibility for hiring the best person for the job is the principal's.

♦ **Knowledge of the job.** Interviewers need to know the predetermined criteria for applicant selection in terms of the job requisition and description, and in terms of how applicants were screened. Everyone must be clear as to what is being sought from the candidates.

♦ **Rules of the district for interviewing.** Each district may have established rules for the interview that it has found to be effective. Such rules could include: statements and questions not to ask according to district rules as well as the law, what information can and cannot be referred to, whether to ask additional questions besides those assigned, what role the interviewer should play, and so on.

♦ **Personal attributes and skills interviewing.** Individual interview team members should:

  • treat candidates with fairness and respect

- have awareness/avoid stereotypes and biases
- learn to pay attention to body language and visual clues
- have the ability to make fine distinctions and perceive accurately
- have the ability to record accurate records after the interview (not rating, but strengths and weaknesses)
- be willing and committed to using criteria as established
- have the ability to give the candidate every chance to be successful
- maintain eye contact
- become familiar with interview questions and structure
- know what to expect as an appropriate answer to a question and how to delve further
- know how to paraphrase an applicant's answers
- stay focused
- make the candidate feel welcome and at ease

Cautions for the interviewer to be alert to:

- making judgments too early
- putting too much merit on unfavorable information versus favorable information
- being influenced by comparisons between one candidate and another
- using your "version" of the criteria to judge
- imposing personal biases (e.g., looks like old boss, hair color, etc.) that may turn you off

It cannot be assumed that interviewers know and understand the above items. They must be taught extensively to arrive at the best decision through shared vision and expectations.

Interviewer Training Workshop

- The Interviewer Training Workshop will include:
  - How to screen applicants' résumés and cover letters
  - How to confirm information from the résumé and cover letter
  - How to maintain eye contact and flow during the interview

- How to become familiar with the oral and written structure of the interview questions

- How to know what to expect as an appropriate or inappropriate answer and how to respond with additional questions

- How to paraphrase an applicant's answers

- How to note body language and visual cues

- How to STAY FOCUSED!

♦ The Interviewer Training Workshop is typically three hours long. It is best to use the room for the training in which the interviews will actually take place.

Key Idea

Have one person sit unobtrusively to the side of the interview team with a laptop computer and record the questions and the responses of the candidate. In the break between candidates, the recorder can print the responses from a portable printer and make copies for the entire group. This frees the team to concentrate on the nonverbal cues and maintain eye contact with the candidate.

Interview Logistics and Protocol

♦ Suggested set up as shown in Figure 4.8:

- U-shaped tables for interview team with "modesty shield"

- host seated at mouth of "U"

- table tents for each person's name and position

- pertinent data and interview questions and rating form for interview team

- recorder designated to take down candidate's responses

- interview team focuses on candidate

Figure 4.8 Setting Up the Interview Room

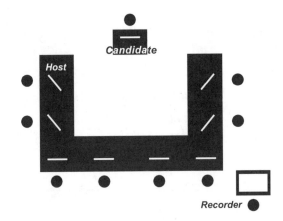

The Interview

Key Idea

Have a host or hostess meet the candidate, describe the process, give printed information (salary benefits, education association contract, brochure about the district programs, etc.), and be cordial to the candidate. Important impressions are made at this juncture.

Now that the interview team has been selected and trained, preparation for the interview itself takes place. In the process of preparation there are six steps to include:

♦ **Planning the interview (format, questions, roles)**

In this stage, the team determines who will design questions (individuals, team, or principal). The questions should be focused and should be based on agreed upon criteria. Each question should meet the following criteria:

- be open-ended
- have a clear purpose tied to criteria
- be tied to job requirements
- be focused and clear
- be repeatable
- have a meaningful place in the entire interview sequence

The interview schedule should be developed with these questions in mind:

- What is the best time to conduct the interview?
- How long will the interview last?
- How will the room be set up?
- Who will introduce and welcome each candidate?
- What is the order of questions?
- Who will ask what questions?
- What will be happening while individuals are answering questions?

These details need to be mapped out in advance for the interview process to run smoothly.

The last thing that needs to be planned is the "rating" criteria. This may not mean a literal rating process—although it might—but rather, what you are looking for and what format you will use in recording and comparing that information. You may use a number system, or a statement format in which to write thoughts about each candidate's strengths, weaknesses, and other information.

♦ **Giving information**

You are not only trying to find a match for your school but also a match for the candidate. An unhappy employee who was not well-informed prior to hiring about the job, school, district, and community tends not to be effective. Time needs to be spent planning what specific information to give the candidate about responsibilities, salary, benefits, the culture and the community, how the district and school operate, with whom he or she will work, and so on. How and when this is to be done needs to be determined.

♦ **Getting information**

Strategies and methods for eliciting desired information are to be determined. Questions need to be designed that will solicit specific information being sought based on the interviewee's response. Information will also be acquired from the reference checks to be done by the principal.

♦ **Personal impact**

The candidate is expected to impress the team! Keep in mind that you are also selling your school, district, and community to the candidate as well. An excellent prospect may well have many options for employment and you want to "hook" him or her. To do so, you need to create a positive and memorable impact. Plan your timeline and procedures for notification, and what you can do to leave a positive impression on each candidate so that he or she will want to return to your district even if not hired.

♦ **Responding to the applicant**

Anticipate questions that the applicant may ask, and plan answers and determine who will answer them. Usually, the principal is more prepared to answer these questions.

♦ **Processing the information**

After the interview is complete, you need a way to compile the information on the candidates and a way to compare and reach a decision. Will all have an equal vote in the process, does the principal want it limited to the best two candidates, what format will be used in discussing each, how will it be sifted out, and how will the best candidate be determined?

The interview questions are important sources of information. Figures 4.9 and 4.10 are samples of interview questions and appropriate responses.

Figure 4.9 Sample School District— Certificated Interview

Candidate name _____ Date _____

Interviewer _____ Total points: _____

		Rate
		low → *high*

1. Please review your educational background and preparation as it relates to this position.   1 2 3 4

- Appropriate courses, education
- Continuing education
- MA
- Professional reading

2. Do you want students to like you? (If yes, why is that?)   1 2 3 4

- Yes, for the right reasons
- Sees "liking" as beneficial to student learning
- Emphasizes relationship-building qualities

3. With all the adverse publicity about education today, why did you want to become a teacher? What do you wish to accomplish?   1 2 3 4

   - Wants to do something for students; seeing their growth
   - Satisfaction in helping others
   - Contribution to society
   - Always wanted to be a teacher
   - Experience with students confirmed their interest

4. Some teachers are better than others; what do you think makes the difference?   1 2 3 4

   - Focus on relationships
   - Specific reference to and description of an instructional model
   - Understands planning—goals, objectives, outcomes
   - Applies new ideas and skills
   - Pacing, instructional level, diagnosis and assessment

5. What do you see to be your strongest areas, and share an example that explains why.   1 2 3 4

   - Relationships
   - Organization
   - Ability to diagnose own strengths
   - Goal-oriented
   - Describes how they developed
   - Able to describe specifics

6. How do you provide for individual differences in students?   1 2 3 4

   - Assessment: tools, methods; interest survey
   - Accounts for learning
   - styles
   - Has management strategies

7. As a teacher you are required to interact with administrators, other staff, parents, etc. Please describe how you work with a variety of individuals and describe a situation you were involved in which was difficult and sensitive. How did you handle it?   1 2 3 4

   - Perspective as a team member as well as an individual
   - Courtesy, professionalism
   - Look for support for solution from others

8. Describe your classroom management style and discuss discipline strategies you would use with students at this level.   1 2 3 4

   - Specific strategies
   - Positive reinforcement
   - Preventive methods
   - Communication strategies

9. How have you grown professionally recently, and what areas would you like to develop in yourself? How was this/will this be accomplished?   1 2 3 4

   - Able to diagnose own needs
   - Professional plan for self
   - Actions taken to implement the plan

10. Can teachers be too empathetic—can they put themselves too much into another person's shoes?   1 2 3 4

    - Understands empathy as different from sympathy

11. What do you enjoy most about teaching?   1 2 3 4

    - Student growth

12. A student told another teacher that your class was boring. What would you do?   1 2 3 4

    - Seeks more information based on a concern for student needs

13. A student is constantly out of his/her seat, bothers others constantly, and has difficulty staying on task. What are some possible causes, and possible remedies?   1 2 3 4

    - Content too difficult
    - Medical causes
    - I've had a student like that, and
    - Age-appropriate reasons, strategies

14. Tell me what you do to cause students to be successful.   1 2 3 4

    - Listening
    - Helping students
    - Teaching strategies
    - Identifying needs and interests
    - Positive attitude
    - Building positive relations

15. How do you know when you are doing a good job of listening?   1   2   3   4

    • Looks to person speaking for clues
    • Person continues to share
    • Person comes back another time
    • When the person speaking is helped

16. Follow-up questions, if any?   1   2   3   4

    _____

    _____

17. Please seek the following information:

    _____
    _____
    _____

Summary

Strengths:

_____
_____
_____
_____

Weaknesses:

_____
_____
_____
_____

Total Points:

_____

Figure 4.10 The Interview Questions

The goal of the interview process is to identify leading candidates for employment who are: (1) **best qualified** to produce the results sought in this position, (2) **best equipped** by experience, training, and temperament to perform effectively in this type of job environment, and (3) **most able to perform effectively** the priority actions required in this position. The following are a sample of questions that could be used to evaluate a prospective applicant's teaching abilities. All questions will relate to the Certificated Personnel Requisition and are used to define the skills of teaching as well as evaluate performance.

1. Please review your background and tell us how your educational experiences have prepared you for the teaching profession.

    _____ appropriate educational background: course work, subject area classes

    _____ plans for continuing education

    _____ Master's Degree

    _____ extensive study with age level/subject matter

    _____ professional activities

2. Why did you want to become a teacher and what do you wish to accomplish?

    _____ purpose for being a teacher

    _____ desire to help students learn; commitment *to each* student

    _____ positive statements/feelings about teaching profession

    _____ seeing students grow and develop

    _____ satisfaction in helping others

    _____ contribute to society

    _____ willingness to grow and be the best

3. What experiences have you had that have prepared you to teach middle school students?

    _____ student teaching

    _____ substitute teaching/long-term assignments

    _____ prior contractual experiences

    _____ volunteer work outside of school day

    _____ extra-curricular experiences

    _____ civic experiences

_____ positive experiences with students

4. What instructional skills should an effective teacher demonstrate and what methods should be used to implement these skills?

_____ knowledge and use of instructional techniques

_____ references to specific instructional models

_____ plans and implements effective lesson plans

_____ understands goals and objectives

_____ implements new skills and ideas

_____ uses a variety of learning styles and methods in presenting lessons

_____ ability to assess students' needs and prescribe programs to meet those needs

_____ plans and paces appropriate lessons

5. What is your strongest asset that you will bring to the teaching profession and please share and explain an example of that strength?

_____ self-awareness assessment

_____ ability to diagnose personal strengths

_____ ability to describe

6. What area would you like to develop in yourself and what strategies do you have for improving your own performance?

_____ ability to diagnose own needs

_____ plan for professional growth

_____ plans to implement growth

_____ commitment to education as a profession

7. How and with whom do you see yourself interacting in this teaching assignment? Give an example of how you have worked with individuals and describe how you handled a situation that was difficult or sensitive.

_____ ability to work both as an individual _and_ as part of a **team**

_____ understands complexity and makeup of team members

_____ ability to work within a consensus model of decision making

_____ respectful, sensitive, and understanding of others

_____ development of interactive strategies

_____ professional

8. How would you prepare your classroom and yourself prior to the first day of school?

____ ability to present ideas into logical statements

____ prepared and positive toward assignment

____ demonstrated ability to sequence activities

____ thoroughness of specific plan described

____ demonstrated ambition, involvement, high energy level

____ initiative

____ ability to pace self in activities

____ successful in implementing plans

9. Describe your classroom management style and discuss discipline strategies you would use for middle school students.

____ establishment of clear parameters; teach the rules

____ understands that positive reinforcement and high expectations are vital to student success

____ importance of student individual needs; consistency, fairness

____ appropriate, positive, preventive approach

____ caring, sincere concern for others

____ well-formulated plan

____ provides clear, positive feedback

____ assisting toward self-discipline

____ development of courtesy, self-control, respect, responsibility

We have one more question to ask you and then we will be happy to answer any questions that you may have.

10. What are some ways in which you would enhance our Block Program (Social Studies, Language Arts, and Reading) to make it challenging, interesting, a meaningful learning experience, and popular?

____ demonstrates a depth and breadth of knowledge of theory and content

____ extent and quality of basic preparation

____ evidence of planning and good organization

____ variety of instructional techniques

____ effectively supports curriculum design

_____ knowledge of current and new educational developments

_____ continues professional preparation and growth

11. At this time, do you have any questions for us?

Following the completion of the interview process a designated interviewer should thank the candidate for coming, and should give the candidate guidelines as to the procedures that will follow. A timeline for notification should be given and a personal contact should be made to the candidate, whether or not he or she is hired. Further, the candidate should be told that, "Should any questions arise after you leave here today, please feel free to contact me and I will try to answer your questions."

At this time the interviewing team needs to have an in-depth discussion about the candidate to determine some of the following:

- Overall communication skills
- Evaluation of written materials
- Organization of thoughts
- Clear, on target, thoughtful, appropriate responses to questions
- Enthusiastic, intuitive, caring, knowledgeable, alive, a learner, a risk taker, a team player
- Ability to understand questions without excessive clarification
- Concise in expression

Finally, the key question is: Was the team able to identify a leading candidate who is **best qualified, best equipped, and able to perform effectively** as a teacher in your school?

Interview Protocol and Format

The following is the suggested general format for the actual interview, which is designed to be a positive and productive process.

- Greeting by host and giving of information.
  - Start by making the candidate comfortable: always offer water/coffee; some quick small talk; and introductions. Supply name cards for all members of the team and role (parent, principal, student, 3rd grade teacher, secretary, etc.) as well as for the candidate.
  - Statement to set the tone: "I want to tell you how pleased we are to have you as a candidate. Of 60 applicants, you are one of six chosen to be interviewed."

- Tell the candidate about the position: grade level, school, strengths and weaknesses of situation, teamwork at that location: "We're looking for someone to mold into that team and make Franklin Elementary more effective."

- *Now*: "We're going to ask you some questions, then you can ask us some."

- "Could you tell us about yourself, your experience, education, family, interest areas, so we have a common place to launch into our questions?"

- Ask candidate to tell about a particular lesson he or she has taught in the last few years (months) where he or she really enjoyed the process. You are listening for details, connections, kids' learning. (Use of Personnel Requisition can guide you.)

- "If I were to come into your room sometime during the year, tell me what I'd see; what the students would be doing, what your role would be, what the room would look like."

- *Strengths*: "If I were to call your principal or someone who knows your work, what would they tell me about you *and* your work at…?" (Record mentally, as interviewee doesn't know if you've called or not.)

- *Weaknesses*: "I have one more question. Then I'll give you an opportunity to ask some of us.…What is it you are working on as a teacher that I could help you with, if you were hired?" This gives you as administrator a beginning place for later reference checks or assistance that you need to provide.

- *Close*: Candidate asks questions; then you express your thanks to him or her, state when you'll be doing your reference checks, and the day when you will be calling finalists. Also: "If you have questions in the meantime, please call me at.…" Reaffirm by telling candidate that all of the candidates *could* fill the position, that you are simply looking for the *best match*. Candidates can now leave with a positive feeling about themselves and the district.

Principal Selection Criteria and Procedures

The selection procedures for principals parallel that for teachers, but with some differences. For one, the process is more public, often involving the community as well as parents. Second, the district office and superintendent are intimately involved because the principal, besides being the leader of the building also becomes a member of the district leadership team. Third, there almost always is an assessment phase. This can range from a formal presentation on such topics as improving student learning to viewing of a video of a teacher lesson and writing an evaluation.

Criteria for Principal Selection

Education

- Master's degree in educational administration or related field, and appropriate state principal certification
- Academic background in clinical supervision, curriculum, instruction, and staff development

Successful Experience

- Supervising instructional and support staff
- Supervising and evaluating educational programs as an administrator
- Classroom instruction

Demonstrated Proficiencies

- Participating team member in district-level policy decisions
- Effective use of written and oral communication
- Proven positive and productive interactions with students, staff, parents, and community
- Strong academic preparation and leadership in school program and instructional improvement, including current best practices in core academic disciplines
- Skills in collaborative decision making and consensus building
- Knowledge of, and leadership in staff supervision, including ability to effectively evaluate classroom instruction and to help teachers improve instruction
- Evidence of leadership in improving student achievement and being accountable for results

Primary Responsibilities

- Serve as the instructional leader.
- Help staff members place emphasis on performance-based education, curriculum, and instructional practices that teach academic skills and encourage analytical and creative thinking, problem solving, communication, and citizenship in students.

- Utilize research-based decision making and effective practices consistent with the school district strategic plan.

- Work with students, staff, and the community to maintain a school climate that provides for the educational needs of students while expanding the use of technology and implementing an enriched, culturally-diverse curriculum at all grade levels.

- Maintain knowledge of district policies and procedures, state and federal law, and organizational goals as they relate to areas of responsibility.

- Collaborate with staff and parents in designing and scheduling programs to meet building and district objectives, in establishing the necessary budget allocations for the school program, and in recommending personnel for positions within the building.

- Ensure student and staff safety and security, including the discipline and management of students in all phases of the school program.

Maintain positive relationships and involvement of staff, parents, and the school community in meeting the needs of a diverse student population.

A Special Case—Applicants With Disabilities

The Americans with Disabilities Act (ADA) was signed into law on July 10, 1990. It affects every employer with 15 or more employees as of July 26, 1994.

The intent of the ADA is to prevent discrimination against qualified people with disabilities. The law requires that employers no longer screen out disabled individuals solely on the basis of their disability. School districts may no longer conduct preemployment inquiries into the nature of the applicant's disability, but can inquire about the candidate's ability to complete job tasks that are part of the job description. School districts generally make sure that the physical facilities are handicap-accessible but should also provide current, accurate, and relevant job descriptions.

The interview process must also be handled appropriately:

- make the interview accessible

- do not automatically assume that the applicant needs assistance, but be ready to provide it

- ask all questions in a professional and straightforward manner

During the interview process, questions should not be asked about:

- the nature of the disability

- the severity of the disability

- the condition causing the disability
- any prognosis or expectation regarding the disability
- whether the applicant will need special treatment or special leave because of the disability

---

Key Idea

- Provide the applicant with the job description and ask if there is any reason why he or she cannot perform the essential functions of the job.
- Further, provide the previous employer or student treacher supervisor with the job description and ask the above question.

Reference Checks

When making reference calls, listen for specific areas the previous principal might mention, which are critical, such as discipline/management. Asking a question such as "Since you know Miss J. better than I, what question should I ask that I haven't asked?" This part encompasses part of "Getting Information"—the reading between the lines, or listening for what is *not* said.

In some cases, a district has prepared job-related questions as part of its "Verifying References" step. At this point it is common for a district to use a telephone reference check form. Such a form is shown here as Background Reference Check (Figure 4.11). Another excellent suggestion for checking references is to visit the candidate's current place of employment.

FIGURE 4.11 Background Reference Check

This review is to be completed and submitted to the Human Resources Office prior to recommending an applicant for hire.

Applicant: _____

Checked by: _____ Date: _____

Name of Agency: _____

Name of Reference and Position: _____

Procedure:

♦ Identify yourself by name and position

♦ Indicate you are considering hiring this applicant and that all information given will be confidential.

♦ Indicate N/A if question does not apply.

♦ Complete the following by verifying it:

1. Verify dates of employment from application and/or résumé.

   _____

2. How do you know this applicant and did you evaluate him/her?

   _____

3. Why did applicant leave employment with your organization?

   _____

4. Do you know of any health conditions that would interfere with job performance or attendance?

   _____ No   _____ Yes (if yes, indicate reasons.)

   _____

5. What is this person's greatest strength?

   _____

6. What is this person's greatest weakness?

   _____

7. Would you rehire this person? If no, why?

   _____

8. Are you aware of any circumstances or activities where this applicant has been involved in substance abuse, addictions, or sexual misconduct?

   _____ No   _____ Yes If yes, give details.

   _____

9. How would you rate this applicant on a ten-point scale (1 = low, 10 = high) in the following areas? Indicate number given after each area.

- Effort to improve _____
- Degree of adaptability/flexibility_____
- Level of cooperation with others _____
- Instructional abilities _____
- Strengths of teacher _____
- Staff relationships _____

10. Since you know the candidate better than I, what question should I ask that I haven't asked?

Additional Questions and Answers

11. Question:_____

    Answer: _____

12. Question: _____

    Answer: _____

Thank the reference, affirm confidentiality, and practice it.

Position Description

An effective instrument for the principal's use is the Position Description. It is similar to the Position Announcement, but serves as a communication piece between the principal and the teacher at time of hiring and induction. It can be discussed between the two individuals, and further defines the required and desired qualifications and duties of the position. When the two parties complete discussion about this description, both will sign and date the form to make a collaborative agreement. Figure 4.12 is a sample of a position description.

Figure 4.12 Position Description

1. Position Title: Primary Teacher
2. Division Title: Multi-Age Program
3. Department or School: Elementary School
4. Title of Immediate Supervisor: Principal
5. General Duties:
   - Teach primary students in a contained, nongraded classroom setting, planning instruction that meets individual needs, interests, and abilities of students
   - Cooperatively plan with the multi-age teacher team
6. Specific Duties:
   - Teach language arts, math, science, social studies, health, art, and P.E. per district-adopted curriculum
   - Assist in the teaching of music, computers, and library skills
   - Create a safe learning environment by establishing clear learning and behavioral expectations
   - Keep appropriate records on students' progress
   - Evaluate students' academic and social growth
   - Communicate students' progress with parents through report cards and conferences, or at times when the rate of learning/behavior changes significantly
   - Attend and participate in staff meetings
   - Participate in staff development sessions for personal/professional growth
   - Work with multi-age staff on learning themes, curriculum spirals, and discipline model for the school
   - Keep the principal informed
7. Qualifications:
   - Current State Teaching Certificate with an elementary endorsement (*Required*)
   - Training in Developmentally appropriate Science and Health Curriculum (Desired)
   - Training in Math-Their-Way (Desired)
   - Experience in integrating the curriculum (Desired)

- Experience in dealing with multiple ages, developmental stages, and abilities in a contained classroom setting (Desired)

8. Discussed and agreed to this _____ day of _____, 20__

Between _____ & _____

Improving the Process

It is important to seek feedback from those interviewed in order to improve the interview process. This feedback should be sought from all interviewed candidates. Figure 4.13 is an example of such a form.

Figure 4.13 Sample School District
Personnel Department Candidate's Evaluation
of School District Interview Team

As we continually strive to refine our selection process, we are interested in feedback from you, the candidate, who are obviously a key participant in the process. We do not ask for your name to protect your right to confidentiality. Please complete your rating following the directions noted below. You may leave this form with the building secretary or send it directly to the School District, Attention: Human Resources Department.

Position: _____ Location: _____

Directions: Please rate your interview team on a scale from 1-6, 6 representing the most positive rating. Place the numeric rating in the blank line.

_____ Were you appropriately introduced to the interview team?

_____ Was the size of the interview team appropriate?

_____ Was the interview conducted in a professional but congenial manner?

_____ Were all questions job-related?

_____ Through both questions and answers, did you feel well informed about the position and its expectations?

_____ Were you provided ample opportunity to ask questions?

_____ Did the team adequately respond to your questions?

_____ Did the team explain the timeline(s) for selection and future notification to you?

_____ Your overall assessment of your interview.

_____ Your overall assessment and rating of the team.

Other Comments: _____

_____

Thank you for completing this evaluation and for your interest in the School District.

Recommendation

Once the committee has determined a candidate for selection, the district personnel office takes responsibility to review the committee's work. This review is the formal checking of legal and other information, including:

+ credentials such as training and recommendations
+ letters of application
+ responses to topics on supplementary application
+ responses to interview questions
+ contact with previous supervisors

The chosen candidate often must have a final interview with the principal or district personnel officer. This final interview is intended to verify that the candidate meets all the district requirements for employment. If this interview confirms the earlier finding of the interview team, then the candidate is recommended to the superintendent and/or board for hire.

Supporting documentation in behalf of the candidate along with the screening evaluation, interview evaluation, and telephone reference check reports go on file for future reference. Upon candidate acceptance of the offer, the personnel officer reviews the written recommendation and supporting information from the interviewers and informs the candidate that he or she will

+ be recommended for the position
+ receive a general statement about the type of contract that will be issued (Letter of Intent)
+ be expected to verify in writing his or her willingness to accept a contract if offered
+ be expected to present documents, as per P.L. 99-603, which establish eligibility to work, and attest, in writing, his or her eligibility to work.

The personnel office then proceeds with securing official statements from previous employers, evaluating transcripts for salary schedule placement, issuing the appropriate contract, and taking care of the business issues of payroll information and teaching certificate registration. Usually the new teacher's principal or district office will also proceed with issuing standard handbooks and other policy information, performance standards and expectations, and responsibilities.

Technology in the Selection Process

In today's computer age, some school districts are electronically scanning resumes to maximize efficiency in their search for new employees. In addition there are some excellent resources on the internet regarding the selection process.

- ◆ www.teacherhiring.net

  This is a comprehensive and excellent site that has been adapted from *Effective Teacher Hiring: A Guide to Getting the Best* by Kenneth Peterson (2002). Select an information page from the following topics on teacher selection and hiring:

  - Bibliography on Teacher Hiring, Interviewing, Employment
  - Principles of Effective Teacher Hiring
  - Tips for Interviewing Teacher Candidates
  - A Taxonomy and Examples of Teacher Interview Questions
  - Study Guide for Expertise on Teacher Hiring
  - A Bill of Rights for Teacher Hiring
  - Topics for Training Teacher Selectors
  - Forms for Teacher Selection and Hiring
  - Links to Information on Teacher Hiring
  - Sample Job Description
  - **Reference Book on Teacher Hiring**
  - **Reference Book on Teacher Evaluation**
  - Web Site on Teacher Evaluation

- ◆ www.educationworld.com "P-files"

  This is an internet site that asks volunteer principals to share information regarding a posed question. One such question that involves selection is: What are the ten most important qualities principals look for in new teachers?

- ◆ www.teachinla.coml

  This site is a very comprehensive site for human resources forms and details the teacher application process in Los Angeles, CA.

Conclusion

Teacher selection is such a complex process and an important administrative task. In selecting the most capable professionals for teaching positions, interviewers must be wise appraisers of candidates and astute forecasters of future teacher performance. Selection and staffing is only one part of the human resources continuum. It is about matching people as well as their career needs and capabilities with the positions and career paths that a particular district has available. It is just the beginning of what should be a productive relationship for both the new staff member and the district. Yes, you want *top-notch* teachers, but it takes top-notch selection processes to get them. It is a growth process, where the teams are trained for interviewing, questions are meaningful and attuned to the "match" desired, and the resulting assignment is evaluated for staff development and analysis. Thus, the Human Resources Staffing Function Cycle, as illustrated in Figure 4.14, never stops!

Figure 4.14 Human Resources Staffing Function Cycle

Selection—Case Study

Mr. Menzies, as the new principal, had completed the interview process. Yet he intuitively thought something was not quite right. He wanted Mr. Cowan as math teacher and the committee consisting of staff, students, and community members had unanimously wanted Mr. Lorentz. As the new principal he was unsure of his next move. He could recommend Mr. Lorentz and live with the decision, or he could hire Mr. Cowan and try to explain his decision to the committee and the rest of the staff.

Mr. Menzies decided to do more comprehensive reference checking by calling principals, superintendents and others who were not on the reference lists of the Mr. Lorentz or Mr. Cowan. After making many calls including some calls to the next-to-last districts, it became clear to him that Mr. Cowan was indeed the superior choice. He had promised his colleagues in the other districts that the information given to him was confidential and he would treat it as such.

Questions for the prospective principal:

1. Whose decision is it to hire the teachers in a school?
2. What is the appropriate role of the committee and how should this be communicated?
3.. What should Mr. Menzies do now? Violate the confidences of others or risk the potential lack of support of the committee process?

Comprehensive Questions

1. Reflect on interviews of which you have been a participant as an interviewer or interviewee. What were the most effective elements of these interviews?

2. Assessments labs are becoming increasingly popular. What would you ask a candidate to do in order to determine effectiveness?

3. Develop a plan for the training of the interview team.

Extended Activities

1. Determine the difference between an excellent candidate and a good candidate by reviewing application materials.

2. Participate in the selection and interviewing process as part of your last term of internship.

3. Perform/develop hiring procedures as if you are already a principal and will need to hire individuals for your building next year.

References

Al-Tubaiy, K. (1993). Five steps to better hiring, *The Executive Educator, 15*(8), 21–22.

Bateman, C. F. (1986). Want superstar teachers? Scout for talent and recruit like crazy. *American School Board Journal, 173*(6), 27.

Buffie, E. G. (1989). *The principal and leadership.* Bloomington, IN: Phi Delta Kappa.

Coastal Human Resources (1996). *Legal and effective interviewing.* Virginia Beach, VA: Coastal Video Communication Corp.

Collier, B. H. (1987). Don't let employees slip away unnoticed: Learn from them. *Executive Educator, 9*(5), 17–19.

DeLandsheere, G. (1980). Teacher selection. *Prospects: Quarterly Review of Education, 10*(3), 318–324.

Fear, R. A. (1984). *The evaluation interview,* 3rd ed. New York: McGraw-Hill.

Goldstein, W. (1986*). Recruiting superior teachers: The interview process.* Bloomington, IN: Phi Delta Kappa.

Greathouse, C. L. (1992, January). 10 Common hiring mistakes. *Industry Week, 20,* 22–24.

Herman, S. J. (1993). *Hiring right: A practical guide.* Thousand Oaks, CA: Sage Publishing.

Niece, R. (1983). The interview and personnel selection: Is the process valid and reliable? *Clearing House, 56,* 234.

Paulk, L. J. (1984). Employee exit interviews. *Spectrum, 2*(1), 7–13.

Saville, A., and J. Hill (1989). *The exit interview: A generic model.* Non-Classroom Material. (ERIC Document Reproduction Service No. ED 310-523.)

5

Orientation and Induction

Reasons for Studying Orientation and Induction

- After recruitment and selection, induction is the next major human resources activity geared to enable the teacher to be a success.
- Induction is often not well done in schools, or not done at all.
- Time proactively invested during the induction period will pay off handsomely during the career of the teacher.
- High expectations for teachers are very important. The induction period is the time to communicate those expectations.
- A third of beginning teachers quit within their first three years on the job. We don't stand for this dropout rate among students and we can no longer afford it among our teachers.

> *An effective induction program is the mortar that cements pre-service training to professional development and leads to teacher success and student achievement.*

ISLLC Standards Covered in this Chapter

Standard 2:

- A school administrator is an educational leader who promotes the success of all students by advocating, nurturing, and sustaining a school culture and instructional program conducive to student learning and staff professional growth.

Introduction

The recruitment and selection process is time-consuming and expensive. After reading through hundreds of applications, sitting through interviews, calling to check references, recommending a candidate for the position, and the principal and selection committee have obtained the employee of their choice, what should the principal do to ensure the success and retention of this new staff member?

The ideal induction program assists in the successful assimilation and development of the beginning teacher, the veteran teacher newly hired into the district, the teacher transferred from other buildings within the same district, and the teacher transferred into different grade or content areas within the same building. Induction is the process designed to acquaint the newly employed teacher with the community, the school district, the school, the program and their colleagues.

Most school districts provide an *orientation program* designed to inform new employees about payroll, health and insurance plans, rules and regulations, and locations of district buildings. These orientation programs also introduce district administrative staff and give an overview of the community. *Induction programs*, on the other hand, are designed to include the information given during orientation as well as provide collegial connections; instructional support; and acculturation to the community, school, and classroom throughout at least the first year as a new employee.

Research shows that in the United States a gradual systematic induction of new teachers is the exception. This is a problem because the teaching profession is one of the few in which beginners are expected to fulfill the same responsibilities as veterans (Reinhartz, 1989). Consider what the research literature has to say about new teachers:

♦ Almost 15% leave teaching after 1 year.

♦ Between 40 and 50% leave after fewer than 7 years.

♦ As a group, the most academically talented teachers are the least likely to stay in the profession.

♦ Younger teachers, when compared to more experienced teachers, report more emotional exhaustion and a greater degree of depersonalization. (Tonneson and Patterson, 1992)

New teachers often enter the teaching profession possessing three characteristics: they are often *unfocused workers,* meaning that they are unable to think of appropriate ways to improve their teaching; they are *highly* motivated and coachable; and they tend to be *idealistic,* with their expectations often exceeding what they can reasonably achieve. These characteristics point to the need and possibilities for teacher induction programs (Young et al., 1993). Additionally, first-year teachers share common problems. According to Kevin Ryan (1986), there are six common problems facing the beginning teacher:

♦ **Shock of the familiar:** Teachers have to meet many unexpected demands now that they are "on the other side of the desk." These demands include paperwork, a need for information by the administration, communication with parents and colleagues, managing several activities and students at one time, lesson plans, and lesson implementation. An additional demand is created by the difference between being a student-teacher and the teacher in charge of everything from instruction and discipline to assessment, organization, and room decorations.

♦ **Students:** Teachers usually enter the profession because they are concerned for children and want to be an effective force in the lives of young people. However, new teachers are unfamiliar and discouraged by the reality of students' attitudes and behaviors that are incongruent with the teachers' personal experiences and views of school culture. Teachers are also confused and discouraged by the social distance that students want in the student-teacher relationship. Students do not want another buddy; they want an effective teacher. This role confusion may cause discipline problems in the classroom. Student discipline for new teachers is sometimes a problem because they must learn to be comfortable with their new authority, plus learn to deal with students respectfully. Beginning teachers also need to learn how to deal with misbehavior quickly and effectively.

♦ **Parents:** Teachers usually aren't taught how to deal with parents. They often expect to find the "June and Ward Cleaver" support from the 1950s, but instead they find conflict due to parents' concerns about their competency, or the "my child can do no wrong" attitude. Also of concern to beginning teachers is the stability of the home life of students. New teachers may have a difficult time relating to the feelings and pressures of the parents, interpreting shortness of time or money as neglect.

♦ **Administrators:** Beginning teachers may have ambivalent feelings about the principal. On one hand, they feel indebted to the principal for their job; on the other hand, they feel anxious because of the authority the principal has over them. It takes time to build trust.

♦ **Fellow teachers:** Beginning teachers often feel isolated because of jealousy or pettiness stemming from rumored or feared talents and energy of beginning teachers. Neglect and social differences stemming from already developed social groups is another source of isolation.

♦ **Instruction:** Beginning teachers are expected to know what to teach and when to teach it. However, district-provided resources are often lacking and because of generic preservice preparation, they may lack the specific skills to develop effective lessons, presentation, and assessment materials for their assignment.

Several of these same problems, such as obtaining resources, authority conflict, collegial relations, and parent/student relationships, also affect veteran teachers in transition.

Awareness of these problems is the first step in developing a solution that can be pursued by the individual teacher, the training institutions, and the school district. This chapter will focus on the following components for an effective induction program:

♦ Purpose
♦ Implications
♦ District Orientation Programs
♦ School Orientation Programs
♦ Role of the Principal
♦ Mentorships
♦ Models and Frameworks of Induction Programs

Purposes of Induction Programs

Wilkinson (1997) in a survey of 201 new teachers in Missouri found that beginning teachers wanted:

♦ Assistance when making some decisions; e.g., dealing with angry parents.

♦ Assistance with teaching responsibilities; e.g., help in finding materials and teaching supplies.

♦ To select their assistance and teaching conditions; e.g., I would have appreciated more feedback on my performance.

♦ An individual professional development plan; e.g., 94% wanted a mentor teacher.

♦ Information about facilities, policies, and procedures; e.g., one-third of the respondents said they started teaching without having basic information about school facilities, rules, procedures, and expectations for their teaching.

The single most important thing you can do in administration is to hire good teachers; the second most important thing is to find ways to keep them (Tomlin, 1993). The main purpose of a teacher induction program is to acculturate the new employee into a specific school district and/or teaching position. School districts usually begin this process by formally welcoming the new employee and providing information about the district. Information regarding demographics, payroll, district rules and policies, and the introduction of district administrators are key elements to the orientation session. It may also include visits to district school buildings, a tour of the community, and visits with their principals and department or grade-level chair. Figures 5.1 and 5.2 list objectives of induction programs.

Figure 5.1 Objectives Common to All School Induction Programs

1. To make teachers feel welcome and secure
2. To enable teachers to become members of the faculty team
3. To offer all newly hired and transfer teachers instructional support and collegial connections
4. To assist teachers to adjust to the work environment
5. To provide information and orientation about:
   - the community
   - the school district
   - the school
   - the faculty and staff
   - the students
   - the educational program
6. To facilitate the opening of the school year
7. To assist teachers in having a successful year—personally and professionally

---

**Figure 5.2 Objectives for Helping
the First-Year Teacher**

1. To explain the school and community culture
2. To aid in gathering materials and equipment
3. To provide a mentor to support and assist
4. To carefully arrange class size and students for success <end>

The induction process should be ongoing and is planned based on district educational goals and expectations. It encourages experienced staff to mentor new teachers in the areas of building processes and procedures, curriculum implementation, and collegial networking. The principal's role is to help develop professional skills in the form of knowledge, attitudes and values necessary for the new employee to become an effective teacher within the school district and the specific building.

Implications

School districts, teachers, and students will all benefit from a well-developed induction program specific to the needs of the community, the district, and the teacher. The program will also help weed out ineffective teachers and teaching practices while developing a context-specific vision of effective teaching practices for promising teachers.

An induction program fosters professional growth of the individual through staff development and collegial relationships. To meet the goal of professional growth for teaching staff, the district must have in place good instructional supervision procedures complete with formative and summative evaluation systems. Also, mentoring and networking, both contrived through district assignment and naturally occurring, will provide good teaching models and strategies for the employee, resulting in professional growth.

Positive outcomes and/or implications include:

♦ Organized mentorships improve communication and facilitate the acculturation into the school community.

♦ Teachers who feel that they belong, that they are learning and improving, and who feel good about themselves and their teaching will be more successful.

♦ Teacher performance will be improved.

♦ Retention rate of promising beginning teachers will increase.

♦ Mandated state requirements for orientation, mentorships, and continuing education for certification will be satisfied.

- Trusting relationships will develop between staff and administrators.

- Teachers will be involved in associations and community organizations.

- People skills will improve.

- Open communication will improve as new teachers are able to speak openly (negatively or positively), without fear of reprisal, at cohort group meeting or with mentor/team groups.

Implementation

There are several ways to implement an effective induction program. Provided here is an exemplary framework. It is only a framework, so adjustments may be made to "fit" the dynamics of individual district and school goals, expectations, and the demographics of the community. Specific models of successful induction programs are included within the framework, with emphasis on mentoring, district orientation responsibilities, and building and administrative responsibilities.

Framework

The staff developer and principal, charged with orientation and induction responsibilities, will encounter groups of anxious beginning teachers each year. How well they orchestrate those activities may determine the length and quality of an individual's professional career, and will also contribute to the level of competence of the district staff.

For beginning school teachers, many questions remain unanswered as they prepare to assume their new professional responsibilities. No matter how thorough the training, how broad the preservice experience, or how successful the student teaching, they approach their first teaching assignment with considerable doubt, concern, and anxiety.

Programs offered by school districts to teachers in the orientation or induction phase of their careers can meet both the needs of the new professionals and the needs of the districts. Based upon findings of research, current practices, and common sense, the following multiphase induction model is presented to assist school districts and staff developers in establishing a program that will achieve positive results. This teacher induction model (see Figure 5.3) has five phases: Definition, Development, Orientation, Operation, and Evaluation.

Figure 5.3 Model Teacher Induction Program as Proposed by Torgeson (1978)

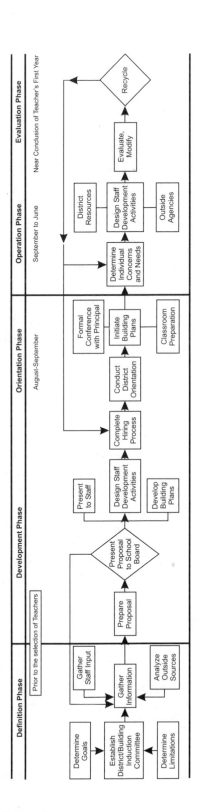

Definition Phase

The first step in developing an effective teacher induction program for a school district is the establishment of a Teacher District Committee. The committee should include a central office administrator such as the director of staff development, an elementary principal, a secondary principal, experienced teachers, and teachers who are completing their first year. A member of the community may be included or, at least, should be available for consultation about appropriate community events and activities.

The committee's first task is to determine the goals for the induction program (see Figure 5.4). Suggested goals include: enhancement of teacher competence, reduction of teacher attrition, improvement of students' instruction, and increased organizational strength for the school.

The committee should also give consideration to the limitations that will influence the committee's proposal. First, budget allocations will indicate funding restrictions. Justify your induction program in terms of the dollars spent as an investment, rather than an expenditure, in the teachers and for the district. Secondly, the committee should note the amount of time projected for involvement by administrators and beginning teachers. In addition, the district's negotiated contract with the local teachers' association should be consulted so that the proposal is in compliance with agreed-upon practices and procedures. And, inevitably, the committee should reflect on various personal philosophies concerning a planned program for induction.

Figure 5.4 Model Teacher Induction Program

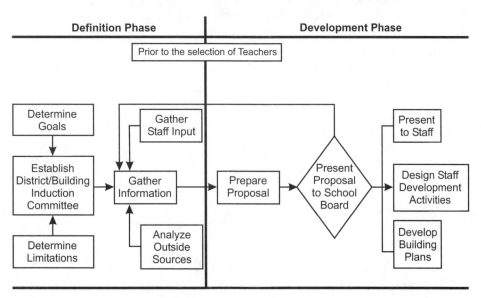

Once the goals of a district induction program have been established, the committee should begin gathering information about similar programs. Even teachers with many years of experience vividly remember their days as beginning teachers and will have suggestions. In nearly every district some induction activities occur each year. The committee needs to be aware of effective past programs. It is appropriate to survey the district's staff about their perspectives concerning their "first year" experiences. A list of questions for the staff might include:

- What information is necessary for a new teacher prior to the beginning of the school year?
- What information should be included during the year?
- How should the information be delivered to the teacher (e.g., small group, large group, handbook, etc.)?
- Who would be best to give the information (e.g., central office, principal, mentor teacher, the teacher's association, etc.)?

Torgeson (1987), in a study of induction in the State of Washington, found that while induction activities occur, some are rated as more effective than others. Figure 5.5 displays the activities and their respective ratings that should be considered as the Induction Committee develops its proposal.

In addition to the district staff, sources outside the district need to be investigated. Other school districts should be contacted to identify their current induction practices. An inquiry sent to the state office of education can determine the availability of state-sponsored programs and/or special funds for beginning teacher programs. Also, the regional educational service district should be contacted about the availability of regional programs. A review of current and professional journals and educational research can ascertain suggested strategies.

Having gathered information from both inside and outside the school district, the committee is ready to begin the process of analyzing the data in light of the previously determined needs and limitations in preparation for designing a teacher induction program. The proposed induction program consists of these phases.

Figure 5.5 Effectiveness of Induction Activities as Rated by Beginning Teachers in Puget Sound (WA) School Districts

Induction Activity	VE	E	SE	NE
Early notification of building and grade assignment	66	24	10	0
Additional time provided to prepare	73	21	6	0
Mentor teacher selected to assist	58	33	7	1
Opportunities to observe experienced teachers	46	25	21	7
Inservice offered throughout the school year	30	58	12	0
Principal observation and feedback	19	61	12	7
Teachers' Association played a role	10	28	42	19
College maintained relationship to support	24	36	19	21
District-wide orientation for new teachers	27	40	24	9
Individual conference with the principal	33	57	7	3
Teacher Handbook was issued	12	43	34	10
Reduced class load was assigned	24	22	27	25

VE = Very Effective   E = Effective
SE = Somewhat Effective   NE = Not Effective

Development Phase

Following this analysis, the committee may begin formulating the induction program for the school district. As the program is being designed, attention is given to coordination with other district programs and/or activities, e.g., the existing staff development program.

The final written proposal includes the goals and objectives of the induction program, an outline of possible activities, and a method of evaluation. With the approval of the superintendent, the proposal is ready to be submited to the school board.

The written proposal should be presented to the school board for approval and/or adoption as a district program. Such a presentation will increase the school board members' awareness of the critical nature of the teachers' first year and demonstrate the need for the district's commitment to support the teachers as they begin their careers.

Once accepted, the induction program is then presented to administrators and staff. They have an opportunity to discuss their roles in the plan and brainstorm strategies to be used. Because, in practice, principals assume the majority of the responsibility for the ongoing induction program, they should develop a formal plan for the coming year (Badertscher, 1978). There are advantages to having principals work together in order to draw from a wider span of experiences and ideas in the development of such a plan. They may also draw from the activities suggested in the adopted program.

The formal plan designed by the principals should be structured to cover the needs of the beginning teachers and the goals of the district. For example, the principals can prioritize areas to be covered during the conference between beginning teacher and their principal. A variety of approaches to disseminate information about areas of concern should be considered to conserve time and avoid overwhelming the beginner. And most importantly, the principal should schedule a specific time for the conference to occur. The length of the conference should be adequate to allow both parties to express themselves.

The district's staff development department may begin developing a year-long program for professional growth. Other groups, such as the local teachers' association, the parent-teacher organization, and the Chamber of Commerce, may participate in the planning. This program may include in-service sessions focusing on district adoption curriculum and/or workshops on the district's instructional model. The staff development department may also wish to request colleges and universities in the area to conduct courses which may be needed by the beginning teacher, for example, classroom management. Another agency with which to coordinate plans would be the regional educational agencies.

Orientation Phase

District Orientation Programs

This step of the orientation phase (Figure 5.6), which is the initial part of the comprehensive program, usually begins with a district-wide session and should take the form of an extended contract for beginning teachers, as they are generally required to report to work before other teachers, often from one to four days. If so, they should be compensated for the additional days.

Figure 5.6 Model Teacher Induction Program— Orientation Phase

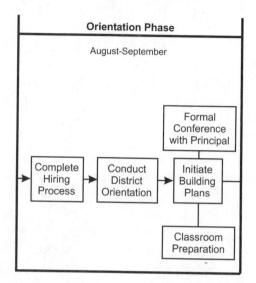

The actual implementation begins as the hiring process is completed. As the decision to hire a specific individual is made, the Director of Human Resources or principal telephones the candidate and welcomes the individual to the district. Written confirmation of selection follows promptly. As soon as possible the newly hired teacher is notified of the specific grade level and building assignment. Once those assignments have been determined, the principal telephones the new teacher and invites the teacher to visit the building and makes curriculum guides available.

The school district has an opportunity to make a favorable first impression on the new employee during the orientation session scheduled before the beginning of the new school year. The district orientation is implemented and designed by the personnel department and the staff development department. The district orientation program serves as a formal welcoming of all new staff members, and provides necessary information regarding the district, community, and schools. Suggested components include: introduction of chief administrators, explanation of necessary business office procedures, a tour or overview of the community, and the statement of district philosophy, vision, and mission. Shelton et al. (1992) offer a six-session orientation plan consisting of:

- **Making contact.** This session gives the new teacher an opportunity to meet the people the teacher will be working with. "Key people" should be introduced, with a description of how each will assist in the transition of the new employee.

- **In school and around town.** This session gives new employees a sightseeing tour of the community and school district building
- **Part of the big picture.** This is the organizational session. An overview of the district's vision, philosophy, goals, and objectives will provide the new employee with a better idea of how his or her efforts will contribute to the school district's mission.
- **Student matters.** During this session topics should include classroom management, positive reinforcement strategies, classroom rules and expectations, grading, corporal punishment or the absence thereof, alternative education programs, and suspension and expulsion.
- **Teacher dos and don'ts.** Review teacher illness procedures for reporting, bad weather days, school closures, and day-to-day procedures.
- **Tools and techniques.** Clarify curriculum expectations, the process for ordering materials, and introduce mentor partnerships.

As an overall component of the teacher induction program, the school district can take the following steps to making the transition easier and more rewarding for new teachers:

- Develop policies that stress the importance of induction programs and that require their implementation.
- Work with local universities to offer classes and programs new teachers can take for college credit. In-service credits are available, as well as college course credit. A booklet with a listing of all courses available is provided to each district employee before the closing of the school year, and employees are encouraged to participate in this staff development and professional growth.
- Reimburse new teachers' tuition for courses designed to help them.
- Provide training for mentor teachers.
- Introduce new teachers to school board members and invite them to attend board meetings.
- Provide an in-depth orientation to the district that begins during the summer, before the hectic opening of school. Include facility and school tours, discussion about the organization, and introductions to key administrators.
- Hire substitute teachers to fill in so new teachers can observe the classes of exemplary teachers.

- Interview new teachers at the end of the first year to find out whether and where they need additional help
  (Tonneson and Patterson, 1992).

Although a beginning teacher induction program may exist in a school district, two groups of beginners may slip through the cracks of even the most structured programs. These groups include teachers employed after the start of the school year and itinerant staff such as speech therapists or music teachers. Because the first of the two groups misses the orientation activities conducted before school and the second group of teachers is not assigned to a specific building, their induction needs may be overlooked. Special efforts should be made to assist these teachers.

Acknowledging the importance of the district-wide orientation session and the conference(s) with the principal, the time for the new teacher to prepare the classroom and plan for instruction must be protected. Torgeson (1987) stated that this task is uppermost in the mind of beginning teachers.

Principal's Role in the Induction Program

In addition to the orientation session, this would be an appropriate time for the principal to confer with the new employee. Time should be made available to hold several shorter conferences rather than one or two longer ones. It would be appropriate at this time for the principal to introduce the staff handbook.

The orientation process now becomes more personalized as the new employees are introduced to those with whom they will be working directly. The same components should apply at the building level as in the district orientation process.

The second segment of the orientation phase occurs upon the return of the experienced staff. During these days before school begins, the tempo of the preparation for the opening of school accelerates. The new teacher, like the veteran, needs to put the finishing touches on the classroom and then direct attention to planning for instruction.

Key Idea

Besides orientation of the beginning teacher by the principal and teachers, provide some time for the school secretary and custodian to meet with the new teachers.

It is during this time that the principal conducts the first staff meeting and reviews the staff handbook containing schedules, building policies, discipline procedures, and so on. The principal should see to it that the beginning teacher is introduced to "key" staff members and parents (Applegate, Flora, & Lasley, 1980). If it was not done earlier, the principal should make certain the new employee knows the location of teaching supplies and curriculum materials and how to requisition them.

As the opening of school approaches, the principal should confer with the beginning teachers about remaining questions, about supplies, and about final plans for the opening of school. This is the time for the principal to express confidence in and support for the new teacher. If ever a pep talk was needed, this is the time.

The principal assumes many roles in the beginning teacher's first-year experience. The role of the principal is vital to the success of the new teacher. Research indicates that inadequate support by administration contributes significantly to teacher attrition. As a principal you play a vital role in the retention of educators.

The first role of the principal is that of master teacher. The principal can ease the process of acculturation by holding regular sessions specifically designed to assist the new employee. These sessions may be held monthly, or weekly, but should be designed to target areas of concern to the beginning/new teacher. As a master teacher, the principal should provide recent information from journals and research, but also refer to experiences others have had during the induction period. Offer the new teacher tools for enhancing instructional techniques. Tools you may suggest to the new teacher include a voice-activated tape recorder or a video recorder. This will allow the teacher an opportunity for informal evaluation. Allan S. Vann (1991) suggested the following topics for orientation/induction meetings. This process may take several months, but helps alleviate the high dropout rate of beginning teachers.

Classroom Management	Classroom rules
	Effective techniques
	Assertive discipline
	Planning for early finishers
Instructional Techniques	Instructional guidelines
	Effective questioning
	Pause/wait time
Home-School	Monthly newsletter
Communication	Phone calls/notes/conferences
Conferencing	Meet the Teacher night
	Parent-teacher conferences
	Positive attitude

Grading and Testing	Frequent assessment
	Comments and reactions
	Checking assignments
Homework	District guidelines
Motivation	Techniques
Time Management	Time guidelines for subjects
	Overplanning vs. underplanning
	Gifted/average/handicapped time needs
Confidentiality	Avoiding gossip
	Maintaining confidentiality
Special Students	Contact with special education teachers
	Pullout assignments
	Referral process
Curriculum Priorities in	Grade-level objectives
Reading and Writing	Journals/silent reading
	Teaching of reading process
Unit/Lesson Planning	Techniques
	Unit plan model
	Sequential development
Curriculum Activity File	Sharing creative ideas
Professionalism	Professional associations
	Professional journals
	Activity beyond classroom

The principal must also serve as an evaluator of the beginning teacher. During the orientation phase, provide the beginning teacher with information that clarifies expectations in the classroom and how these will be evaluated. Establish an observation time with the teacher within the first month of school. Explain how the evaluation process will be implemented using the following cycle:

♦ Preobservation Conference

♦ Observation

♦ Data Analysis and Strategies

- Postobservation Conference
- Postconference Analysis

For this cycle to be effective, it is critical that the principal establish trusting relationships and furnish the teacher with objective data. Observations and evaluations should be timely and effective, providing the teacher with meaningful and applicable feedback for improvement.

Further, the principal needs to be a "guardian angel" for the new staff member. It is the principal's responsibility to limit the new teacher's co-curricular activities, committee involvement, teaching responsibilities, and student load. There will be plenty of time in the future to get involved.

Key Idea

Place new teachers in situations that give them a high probability of success. We have all heard the horror stories. The new teacher who has four "preps," 50% special needs students, works in the portable that was picked bare of any curriculum materials or supplies, and serves as cheerleader advisor, PTA liaison, and building union representative. Is it any wonder that so many new teachers leave the building or profession?

An effective principal will invest time and commitment to the beginning teacher. If you consider this investment as one which affects the lives of hundreds of children each year, it is definitely worthwhile.

Key Idea

Limit the role of the new teacher in extracurricular activities so that the focus can be on becoming successful in the classroom.

Mentor Programs

Early in the orientation phase, a mentor teacher should be identified for the beginning teacher. The most important qualities for effective mentors are good communication skills, outstanding classroom skills, respect of their peers, and desire to participate (Loucks, 1993). Mentors are a source of support and advice to the new employee. Mentors serve as coaches, observing and providing feedback, while demonstrating effective techniques and strategies. Studies found that mentoring programs improve teaching, raise teachers' self-confidence, and increase teacher retention (Ladestro, 1991). Preparation of the mentor teacher is vital to the success of the mentorship, and should be addressed as a priority of the induction program.

Key Idea

Select one of the best teacher mentors from your staff, preferrably not the same grade or subject as the mentee. The new teacher will have plenty of opportunity to obtain assistance from teachers in the same grade or subject area.

It is important that the district provide training for the mentor prior to the assumption of the new responsibility and continue that training throughout the mentoring process. Training of mentor teachers in relation to teacher induction programs should include school district philosophy, needs, and priorities; district policies and operating procedures; working with the adult learner; stages of teacher development; concerns and needs of beginning teachers; clinical supervision, classroom observation, and conferencing skills; teacher reflection, and fostering self-esteem and self-reliance in the novice teacher.

The mentor needs more than pedagogical skills; he or she must be able to communicate with the newcomer openly and supportively. Ideally, the mentor should be someone who enjoys the chance to learn from the helping relationship and who considers working with a newly trained teacher an opportunity to enhance his or her own skills. The mentor teacher is likely to influence more than the new teacher"s instructional skills; the mentor can have a powerful impact upon the values and norms of the new teacher (Fagan and Walter, 1982).

Key Idea

Mentoring is a relationship not an activity.

A. Collin

Developmental relationships such as between a mentor teacher and protégé can be powerful stimuli for change and learning. Research indicates that mentors as well as beginning teachers find that the program enhances their classroom abilities, increases their enthusiasm for teaching, and that they experience positive results involving their teaching, professional growth, and impact on the profession. Teacher retention, collegial relationships, important decision making, development of visions, active learning, support of new professionals, promotion and maintenance of professional standards and emotional support are evidence of the impact a mentor program can have as part of the overall induction program.

With the grim reality of budget cuts, it is evident that the principal must pursue other means of support for the survival of mentorship programs.

Other alternatives to funding mentor programs include utilizing retired teachers to serve as mentors, principal coverage of teacher's classroom to allow the teacher to observe other teachers, and the Collaborative Induction Model, a zero-based budget program undertaken by the state of Texas. However it is funded, the importance of maintaining a mentor program is vital to the success and retention of the beginning teacher.

Key Idea

The principal should monitor the mentoring program throughout the year.

The Quakertown Community School District (Beerer, 2002) decided that time was a critical factor in the induction program and carved out fifteen (15) contractual days each year during the first five years to be spent in the New Teacher Academy. During these 15 days each year, teachers take part in workshops specifically designed for them personal choice staff development, graduate course work, and provide students with enrichment and/or remediation. The responses to this commitment by the district can be captured by Andy Boquist, a third-year teacher who stated "[A]ny district willing to bring its new teachers for two weeks in the summer to help endure a successful start to their teaching career (or an experienced teacher's transition to a new district) was the right district for me (Beerer, 2002)." The following figure (Figure 5.7) illustrates the time commitment to the induction program in Quakertown.

Figure 5.7 Five-Year Induction Plan
Quakertown Community School District, PA—
New Teacher Academy

Year	Summer Academy and Follow-up Days	Staff Development (Personal Choice)	Enrichment/ Remediation	Graduate Degree Program
	Required	Select from Each Column to Complete Day		
1	12 days	0–3 days	0–3 days	None
2	6 days	0–9 days	0–9 days	0–5 days
3	5 days	0–5 days	5–10 days	0–5 days
4	None	0–10 days	5–15 days	0–5 days
5	None	0–10 days	5–15 days	0–5 days

Operation Phase

During the first month of school, the principal should monitor the performance of the beginning teacher carefully by visiting the teacher's classroom and initiating regular discussions with the new teacher. By the end of the month, both parties should begin to identify areas of interest and/or concern which may be addressed in an individually designed program for professional growth (see Figure 5.8).

Figure 5.8 Model Teacher Induction Program— Operation Phase

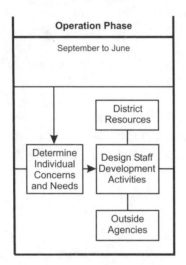

With the teacher's needs identified, appropriate staff development activities may be selected. The principal may have already generated a list of possibilities he or she considered during the development phase of the building level induction program. Resources from both within and outside the school district need to be considered. In North Carolina the State Department of Public Instruction recognizes the need state-wide for induction programs and is creating a training packet to standardize mentoring programs for all school districts (Brown, 2003).

Within the district, the principal and beginning teacher may select from available curriculum and instruction in-services. Observation of experienced teachers may be scheduled as well as a day or two of released time during which the beginner could do long-range planning. The principal should be committed to observations of classroom performance with prompt feedback. New teachers are not best left alone to learn (Ryan, 1979). Classroom visits and conferences support the beginner's instructional goals and prevent the teacher from repeating costly errors. The frequency of the visits, however, should be determined by the individual needs of the beginning teacher.

Sources independent of the school district may once again be used. For example, the local teachers' association may be encouraged to conduct sessions that explain the negotiated agreement and the goals of the organization. College and university bulletins may reveal worthwhile classes that are available locally. It may not be too early for the new teacher to inquire about advanced educational degrees or, at least, about requirements for permanent certification. The regional educational service districts that also conduct workshops and in-service sessions should be consulted. Lastly, community agencies may offer activities that provide information about the community as well as recreational benefits.

Once the list of appropriate activities has been selected, attention should be given to scheduling them in a balanced manner throughout the school year. By individualizing the selection, and jointly determining the schedule, the principal and beginning teacher have developed a long-range program of induction.

Throughout the implementation of this plan, the principal needs to closely monitor the progress being made by the beginning teacher. The principal should caution the new teacher to limit the building and district committee assignments during this busy first year and help the new teacher to say "no" when that response is in the best interest of the teacher and the instructional program.

Evaluation Phase

The final phase of the induction program is the evaluation phase (see Figure 5.9). This phase is important to provide data upon which to base improvements to the program. The plan is then ready for recycling for the incoming group of teachers.

Figure 5.9 Model Teacher Induction Program—Evaluation Phase

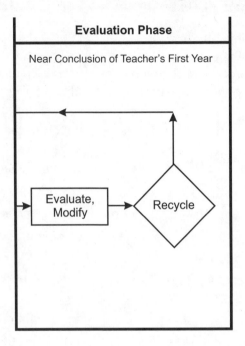

Evaluation Phase

Near Conclusion of Teacher's First Year

Evaluate, Modify

Recycle

Before the end of the school year, both the district and the building induction programs need to be evaluated. On the district level, all beginning teachers need to be surveyed regarding their impressions of the components of the induction program at the district building, a New Teacher Induction Questionnaire (Figure 5.10) is provided to serve as a model for receiving information. The comments and suggestions from this questionnaire should be used along with data from administrators to make needed improvements in the program.

Figure 5.10 Sample New Teacher
Induction Questionnaire—Part I, District

The purpose of this survey, Part I, is to help us determine whether we've provided the needed support and orientation for you to assume successfully your new role as a professional teacher in our school district.

Your candid thoughts and comments are welcome. Please do not sign this form. Thank you.

1. After you were hired, but before you moved to the district, your contact with school personnel made you feel:

    ___ very welcome   ___ somewhat welcome

    ___ somewhat unwelcome   ___ not welcome

2. How helpful were district personnel with your move?

    ___ very helpful   ___ somewhat helpful

    ___ not helpful at all

3. What was your initial impression of the district's overall attitude to teaching and learning?

    ___ very professional   ___ somewhat professional

    ___ somewhat unprofessional ___ very unprofessional

4. What is your current impression of the district's overall attitude to teaching and learning?

    ___ very professional   ___ somewhat professional

    ___ somewhat unprofessional ___ very unprofessional

5. Has the district lived up to your expectations?

    ___ very much so   ___ somewhat

    ___ not really   ___ not at all

6. Please describe what we did best to help you move to and join our school district from the moment you were hired until school started.

    _____

    _____

7. Please describe what we should have done better to help you move to and join our school district from the moment you were hired until school started.

    _____

    _____

8. Please describe in general terms how well we have done in supporting your first two months of teaching in the district.

_____

9. Other comments: _____

_____

_____

Please complete Part II and return both parts to the Superintendent's office.

At the building level, the principal and the beginning teacher need to evaluate the growth achieved and discuss future plans. Together they may decide there is less need for a formalized plan during the second year and may identify only a limited number of activities. Or there may be apparent needs that still need addressing through such a plan. In that case, a new individualized plan may be developed. Figure 5.11 is the outline of a plan designed to help principals seek information from the new teacher regarding the induction program.

Figure 5.11 Sample New Teacher Survey— Part II, School

The purpose of this survey, Part II, is to determine whether school personnel has provided you the needed support and orientation for you to successfully assume your new role as a professional teacher in your assigned school.

		Very Favorable		Neutral Neutral	Very Unfavorable	
1.	What was your initial impression of the building?	5	4	3	2	1
2.	How helpful were building personnel in your orientation?	5	4	3	2	1
3.	I felt welcome and secure	5	4	3	2	1
4.	I had collegial support.	5	4	3	2	1
5.	I had assistance adjusting to the work environment.	5	4	3	2	1
6.	I was given information about the community.	5	4	3	2	1
7.	I was given information about the building.	5	4	3	2	1
8.	I was given sufficient information about the students.	5	4	3	2	1

9.	I was given sufficient information about the programs.	5	4	3	2	1

School Mission

	Training in technology	5	4	3	2	1
	The availability of a mentor	5	4	3	2	1
	Building learning goals	5	4	3	2	1
	Curriculum training	5	4	3	2	1
10.	The facilities were adequate	5	4	3	2	1
11.	School policies were explained	5	4	3	2	1
	Grading	5	4	3	2	1
	Parent/Teacher conferencing	5	4	3	2	1
	Remediation	5	4	3	2	1
	Summer School	5	4	3	2	1
	Professional Development	5	4	3	2	1
	Classroom Management	5	4	3	2	1
	Extra-curricular activities	5	4	3	2	1
12.	I felt the mentor program was very helpful.	5	4	3	2	1
13.	The staff was very helpful.	5	4	3	2	1
14.	The Administration was very helpful.	5	4	3	2	1
15.	Staff development was very helpful.	5	4	3	2	1
16.	The attitude to teaching and learning is very professional.	5	4	3	2	1

17. Please describe what we did well to help you join our staff.

_____

_____

18. Please describe what we did not do as well to help you join our staff.

_____

_____

19. Please describe in general terms how well we have done in supporting your teaching in the building.

_____

_____

20. Other comments:

_____

_____

_____

Thank you very much for your response.

Recommendations

The following activities are recommended for an effective induction program:

- Give teachers ample paid time to work in their classroom prior to the beginning of the school year—minimum of two days.

- Select, train, and compensate mentor teachers.

- Notify beginning teachers of grade and building assignment early. For teachers hired in spring or early summer, notification should occur no later than August 1.

- Provide the equivalent of five days of release time opportunities for the beginning teacher to observe other teachers, participate in joint planning, collaborate with mentor teacher, and participate in building and district level in-service aimed at assisting the teacher.

- Induction activities should be scheduled throughout the first year. The activities scheduled at the beginning of the year are necessary but not sufficient.

- Observe the beginning teacher early in the school year. This allows the principal to assist before the problems become great.

- Invite the local teachers' association and colleges to assist in the planning and implementation of induction activities. Look for ways to reduce the workload of the beginning teacher. For example, limit committee assignments. However, be cautious. Beginning teachers want to be considered as full participating members of the school team.

In the personnel selection process, teachers are reminded that they have only one opportunity to make a good first impression. Likewise, in inducting new teachers the district has only one such opportunity. A carefully designed induction program will not only create that kind of impression but also launch a productive, positive, and professional career teacher. The beginning teacher will be alert to even the minor courtesies. Figure 5.12 lists some practical ideas for both the principal and the central office staff to consider in making a positive impact on the new and/or transitioning teacher.

Figure 5.12 Some Practical Ideas to Consider—
Little Things Mean a Lot

Central Office

- Lunch/Banquet sponsored by Chamber of Commerce or local service club
- Subscription to local newspaper
- Housing Information
- Welcome by community leader
- Extended contract
- Introduction at board meeting
- Presentation by business and/or personnel office
- Frame for diploma/certificate

Principal

- Tour of school neighborhood
- Name tags for all staff during first week
- Get-acquainted potluck dinner with the new teachers as invited guests
- Visit new teacher's classroom within two weeks
- Schedule meeting for new teachers with secretary to discuss office procedures
- Bulletin board with pictures and names of all staff title "Staffed for Excellence"
- Send teacher's editins and curriculum guides during summer
- Provide complimentary membership in PTA

A Comprehensive Year-Long Calendar of Induction Activities

The induction program costs money but it should be considered an investment in both the teacher and the instructional program. The following is a list of some possible activities for the year-long induction program.

August

- Mentor teams selected
- Mentor teams meet for introductory activities and program overview
- Mentor teams discuss school procedures
- Staff retreat (2 days)
  - New staff introductions
  - Get acquainted activities
  - Review of building goals
  - Committees and calendar
  - Staff development goals and activities
  - Social time for staff

- Staff meeting at end of first day of school to discuss needs and celebrations
- Mentor meets informally with mentee to discuss first day

September
- Mentor seminar
  - Process for mentor training
  - Peer coaching
  - Observation/feedback techniques
  - Classroom management/organization/discipline

    Assignment: Mentor/mentee observe each other at least twice and engage in feedback discussions regarding management/organization/discipline
- Informal mentor/mentee meetings as needed
- Informal observations of mentee by building principal
- Mentor/mentee open house planning
- Principal/mentor program feedback meeting
- Principal/mentee program feedback meeting

October
- Mentor seminar
  - Classroom management/organization/discipline review and feedback
  - Curriculum and lesson planning (daily and long-range)

    Assignment: Mentee to observe a variety of methods for daily and long-range planning from at least three other staff members in addition to mentor
- Informal mentor/mentee meetings as needed
- Informal observations of mentee by building principal
- Principal/mentor program feedback meeting
- Principal/mentee program feedback meeting

November
- Mentor seminar
  - Daily and long-range curriculum planning review and feedback
  - Student evaluation

Assignment: Mentee to observe a variety of assessment and record-keeping strategies from at least three other staff members in addition to mentor

- Mentor/mentee report card planning and procedures
- Mentor/mentee parent conference planning and procedures
- Goal setting and planning for formal observation by building principal
- Preobservation conferences with building principal
- Formal observations of mentee by building principal
- Postobservation conferences with building principal
- Informal mentor/mentee meetings as needed
- Staff Development In-service (all staff)
  - Authentic assessment
  - Performance-based criteria
  - State guidelines
  - District guidelines
  - SLIG grant decisions
  - Blending of learning objectives and exit outcomes

December

- Mentor seminar
  - Student evaluation review and feedback
  - Parent communication and involvement

    Assignment: Mentee to meet and discuss parent involvement and communication strategies with at least three other staff members in addition to the mentor
- Informal Mentor/mentee meetings as needed
- Informal observations of mentee by building principal and mentor
- Mentor/mentee meet to discuss management and discipline progress

January

- Mentor seminar
  - Parent communication and involvement review and feedback
  - Building a professional network of support

Assignment: Mentee to observe teachers of same grade level or subject area in same building or other district sites. Mentee given release time to observe. Mentor/mentee meet to discuss observations and share ideas for building professional network

♦ Mentee makes contacts with others not observed to add to network

♦ Informal mentor/mentee meetings as needed

♦ Informal observations of mentee by building principal and mentor

♦ Mentor/mentee discuss semester grading procedures

♦ Mentor/mentee discuss daily and long-range curriculum planning progress

♦ Principal/mentor program feedback meeting

♦ Principal/mentee program feedback meeting

♦ Mentee builds network with classified staff and other administrators in the district

♦ Mentee attends regional workshop or other professional growth in-service to expand knowledge and network

February

♦ Mentor seminar

  • Building a network of support review and feedback

  • Goal setting and planning for improvement

    Assignment: Mentor/mentee set goals for improvement. Mentor/mentee to plan changes. Mentee to implement changes. Mentor to observe mentee again. Mentor to provide feedback to mentee for self-reflection.

♦ Informal mentor/mentee meetings as needed

♦ Mentor/mentee to discuss student evaluation progress

♦ Informal observation of mentee by building principal

♦ Staff Development In-service (all staff)

  • Student assessment continued

  • Portfolios presentation by outside expert

  • Alternative assessment strategies

  • Pilot program developments discussed

  • Attendance at assessment workshop opportunities discussed

March

♦ Mentor seminar

  • Goal setting and planning for improvement review and feed-back

  • Meeting the needs of culturally diverse students

    Assignment: Mentee to observe culturally diverse classrooms in district or out of district. Mentor/mentee discuss methods for meeting the diverse needs of all students in class. Mentee brings in outside visitors to bring cultural diversity opportunities to class. Mentee becomes sensitive to diversity issue.

♦ Informal mentor/mentee meetings as needed

♦ Informal observations by building principal and mentor

♦ Mentor/mentee to discuss parent communication and involvement progress

♦ Principal/mentor program feedback meeting

♦ Principal/mentee program feedback meeting

April

♦ Mentor seminar

  • Meeting the needs of culturally diverse students review and feedback

  • Meeting the needs of inclusion students

    Assignment: Mentee to spend time with and observe resource, chapter, behavioral, and functional teachers. Mentee to discuss strategies for meeting needs of inclusion students with both special education and regular education staff members. Mentor/mentee to discuss specific strategies and plans.

♦ Informal Mentor/mentee meetings as needed

♦ Mentor/mentee meet to discuss goal setting/improvement progress

♦ Informal observations by building principal and mentor

♦ Mentor/mentee meet to plan third quarter report cards and conferences

♦ Principal/mentor program feedback meeting

♦ Principal/mentee program feedback meeting

May

♦ Mentor seminar

- Meeting the needs of inclusion students review and feedback
- Conflict resolution techniques

  Assignment: Mentee to meet with intervention specialist to discuss conflict resolution techniques. Mentee to attend in-service on conflict resolution. Mentor/mentee develop plan for implementing conflict resolution strategies.

- Informal mentor/mentee meetings as needed
- Mentor/mentee discuss culturally diverse and inclusion progress
- Mentor/mentee discuss end-of-year discipline and management
- Principal/mentor program feedback meeting
- Principal/mentee program feedback meeting
- Informal observations by building principal and mentor
- Staff Development In-service (all staff)
  - Assessment continued
  - Planning for changes in assessment for next year
  - Analyze improvements made this year
  - Committees for continued progress formed
  - Staff retreat agenda planned

June

- Mentor/mentee/principal discuss summative issues for mentor program
- Mentor/mentee discuss year-end procedures
- Mentor/mentee plan year-end report card and student placement
- Mentor/mentee develop plan for ongoing informal support next year
- Mentor/mentee celebrate a successful year
- Building principal/mentee discuss ongoing educational opportunities for continued growth

July

- Mentee rests and starts thinking with excitement about next year

Technology in the Induction Process

There are excellent sources on the internet for ideas and resources regarding teacher induction. One serious word of caution is needed here regarding use of technology. The principal must make sure that the teacher and all new employees understand the dangers of illegal and unethical use of the internet. One example will suffice to illustrate the significance. A state teacher of the year in 2001 was accused of illegal and unethical use of the internet in 2003. Shortly after being confronted, the teacher committed suicide.

1. www.ets.org/pathwise/mentoring

   The PATHWISE© Framework Induction Program prepares mentors to assist beginning teachers as they transition for the university or other environments to classroom practice. The program includes training for the mentors and materials for both mentors and beginning teachers to guide the growth process.

2. www.doe.mass.edu/eq/mentor/r_mentor.html

3. www.nsdc.org/library/jsd/234.html

4. www.WestEd.org/cs/wew/view/rs/212

5. www.newteachercenter.org

6. www.ccsd.net/jobs/PDNTIindex.htm

   This site has instructional videos such as "Preparing for the First week of School" and "Establishing Classroom Rules and Procedures" among others (You will need to have RealPlayer to view them). It is a very comprehensive site.

7. www.lausd.k12.ca.us/lausd.offices.tsu.tsu/htm

8. www.boiseschools.org/employee.html Click on Professional Development.

9. www.jeffco.k12.co.us/isu/induction.index.html

   Colorado's state mandated teacher induction program is a two-year program for new teachers. Included on the website is an explanation of the mentor teacher program, orientation and induction activities, mentor teacher application and stipend information, new teacher unit and lesson planner and a professional growth application.

10. www.ed.gov/pubs/PromPractice/chapter5.html

    This site discusses the induction of teachers. Topics covered include case studies from Delaware, Columbus, OH, and Omaha, NB.

11. www.ed.gov/pub/survivalguide/message.thml

    This is a survival guide for new teachers.

Conclusion

Orientation and the induction of the new teacher is a critical component of an effective human resources program. Considerable time and money is often spent in the recruiting and selection phase, whereas, orientation and induction are often not well done or not done at all. The components of an effective induction program include:

- ample time prior to and throughout the induction program
- orientation
- mentorships/cohort groups
- timely and frequent formative evaluations
- in-service workshops on effective teaching, assessment methods, and classroom management techniques
- ongoing staff development
- reasonable workload assignments (i.e., manageable preps, a balanced heterogeneous mix of students, gradual inclusion into committee or extracurricular responsibilities, and possibly extra planning time built into the daily schedule)
- opportunities to observe other effective teachers
- opportunities for team teaching
- clear expectations

Induction—Case Study

Filling the Bronzed Shoes

Mr. Lint was the outgoing choir director. He had been directing this program for about twelve years. He was a dynamic and enthusiastic teacher. Mr. Lint was also highly regarded as a leader in his church. Students felt honored to be part of his choirs. Parents and community members supported his program and teaching methods for years by donating money and volunteering time.

Mr. Olson was the principal of the high school. He loved and appreciated Mr. Lint as a teacher. He gave Mr. Lint excellent evaluations.

The community was shaken by Mr. Lint's leaving and worried about who the principal would hire to replace Mr. Lint.

Mr. Laster was the music teacher hired to replace Mr. Lint. Mr. Laster was older and not as enthusiastic as Mr. Lint, but he worked very hard to continue the tradition of excellence in the music program. During the first year, Mr. Laster was beginning to show signs of stress.

He had desperately tried to fill the shoes of his predecessor. He worked extremely hard to become a "Mr. Lint," but the students and the community just did not accept him. Students were dropping out of choir and the once prestigious musical department was turning into an embarrassment. Parents complained, students begged for a replacement and the community did not open its arms to Mr. Laster.

In spite of all Mr. Laster's efforts, he quit after two years of trying to fill the bronzed shoes of a well-liked teacher.

Questions for the prospective principal:

1. What would you have done to support Mr. Laster knowing that he had a difficult task ahead of him?

2. How would you have helped the students and parents accept Mr. Laster?

3. What elements of an induction program would you have in place for the next music teacher?

Comprehensive Questions

1. How can a well planned induction program help a new teacher?

2. What is the principal's role in regard to the success of a new teacher?

3. What attributes depict an effective mentor teacher?

Extended Activities

1. Write a proposal for the superintendent/school board which outlines an induction process for your district.

2. Describe how you would select and train a mentor teacher.

3. Interview a teacher who has recently completed the first year in teaching. Ask what the teacher found helpful during the first year; what was not helpful; and what the principal could do to assist during the first year of teaching.

References

Applegate, J. H., V. R. Flora, and T. J. Lasley (1980). New teachers seek support. *Educational Leadership*, 38(1), 74–76.

Armstrong, C. (1993, Sept.). Do's and don'ts for beginning teachers. *Principal*, 73(1), 30–31.

Badertscher, J. A. (1978). *Inducting newly placed teachers: Orientation responsibilities of the school administrator.* U.S. Educational Resources Information Center, ERIC Document No. ED 155 805.

Beerer, K. M. (2002, Fall) District carves out time for new teachers to learn. *Journal of Staff Development*, 46-49.

Bradley, H. W., and J. F. Eggleston (1978). An induction year experiment. *Educational Research, 20*(2).

Brown, L. (2003, August 20). Old hands help new teachers. Raleigh, NC: *News and Observer*.

Callari, C. L. (1990, Winter). Beginning teacher induction: The bridge to lifelong learning. *Education, 111*, 260–264.

Collin, A. (1988). Mentoring. *Industrial and Commercial Training*. (March/April).

Fagan, M., and G. Walter (1982). Mentoring among teachers. *Journal of Educational Research, 76*(2), 112–118.

Freshhour, D., and R. Hollman (1990, Sept.). Orienting new teachers for maximum effectiveness. *NASSP Bulletin, 74*(527), 78–83.

Garten, T., et al. (1993, Sept.). Teacher induction using a shared lesson design model. *NASSP Bulletin, 77*(554), 76–81.

Goldman, P. (1988, Winter). Introducing the new teacher to the school: Lessons for administrators. *OSSC Report, 28*(2), 1–7.

Hadaway, N. (1993, Winter). Circumventing the funding issues in induction. *Action in Teacher Education, 14*(4), 24–29.

Harris, B. H., and B. J. Monk (1992). *Personnel administration in education*. Boston: Allyn and Bacon.

Heck, R. (1988, Nov.–Dec.). Planning and implementing a teacher induction program. *Thrust, 18*(3), 50–52.

Helping newcomers adjust. (1992, May). *Front Line Supervisor's Bulletin*.

Hofman, J., and H. Feldlaufer (1992, Nov.–Dec.). Involving veteran teachers in a state induction program. *Clearing House, 66*(2), 101–103.

Huling-Austin, L. (1992, May-June). Research on learning to teach: Implications for teacher induction and mentoring programs. *Journal of Teacher Education, 43*(3), 173–180.

Huling-Austin, L. (1986, Jan.–Feb.). What can and cannot reasonably be expected from teacher induction programs. *Journal of Teacher Education, 37*(1), 2–5.

Jensen, M. C. (1987). *How to recruit, induct and retain the very best teachers*. Eugene, OR: ERIC Clearinghouse on Educational Management.

Ladestro, D. (1991, Oct.). Learning from the experienced. *Teacher Magazine, 3*(2), 20–21.

Lawson, H. A. (1992, May–June). Beyond the new conception of teacher induction. *Journal of Teacher Education, 43*(3), 163–172.

Loucks, H. E. (1993, Sept.). Teacher induction: A success story. *Principal, 73*(1), 27–29.

Natale, J. (1993, July). Why teachers leave. *Executive Educator, 15*(7), 14–18.

Newcombe, E. (1990). *Perspectives on teacher induction*. Philadelphia: Research for Better Schools.

Odell, S., and D. Ferraro (1992, May–June). Teacher mentoring and teacher retention. *Journal of Teacher Education, 43*(3), 200–204.

Rebore, R. W. (1987). *Personnel administration in education: A management approach,* 2nd ed. Englewood Cliffs, NJ: Prentice-Hall.

Pardini, P. (2002, Summer). Stitching new teachers into the school's fabric. *Journal of Staff Development, 23*(3).

Reinhartz, J. (Ed.) (1989). *Teacher induction*. Washington, DC: NEA.

Rosenholtz, S. J. (1989, March). Workplace conditions that affect teacher quality and commitment: Implications for teacher induction programs. *The Elementary School Journal, 89*(4), 421–439.

Ryan, K., et al. (1979). My teacher education program? Well…first year teachers reflect and react. *Peabody Journal of Education, 59*(2), 267–271.

Ryan, K. (1986). *The induction of new teachers*. Bloomington, IN: Phi Delta Kappa.

Schempp, P. G., A. C. Sparkes, and T. J. Templin (1993, Fall). The micropolitics of teacher induction. *American Educational Research Journal, 30*(3), 447–472.

Schaffer, E., S. Stingfield, and D. Wolfe (1992, May–June). An innovative beginning teacher induction program: A two-year analysis of classroom interactions. *Journal of Teacher Education, 43*(3), 181–192.

Schell, L. M., and P. Burden (1992). *Countdown to the first day of school*. Washington, DC: NEA.

Shelton, M., et al. (1992, Jan). Great beginnings. *Executive Educator, 14*(1), 27–29.

Tomlin, M. (1993, March). The evolution of new teachers. *Executive Educator, 15*(2), 39–40.

Tonnsen, S., and S. Patterson (1992, Jan.). Fighting first year jitters. *Executive Educator, 14*(1), 29–30.

Torgeson, L. M. (1987). Teacher induction: A study of practices involving beginning elementary teachers in the greater Puget Sound area with a recommended model for implementation. Ed.D. Dissertation, Seattle University.

Vann, A. (1991, Sept.). A guide to orienting new teachers. *Principal, 71*(1), 14–16.

Webb, L. D., et al. (1987). *Personnel administration in education: New issues and new needs in human resource management*. New York: Merrill.

Wilkinson, G. A. (1997, Spring). Beginning Teachers Identify Gaps in their Induction Programs. *Journal of Staff Development, 18*(2), 48–51.

Wisley, E. A. (1984). A comparison of the perceptions of beginning elementary teachers and their principals of the forms of assistance for beginning teachers. Ed.D. Dissertation, Oklahoma State University.

Young, T., et. al. (1993, Jan.–Feb.). Helping new teachers: The performance enhancement model. *Clearing House, 66*(3), 174–176.

6

Supervision and Evaluation

Reasons for Studying Supervision and Evaluation

◆ The supervision of the instructional process is the "quality control" element of student learning for which the principal is accountable.

◆ The failure of the principal to evaluate is in many instances *prima facie* evidence for the principal's dismissal.

◆ Teachers need feedback on their performance. If they are doing well they need to be told. If they are not doing well, they need to be told *and helped*!

◆ Doesn't it make sense that if you are the instructional leader, you need to be very involved with the instructional process?

> *We can't press teachers to develop [new] and alternative sources of assessment [for students] and then evaluate teachers the same way we did in 1950.*
>
> McGreal, 1996

ISLLC Standards Covered in this Chapter

Standard 2:

◆ A school administrator is an educational leader who promotes the success of all students by advocating, nurturing, and sustaining a school culture and instructional program conducive to student learning and staff professional growth.

Standard 3:

◆ A school administrator is an educational leader who promotes the success of all students by ensuring management of the organization, operations, and resources for a safe, efficient, and effective learning environment.

Standard 5:

♦ A school administrator is an education leader who promotes the success of all students by acting with integrity, fairness and in an ethical manner.

Introduction

This chapter deals with a critical area of human resources: supervision and evaluation. It is recognized that most university programs have entire courses on supervision and evaluation. This chapter is not meant to supplant those courses. If it precedes that course, it should be viewed as an introduction; if it follows such a course it should be viewed as reinforcement. In all cases, supervision and evaluation are important enough to the field of human resources and to the principal to warrant this treatment.

Aside from selection, teacher evaluation may be the principal's single most important activity. The evaluation process presents the principal with the opportunity to stimulate growth and improve teacher performance as well as to recognize quality instruction. The improvement of teacher performance is critical since it is directly correlated to improved student performance. This connection cannot be stressed too much. The success of students depends on the success of the teacher. This chapter is designed to give principals greater understanding of this important process and provide several useful hands-on tools to make the process of evaluation easier to understand and accomplish.

The following quote from "Teacher Evaluation as a Strategy for Improving Instruction" (Weber, 1987) provides a very useful introduction and sets the stage for the presentation of current information and strategies to help the principal perform in a more competent and professional manner.

> The history of teacher evaluation in the public schools of the United States has been marred by a tension between including teachers' input and applying standards from administrative criteria. From the last decade of the nineteenth century, teacher education has been increasingly humanized by including more concerns for the development of teachers' skills.
>
> Before the turn of the century, teacher "inspection" was the evaluation method most frequently practiced. Administrators, who did not need to be trained in teaching or observing, observed teachers for their conformity to district expectations. These expectations could be personal as well as professional. Evaluations might focus

on critiques of student behavior for instance, or on a teacher's personality—including out-of-class activities.

The emphasis then shifted to the efficiency of teaching and the "scientific management" of students and school personnel. After this interest in efficiency and economy of effort, however, administrators began to see the need to cooperate with teachers in evaluations. Researchers, too, began to isolate significant teaching behaviors, warranting the belief that good teaching can be developed with adequate attention and effort. By the post World War II period, cooperation between supervisors and teachers was an assumption in the research, if not in the majority of schools (Peterson 1982). Through the influence of clinical supervision approaches, concern for mutual effort and reciprocity are features of nearly all new models of supervision.

On the other hand, as evaluation turned more democratic in theory (if not in the practice of most schools), it has been matched by a growing public pressure for teacher accountability. The result has been numerous programs that combine the historical gains in development-centered evaluations with accountability strategies aimed at ensuring minimum standards and encouraging maximum effort.

In the effort to improve teaching, a great deal of energy has recently been directed at improving teacher evaluations. At the policy-making level, states and school districts have been initiating programs to accelerate schools' procedures for dismissing incompetent teachers or improving competent teachers. For example, in 1985 Kansas began a state-wide, legislatively approved internship program for teachers. Local committees, consisting of administrators and senior teachers (assessed, assisted, and supported) all first-year teachers.

When the teacher evaluation process is carried out effectively and sensitively, the teacher can grow and become more productive. But when the evaluation is conducted ineffectively or insensitively, there are usually troublesome consequences. Teachers can feel insulted or misunderstood; their self-esteem and sense of job security are threatened. Students lose out because their teachers are less effective than they could be. The entire school organization can become tense, and its members can become overly competitive, and distrustful. The entire ambiance can be adversely affected by poorly conducted teacher evaluations.

It is essential, therefore, that the principal develop a thorough understanding of this process and an ability to accomplish it in a competent and professional manner.

The process of teacher evaluation has evolved significantly in the United States in the past century. As Weber noted, in the public schools of the 1800s the process was primarily known as "teacher inspection." As the name implies, it consisted of the administrator periodically observing the teacher to see if the rules were being followed and the established expectations were being met. The observers were the school officials, people who usually were not trained in teaching or supervising.

Predictably, these supervisors scrutinized the teacher's professional and personal behavior in and out of the classroom, as well as values and ideologies. There was generally no sense of reciprocity in which the teacher's viewpoint or professional creativity might have been considered, nor was there any particular effort to enhance the teacher's capacities to do a better job. In such a climate there was little opportunity for professional growth and development, but there was considerable fear, and reluctance to learn or try innovative teaching strategies.

Gradually through the early decades of the twentieth century, changes in supervision and evaluation methods took place as teaching and educational administration became established as professions. The first shift accompanied the trends toward "scientific management" in education, when a primary consideration was gaining the maximum efficiency from teachers. Ultimately supervisors came to recognize the importance of cooperation with teachers in their evaluations.

The components of a successful evaluation process consist of (1) a preobservation conference, (2) the classroom observation, (3) the analysis of data from the lesson and planning of postobservation conference, (4) the postobservation conference, and (5) the conference check-up (Goldhammer et al., 1993). See Figure 6.1.

Figure 6.1 Teacher Evaluation Process

Task   **(Suggested Deadline Date)**

First Teachers' Meeting   (August–September)

At the first teachers' meeting the principal should review the evaluation process with the staff:

◆ This should be completed before the preobservation conference

- ◆ Review the general job description with teachers and cocurricular supervisors
- ◆ Review Code of Professional Conduct or Code of Ethics for Teachers and School Employees—give to all employees

First Observation

- ◆ Preobservation conference   (October/November)
  - • Collect information about the lesson and the class
  - • Discuss the teacher's lesson plans/objectives for the lesson
- ◆ Classroom observation   (October/November)
  - • Collect data based on questions posed in the preobservation conference
- ◆ Analysis of the lesson in detail   (Within 24 Hrs.)
  - • Cite evidence from the anecdotal record
  - • Discuss the strengths and weaknesses of the lesson
- ◆ Postobservation conference   (Within 24 Hrs.)
  - • The purpose of the conference is to review the lesson.
  - • Discuss the lesson with the teacher and assist the teacher in reflecting on the lesson.
  - • Affirm positive teaching techniques and assist in identification of techniques that will improve instruction and student learning.
- ◆ Follow-up observations and conferences as needed

Second Observation   (February–March)

- • Same process as first observation
- • Teacher shares progress with yearly goals

Formal Evaluation   (April–May 15)

- ◆ The formal evaluation is written sometime after the second observation and before May 15. (Check the laws and requirements of your state and/or district. They may be different.)
- ◆ Evaluation conference
  - • Share the formal written evaluation with the teacher.
  - • Initiate preliminary discussion regarding goals for the next school year.

The Preobservation Conference

Key Idea

Good principals remember what it was like to be a teacher.

Most teachers remember the first time they were officially observed. They remember because the event was pivotal in their careers, their professional development, and especially because they weren't really sure what the process or result would be. The event is so important in the lives of most young teachers that it is usually anticipated with heightened emotions. Some regard it with dread, anxiety, or even fear, while others look forward to it as an opportunity to receive feedback from their principal.

Because the first official observation is so crucial and filled with so many uncertainties, it is possible, maybe even probable, that the conference will provide a distorted picture of what the teacher can and is doing. To make an assessment based on the data thus acquired could be inaccurate and ultimately damaging to the teacher, the students, and the entire school. On the other hand, when the principal is helpful and supportive, the teacher's acceptance of an appraisal and satisfaction with the principal increases.

Key Idea

The ability of the principal to establish a trusting relationship with the teacher is a crucial element in the evaluation process.

A competent and careful principal wants to minimize these risks and get the most accurate picture possible in the observation. One of the most effective techniques to achieve this is the preobservation conference.

Such a conference has the same function and procedure as a rehearsal has for an actor or public speaker. It is analogous to a teacher giving a sample test to students to help them know what to expect. The preobservation conference can assuage anxiety and enable the teacher to focus on the task at hand rather than on peripheral issues. It shows the teacher that the principal wants the process to be fair and wants to give the teacher every chance to do well. It demonstrates the fact that the principal and the teacher are in a collaboration to achieve the best possible outcome, rather than in an adversarial relationship whose purpose is ultimately to dismiss or humiliate the teacher.

Preobservation conferences have many other benefits, both for the teacher and the observer (Sweeney, 1989). They promote trust and positive relationships; clarify the lesson objectives; identify the teaching/learning activities that will be utilized to reach those objectives; and provide insight into follow-up lessons. The teacher can inform the principal in advance about the classroom environment and any individuals who might require special attention. The preobservation conference also affords teachers the opportunity to indicate the specific areas on which they want the principal to provide feedback.

The principal can use the preobservation conference to provide the teacher with specific information about what topics, characteristics, or issues will be focused on in both the observation and postobservation conference. Figure 6.2 is a comprehensive guide to the preobservation process which the beginning principal would do well to follow. Figure 6.3 is an abbreviated form that the more experienced principal might want to use.

Figure 6.2 Preobservation Planning Questionnaire—for Principal's Use with the Teacher in the Preobservation Conference

1. Objective:
   - What do you plan to teach in this period of instruction?
   - What should the students know or be able to do as a result of instruction of this content?
2. Content:
   - What factors were considered in selecting content for this lesson?
   - How did you determine that students were ready for this lesson?
   - How did you decide how much content would be taught in this period of instruction?
   - How is the content related to previous and/or future lessons?
   - What elements of content will be emphasized in this lesson?
3. Materials:
   - What materials are to be used for instruction and why were these selected?
   - What preparation of materials is required prior to the beginning of the lesson?
   - What plans have you made for managing materials during instruction?
4. Activities:
   - What activities will be included in this lesson and for what purpose?

- How will you conduct each of these activities?
- What is the sequence of activities to be used?
- How will the classes be organized for instructional activities?

After the preconference, the principal should use the following steps and concepts in order to provide for the professional growth of the teacher.

5. Evaluation: How will you determine that the intended learning has taken place?

   - Analyze and label the data using the elements of instruction as the criteria.
   - Can the teacher:

     ___ Teach to an objective?
     ___ Select the correct level of difficulty for the learners?
     ___ Monitor the learner and adjust the teaching?
     ___ Use (not abuse) the principles of learning?

   - c. Look for:

     ___ Elements of lesson design
     ___ Organization of the materials
     ___ Effective use of audio-visuals
     ___ Good questioning techniques, wait time, delving, some higher thinking level questions
     ___ Clear directions
     ___ Recognition of learning styles
     ___ Classroom management techniques
     ___ Time-on-task
     ___ Student participation, amount and variety of students

   - Cite evidence for reinforcing (label +) and evidence for those things that need to be refined (label −).

6. The conference takes place between the principal and the teacher. The purpose of the conference is to review the lesson and to point out methods and techniques which enhanced learning and which need to be improved.

7. Follow-up Observation:

   A follow-up observation is made to check improvement in the area of focus decided during the conference.

   The principal can see if the good skills have been maintained and if the new skill has been incorporated into the lesson. If change is not achieved for a new skill, the principal keeps teaching in an effort to reach the desired outcome.

A conference with the teacher should follow this observation.

8. The important keys to the success of teacher evaluations lie in the relationship of the principal to the staff (feelings of trust) and the ability of the principal to furnish the teacher with objective (hard) data.

9. Furthermore, principals intent on improving instruction will make sure they have the following components included in the evaluation program each year:

- The preobservation conference

- The observation

- The analysis and strategies session.
    ___ What took place?
    ___ How to present your finding to the teacher?

- The postobservation conference
    ___ Formative evaluation
    ___ Summative evaluation

- The conference check-up
    ___ Conclusion

Figure 6.3 Preobservation Information

Teacher: _____

Grade: _____

Subject/Lesson: _____

Time: _____ Date: _____

1. What are the objectives? (skills, attitudes, knowledge)

2. Where are you in the course or lesson? (unit, lesson, page numbers in texts, introductory, middle or culminating activity)

3. What instructional methods are you going to use?

4. How will you know if the students have learned?

5. What particular teaching behaviors do you want monitored?

6. What special characteristics of the students should be noted (unusual behaviors, group interactions, students leaving during class, lab work, etc.)?

Preobservation conferences can take many different formats. Since the needs and experiences of teachers vary, the type of conference that is best suited for one may be ill-suited for another. Moreover, the type of preconferences that are best for teachers at early points in their careers may be contraindicated for the same teachers at later stages. Thus, the wise principal will use the procedure and format that most closely approximates the specific needs of the teacher to be observed.

For example, seasoned veteran teachers who have long known and worked with the principal could be approached more informally. Most of them would probably be more comfortable dropping into the principal's office for an informal discussion about the official observation. On the other hand, a new teacher who has not yet had an extensive relationship with the principal would probably derive greater benefit from a more formal and extensive conference. This gives both the teacher and the principal a chance to learn more about what is to be observed, and about the conditions of the observation.

Whether the preobservation interaction is formal or informal, brief or extensive, the very least it must do is establish clearly when the evaluation is to take place and the purpose of the evaluation. In almost all instances the principal also asks for input regarding the purpose and direction of the evaluation. Beyond these minimal requirements of the preobservation, the principal uses professional judgment in determining, providing, and obtaining whatever additional information is necessary to make the evaluation beneficial for all.

Key Idea

Teachers generally do good work and as such should be praised. For those who are experiencing difficulty, they need to be helped. In both cases and especially in the latter, timing is crucial and the principal's skills are on the line. It is recommended that teachers new to the principal and the building be visited during the first two weeks of the school year. Such a visit can save a great deal of time later if the principal must deal with remediation.

The Observation

Instead of solely observing the teacher, I find it more helpful to focus on observing the students for it is their learning that is important.

L. Keylin, High School Principal, 2000

To many less experienced teachers, the principal's direct observation may seem like the beginning and end of the evaluation process. After all, they might think, once it's over, there's nothing to do but go back to normal. While direct observation is important, even essential, it is by no means the whole of it. It is analogous to "data gathering" in the research process. Researchers need the raw data but until they have studied, analyzed, looked at the data from different viewpoints and in different contexts, and compared and interpreted the data objectively, the data are virtually meaningless. It is the same with the observation. It is important, but merely one step in a multistage process. As such, the teacher must be made aware that many more steps must occur for the evaluation to become truly meaningful.

What gives credence to the observation is the fact that all the subsequent interpretations that are made will be based on the information gathered during this phase. If the information is inaccurate, distorted, or unrepresentative, then all the subsequent phases in the evaluation process will also be distorted. Therefore, the careful principal must do everything possible to assure that the data obtained in the observation are valid.

Even the most capable and observant supervisor sometimes fails to get accurate information out of the observation. The teacher, who is usually very capable, might experience a sudden and atypical panic reaction to the unaccustomed scrutiny. A student, who is usually well-behaved, might disrupt the class in a way that no one had anticipated or for which they were not prepared. Or the principal might be overly tired or rushed from the press of other obligations and likely to miss details that would otherwise be noted as important. Such circumstances are common, even inevitable; so too are a myriad of other variables that influence the dynamics of a complex social group such as a classroom, especially when the principal-observer is introduced into that situation to further change it in unforeseeable ways.

While such circumstances are unavoidable, they need not preclude a principal's acquisition of good and accurate data if the right precautions are taken. One precaution is for the principal to always distinguish between events over which the teacher has (or should have) control, and those events which are not controllable by the teacher. After all, the evaluation is about teacher performance, not the degree to which a classroom meets some social ideal. For example, a regular classroom teacher who has no classroom aide but is responsible for the education of a student with a severe disability and 30 other students, should not be compared unfavorably with a teacher who does have an aide or has no students with disabilities.

One tool that is helpful to many principals in acquiring relevant, complete, and accurate data is the use of *scripting*. Several examples of this method are found in Figures 6.4 and 6.5. The principal should keep focused on what is relevant, and to ignore peripheral but distorting side issues. For example, a principal might be attentive to the classroom environment and forget to observe how the class members interact—until reminded by the observational guide to look for it.

Of course, no observational guide can provide the principal with all the cues and reminders of what to watch for. Continuing self-development and self-awareness are as important for the administrator as for the teacher being observed. The principal must be wary of personal biases or blind spots and must have the flexibility to recognize that many different teaching styles can be effective. If the principal has a preconceived notion that only one teaching style is the best and judges every teacher by that standard, an invalid observation may be conducted.

Figure 6.4 Sample Classroom Observation

Teacher: (Elementary)

Subject: Math

Date: _____   Time: 1:50 to 2:22

Observer: _____

When I entered your room, the students were ready to take a timed math test.

- ♦ After the test, the students corrected each other's papers.
- ♦ They turned the papers in to you, at your request.

You moved from that activity to a new lesson.

- ♦ You passed out worksheets for a new lesson.
- ♦ You passed out some beans for the students to use on this activity.
- ♦ You gave directions for the worksheet.

  1. _____, direction-giving is one of the most important aspects of setting the stage for proper and correct learning. When we give directions, it is most important that we do the following:

  - Plan and think through the directions in advance to determine
    - How many different things must the student remember to do?
    - Which of these has been done before, and which are new to him?
    - Can the student do new things if he or she tries?
    - How many directions must be given at one time?
    - When is the best time to give these directions?
    - What is the best sequence for the directions and what must be given at the same time?
    - Should the directions be written or verbal?
  - Giving directions to individual students involves these steps:
    - Getting the students attention

- Giving the directions in a way that reflects conscientious planning
- Checking understanding
- Modeling the behavior desired
- Translating into action the directions
- Redirecting if necessary

When the students started to work after the initial directions, many questions continued to be asked throughout the lesson.

- ◆ I would suggest that you make sure you include these steps when you are teaching a lesson to ensure correct understanding of the intent of the objective:
- ◆ _____, which creates the focus in the mind of the learner on what it is you desire.
- ◆ Where you are going with the information you intend for them to learn.
  - Explain what it is you want them to learn—make clear what is unclear.
  - Model the example so that the students clearly understand what you want.
  - Instruct
  - Your method of presentation of the information
- ◆ Questions:
  - What questions did students ask that offered reassurance that your explanation was clear?
  - Monitor the activity to ensure student understanding of the lesson's objectives; make adjustments as needed.
- ◆ Activities:
  - Monitor progress on the assignment by rotating through the classroom, offering clarification/assistance where needed.
- ◆ Respond positively to the efforts of the learners.
  - Positive reinforcement of students' activity is rewarding and promotes incentive.
- ◆ Closure:
  - Putting it all together—to articulate in the mind of the learner what he or she has learned.
  - Reviewing—to summarize what was learned.

- Putting the learning into practice. What did you want them to learn from this activity? Clarify the import of what they have just learned.
- This type of organization makes sure you have set the stage necessary to get the desired learning from your students.

Class Management

- During this time period, at least 10% of your time was spent correcting students.
- Good class management is important and you should insist on it.
  - When you say I want no talking, mean it.
    - Do not talk over the top of your students. Insist on quiet.
    - If they are not quiet, have a consequence in mind for their actions.
  - You should use more positive reinforcement. I *did not* detect one incident where you praised a student during this lesson.

_____, lesson planning is the most important first step of an effective lesson. I would like you to turn in your plan book to _____ every day as you leave.

Please make an appointment to discuss my observation.

Date _____ Teacher _____

Date _____ Observer _____

Figure 6.5 Sample Observation Report

Teacher: _____   School: Junior High

Date: _____   Subject: Language Arts

Time: 9:50–10:40   Observer: _____

Lesson Objective

The objective of the lesson was to enable students to write a response letter of a minimum of three paragraphs and to use appropriate introductory and closing and addressing procedures.

Lesson Design

After the bell rang at 9:50, students were told about upcoming projects and tasks to be done in ensuing hours and days. You reviewed with the students the results of a previous project, which included an analysis of a book or movie or play, etc. You reminded students that they were supposed to have taken care of adminstrivia, plot, and most importantly, opinion and substantiation for that opinion. Following that, you began a modeling activity that demonstrated how an analysis of a TV show might occur. The example used was the Cosby show; the model was to identify two issues. These issues included family values and humor. On the board, you wrote "family values," underlined it, and next to it wrote "humor" and underlined that. You then requested students to provide specific examples underneath "humor." Family values included such items as family trust, honesty, etc. Following that, you wrote instructions on the board concerning three paragraphs for the project of the day. The instructions included:

- An imaginary response to an imaginary person who had written a letter
- Piece of current news
- An inquiry

Then you gave instructions that you would provide the stationery. On the board also, you provided a block model of the location of the return address, the introductory remarks, the body, and conclusion. Students worked on that project until approximately 10:40.

Lesson Analysis

In analyzing the lesson, it was clear that you had an objective, which was consistent with the previous day's work, and followed that activity, which was logically related to the previous assignment. You developed appropriate models and appropriate input methods to demonstrate the important points of the assignment. You demonstrated appropriate use of feedback and interest-generating devices with frequent utilization of humor. An on-task analysis was developed, and the result of that analysis showed that the class had an average on-task analysis for a ten-minute period of 71%. The on-task behavior varied from a low of 68% to a high of 88% during the appraisal period. The analysis also demonstrated that there was an increase of on-task behavior at each subsequent two-minute checkpoint to where the last checkpoint had the highest on-task behavior of 88%. This information indicates that for the plotted period, the amount of on-task behavior was below what would be wanted in that situation. The recommendation is that the students be given guided opportunity to practice the task prior to assigning the independent work, which should increase the on-task behavior and decrease the number of questions that occurred during the class period. The monitoring that you did was appropriate. However, a number of the questions possibly could have been eliminated by employing one group activity on a specific example prior to assigning the independent work.

Summary

In summary, you demonstrated the ability to select an appropriate objective, to analyze the objective, and to provide appropriate input and models related to that objective. Increased focus on guided practice, or giving the students a specific example from which to work, should increase on-task behavior and decrease questions during the independent phase of the lesson.

Thank you for the opportunity to observe.

Date: _____ Teacher: _____

Date: _____ Observer: _____

Objectivity is crucial in the observation process. It is important for the administrator to keep the overall purpose of the evaluation in mind and recognize that the observation is only to gather data, not to project one's own agenda onto the event being observed. The principal must remember that the data-gathering part of the evaluation is:

◆ concerned with overt observable behaviors and concrete, specific facts rather than inferences, assumptions, or explanations

◆ based on the actual performance of the teacher, rather than the teacher's personality traits or background

◆ related to the present performance only, rather than past performances or reports about past performances made by different supervisors

◆ to determine the teacher's needs rather than the administrator's wants

- focused on specific information that can be useful, not over-whelming, to the teacher

- an attempt to distinguish between observed events that lie within the teacher's control and those over which the teacher has no control

- a process that requires objective, thorough, and well-documented notes

The principal who has taken comprehensive notes of the objective facts can later meet with the teacher and reconstruct the observation with more validity and reliability. Objective notes are important to the next phase in the evaluation process, the analysis.

Analysis

> ...analysis exists for the sake of understanding true events in order to exercise greater control over future events.
>
> Goldhammer, 1969

To *fail to plan* is to *plan to fail*. Since the evaluation is based on performance, the first step after the observation is to analyze what was observed. Thus, during the observation, it is critically important that an inclusive record of events be maintained. This collection of data provides the basis for decisions concerning the performance areas to be covered in the postobservation conference. It is helpful for the principal to think like a teacher during this step of the process. This part is analogous to the planning of the lesson: you know the material and the "student." Now, how are you going to present the material so that teaching effectiveness improves and student learning takes place?

Critical questions for the principal to focus on during the analysis stage include the following:

- What techniques or strategies do I want to reinforce, encourage growth in, or stimulate the teacher to think about?

- What are the answers to the questions and concerns posed during the preobservation conference?

- What behavior or strategy had the greatest impact on teaching/learning behaviors?

- Was the lesson objective clearly stated and did the teacher stay on target by:

- giving directions and explanations relevant to the learning task?
- asking questions relevant to the learning task?
- conducting activities relevant to the learning task?
- responding to learners in ways relevant to the learning task?
- Were teaching opportunities outside of the stated objectives present and if so, did the instructor show flexibility and creativity?
- Did the instructor select objectives that were at the correct level for the students?
- Were there levels of opportunity for learning that met the needs of all students in the class?
- Were most learners able to experience success?
- Were behavior problems present, and if so, did the instructor
  - set standards and praise correct behavior?
  - anticipate and prevent incorrect behavior?

A form that the principal can use to prepare for communicating to the teacher is reproduced in Figure 6.6. The principal in the analysis of the lesson should select two or three items that occurred during the lesson for reinforcement and one item for refinement. If the principal provides more written information, the teacher will not be able to focus on specific areas of improvement. It becomes a case of data-overload and thus paralysis by analysis.

Figure 6.6 Anaylsis and Strategy Session Form to Be Used by the Principal in Planning the Postobservation Conference

Analysis of the lesson

Reinforcement (Choose 2 or 3 Items)	Refinement (Choose 1 Item)

It is important to remember to keep it *simple* and *workable*. Don't try to impress people by digging too deep merely to show off your depth of knowledge in a given area. Work within the area of understanding of the teacher and help the teacher grow. As a principal, your analysis should be for the teacher's benefit rather than for your personal gratification.

Postobservation Conference

> *...I propose that a minimum responsibility incumbent upon the observer is to discuss what he has observed with the teacher. (This) is what earns you your right to observe.*
>
> Goldhammer, 1969

After the lesson has been observed, the data analyzed and the postobservation conference planned, the teacher and observer should get together to analyze the observational data and set goals for improvement. This is an important occasion in the evaluation process because it allows teachers to talk in detail about their work with someone who has been in the classroom and is able to provide feedback and assistance, either directly or indirectly. It is also a time for diplomacy and candor on the part of the observer. No two conferences are going to be alike nor should they be. Teachers are different, and your approach should be designed to elicit the most favorable results from the teacher being observed. Thus, one of the most important decisions that faces a principal preparing for a conference revolves around what approach to use (Sweeney, 1989).

Maureen Zolubos, principal in Westborough, MA, considers four factors in deciding on the approach to use:

- ♦ What is my purpose?

  The supervisor must be very clear about the decision level to employ in discussing performance. Following are four decision levels and a guide to their use:

  - Delegate—leave the decision to change up to the teacher.

    Utilize this choice with a highly skilled, analytical, and knowledgeable teacher.

  - Suggest—suggest possible change, but leave the decision up to the teacher

    Utilize where performance is effective but alternative strategies might be helpful.

- Recommend—clearly communicate the need to change or improve present practices.

  The need for change is stronger, and the teacher *should* change present practices.

  - Direct—clearly communicate that change must be made and set goals and timelines.

    This is typically employed where performance is below the district standards.

♦ What are the needs and communication or behavior style of the person being evaluated?

Augment the golden rule with the platinum rule—Do unto others as they would have you do unto them. A careful examination of the characteristics of the teacher helps to determine the approach to use in the conference.

♦ What are the situational elements to consider?

Situational factors that should be considered in planning the approach include:

- Past observation
- Recent incidents or events in the work environment
- External events

♦ What is my communication/behavioral style, and what strengths do I bring to the conference?

- Rule one in conducting a conference is to be yourself.
- Rule two is to adjust your behavior to meet the other's communication/behavior needs.

You should face this dichotomy by playing to your strengths and adjusting within your comfort zone. Following are three questions to ask in assessing your style:

♦ What behaviors do I bring to the conference that promote success?

♦ Is my primary communication style direct or indirect?

♦ Do I need to flex my basic behavior or communication style to promote success in this conference?

Insincerity and lack of interest will show quickly in a postobservation conference and will severely dampen the interest of those observed and lower their impression of the principal. Superficial observations should never take place; they must be avoided at all costs. If you don't think that it is important enough to do it right, then you should have a quiet little talk with yourself and rethink your priorities. One of your most important goals as a principal should be to develop well-planned and meaningful observations that show your staff that you are really concerned about their professional development, teaching effectiveness and student learning, and personal well-being. Along the same line, it is wrong to assume that feedback from the observation is just the final stage and not an important element in the growth of both parties involved. Feedback should provide results that are revealing, persuasive, caring, and creative.

Principals can make feedback more useful by eliciting information from the teacher about what transpired in the classroom during the observation. It is important to ask questions of the instructors to guide them into the areas that you wish to discuss with them and then to ask further questions that will allow them to develop solutions to their difficulties on their own, thus establishing "ownership" in the process. Questions are the ultimate tool for promoting success in a conference. Barbara Licklider, principal in Council Bluffs, IA, suggests using six types of questions:

- analysis questions
- fact-finding questions
- attitude questions
- checking for understanding questions
- agreement questions
- checking for commitment questions

The principal and staff of Hillcrest Elementary School use the following questions, which focus the postobservation conference on student learning:

Figure 6.7 Hillcrest Elementary Postobservation Reflection Questions

The following questions will guide our postobservation conversation. I will give you a copy of these questions after each observation with observation notes. I do not expect you to write answers to these questions. I simply share them with you to help you focus your reflections regarding your lesson and let you know the direction our dialogue will take.

1. What did you do that enabled students to achieve the lesson objective?

2. What did the students do to indicate that they had achieved or did not achieve the lesson objective?

3. Describe how our method of assessment (performance, selected response, essay/short answer, and personal communication) matched your lesson target (knowledge, reasoning, skill, or application). How will your assessments focus further instruction?

4. What aspects of your classroom management plan supported student achievement?

5. Within your class are students with many developmental levels. Also, students often exhibit a particular learning preference or style such as visual, auditory, or kinesthetic. what did you do that enabled successful learning by all these different learners?

6. If you plan to teach this lesson again, describe changes you might make to improve it. If you do not plan to teach this lesson again, explain why you would not do so.

Another set of questions for the principal to ask the teacher during the postobservation conference is:

♦ What did you do that you liked?

♦ If you were to teach this lesson again, what might you do differently?

♦ How can I help you?

Figure 6.8 Postobservation Conference— Principles of Constructive Feedback

1. Focus on **behavior** rather than on the person. "Monitoring can increase student time on task" rather than "you're not moving around the room checking on students."

2. Focus on behavior that the teacher can do something about. Frustration is only increased when a person is reminded of some shortcoming over which he/she has no control.

3. Be **descriptive** rather than judgmental. Avoiding evaluative language reduces the need for the individual to respond defensively. "It is effective because…" rather than "I like…"

4. Be **specific** rather than general. "When you gave directions for the activity, you wrote them on the board in logical sequential steps and you reinforced them verbally," rather than "you did a good job with your directions."

5. Focus on **sharing** information rather than giving advice. "These are alternatives" or, "can you think of alternatives," rather than "this is the way to do it."

6. Base comments on **observation** rather than hearsay. "I saw you do…" rather than "someone told me that…"

7. Be **helpful** to the teacher rather than destructive. Comments should focus on improvement rather than being a release of your own frustration by "chewing him/her out."

8. Give the teacher the **amount** of information he/she can use rather than the amount you would like to give. To overload is to reduce the possibility of using anything effectively. When you give more than can be used, you are more often than not satisfying some need of your own rather than helping the teacher.

9. Be **timely**. Feedback is most helpful when offered at the earliest opportunity. A tactful delivery at an opportune time will likely ensure receptivity. Excellent feedback presented at an inappropriate time may do more harm than good.

10. Check to ensure **clear communication.** Have the teacher try to rephrase the feedback he/she has received to see if it corresponds to what you had mind. Feedback is often subject to distortion or misinterpretation.

Weber (1987) stated that the most important reasons for asking questions are that they help to increase the participation and involvement of the teacher, and enhance the *trust*, *credibility*, and *rapport* between the principal and teacher. These three items (trust, credibility, and rapport) are critical because they are essential for positive communication and commitment.

- They enable the principal to check perceptions about data collected in the observation.
- They help the principal to assess the receptivity of the other person.
- They help the principal to identify personal needs, beliefs, and values about what the employee wants and believes works best.
- They stimulate the teacher to analyze performance and explore other approaches.
- They enable the principal to check for understanding, agreement, and commitment.

The more *listening* the principal can do the better it will be for the teacher as well as the principal. It is important to keep the feedback going in two directions—being a dialogue rather than a monologue (Weber, 1987). Remember the old adage: you have two ears and only one mouth. Use them in like proportion.

Another method mentioned in the "Program for Quality Teaching" urges observers to listen more and talk less. To do this, Weber suggested that the observer can:

♦ ask for the teacher's feelings

♦ ask for the teacher's inferences

♦ ask for the teacher's opinions

♦ ask for the teacher's suggestions for improvement

The nature of a principal's questions can radically affect the outcome of a conference. While two or three well-chosen, well-placed, and well-asked questions may be effective, it is by no means true that twelve or eighteen questions will be six times as effective (Hyman, 1986). Keep it *short and to the point*. If you do it right, you will be talked about as the administrator who gets it done quickly and efficiently. State your facts, ask your questions, and let the teacher draw the conclusions. If you find you are having trouble coming to an agreement with the teacher, Weber (1987) offers the following principles for consideration:

♦ Shut up and listen. If the other person is frustrated:

  • let him or her vent the anger or frustration

  • take notes and do not interrupt

♦ Enhance or maintain the teacher's self-esteem.

  • praise—effort, competence, and self-worth

  • refrain from criticizing or acting defensively

♦ Listen and respond with empathy.

♦ Ask for the teacher's help in solving the problems that are holding up agreements.

Weber (1987) also offers these seven key strategies that are also helpful in overcoming postobservation conference road blocks:

♦ Determine the nature of the problem and the other's needs.

  • ask questions and listen

  • try to determine the nature of the problem you are dealing with

  • try to understand the other person's feelings and needs

- Explore the nature of the feelings.
  - listen for those feelings
  - reflect them back to the person
  - try to work it so that you can explore the source of the feelings
- Never lose your temper.
  - stay cool on the surface but paddle like mad underneath
  - remember, it is a professional not a personal matter
- Use "I" and not "you" statements.
  - "I" communicates what you need
  - "you" is like pointing a finger in his or her face
- Respect the others' rights and require that they respect yours.
  - set the rules
  - politely hold to the rules fairly and consistently
- Limit behavior/clarify consequences. If the person is behaving inappropriately:
  - communicate that the *behavior* is inappropriate
  - clarify the consequences of this behavior.
- Know when to terminate.
  - calmly terminate the conference if the other person goes beyond the limits set
  - terminate if you feel that you can go no further at the present time
  - terminate when it is evident one or both parties need a break
  - terminate when business is finished

To focus the postobservation conference, the principal gave each teacher a copy of his questions. He did not expect written answers to these questions, but what the teacher to focus reflections regarding the lesson and let them know the direction the dialogue would take. His questions were:

1. What did you do that enabled students to achieve the lesson objective?
2. What did the student do to indicate that they had achieved or did not achieve the lesson objective?
3. Describe how your method of assessment matched your lesson objective? How will your assessment focus further instruction?

4. What aspects of your classroom management plan supported student achievement?

5. What did you do that enabled successful learning by students with different style or ability level?

6. If you were to teach this lesson again, describe the changes you might make. Why would you make hose changes?

Remember that without effective postobservation conferences, classroom observations become perfunctory in nature and produce relatively few instructional improvements because they fail to significantly modify teacher behavior (Dunkleberger, 1987).

It is hoped that eliciting information, being persuasive, and remaining open to alternatives will help instill *motivation* for the improvement within the teacher. All of the observation data is not worth much without it, as *self-motivation* is one of the critical forces in any improvement strategy. Ideally, the feedback should contribute to the accuracy of a teacher's *self-assessment*—an idea that should appeal to any teacher who wants to become more proficient (Weber, 1987). A format for working with competent and experienced teachers who are self-motivated is the annual goals approach as shown in Figure 6.9.

Figure 6.9 Format for Establishing and Assessing Annual Goals

Teacher _____ Subject(s) _____ Year _____

1. In Column I list three (3) goals for the present school year, one of which may be non-instructional.
2. In Column II list the specific action plans for the teacher to accomplish the goals.
3. In Column III 1ist the ways in which the teacher can determine when all goals have been accomplished.
4. In Column IV list the ways in which the principal can assist.

I. Goal	II. Action Plan	III. Indicators of Success	IV. Comments

Agreed to by _____ Teacher _____ and _____ Principal _____ on _____ Date

Postobservation Conference Check-Up

> *Now is the time for you to model for the teacher that Feedback is the Breakfast of Champions.*

Now that the principal has been through the entire evaluation process, it is important to find out how he or she did. One of the best ways to accomplish this is by doing a supervisory evaluation check-up. This involves asking those who have been evaluated to let you know how they feel you are doing. It is a check-up on the principal. Following is a list of questions from Jerry Braden, a principal in the Key West (FL) School District, that he uses to help him modify his approach to future conferences:

- During the conference did my supervisor
  - clearly communicate the purpose of the conference?
  - involve me in the discussion?
  - listen thoughtfully and open-mindedly?
  - exhibit positive nonverbals—facial expression, body language, etc.?
  - provide specific feedback about my performance?
  - check to see if feedback or suggestions were clear to me?
  - help me to analyze my performance?
  - encourage or allow me to express my opinions?
  - maintain a candid atmosphere?
  - act tactfully in a task-oriented manner?
  - really appear to be interested in my opinion?
  - provide suggestions or provide help if asked?
  - help me consider different strategies or approaches?
  - reinforce what I did well?
  - focus on important aspects of teaching?
  - help me reflect on what I do?
  - give me sufficient time so that I did not feel rushed?

Three other evaluation techniques hold promise for the improvement of teaching and student learning. They are peer review, self-evaluation, and portfolios.

Peer Review: Peer review is the evaluation of a teacher's performance by a colleague or team of colleagues. These colleagues are recruited from the ranks of teachers and often have the assignment of Teacher on Special Assignment (TOSA) for a period of two years. The term peer suggests that the person doing the reviewing and the person being reviewed have the same organizational title (teacher, counselor, etc.) and often have had the same assignment in terms of grade level (elementary, middle, or high school) and subject (math, science, etc.) (Peterson, 1995). The peer reviewer is selected by a group of teachers and administrators and is often widely accepted as an excellent teacher and a curriculum leader. The peer review does not substitute for the formal evaluation as this is the responsibility of the principal. It is helpful for beginning teachers in that they often feel as if they can be more candid with the peer than with the principal and with the teacher having some difficulty for much the same reason. A further benefit is that the reviewers often gain by observing another teacher in action and thus, can share that information with others and even use it themselves.

Lieberman (1998) in discussing the effectiveness of the peer review states "(n)ot even the most ardent supporters of peer review have been able to cite any improvement in student achievement clearly attributable to peer review that justifies the expenditures." If there is no impact of the achievement of students, then what about peer reviewer's impact on teachers? If the peer review increases the likelihood that poorer teachers would leave the profession, then it can be assumed that the outcome would be increased student achievement. However, research in the most experienced school district regarding peer review Toledo, OH has failed to affirm any claim for the student achievement gains attributable to the peer review process (Lieberman, 1998).

Self-Evaluation: All teachers engage in some form of informal evaluation. Usually it is at the end of day when the teacher is tired and the events of the day blend together into a day that is usually judged to be good or bad without much reflection on what made it a good or bad day. Also lacking is the reflection that if the teacher were to teach the lesson again what might be done differently. This is too bad since if evaluation is to benefit the teacher and ultimately the student then it should be done in a timely fashion and while the teacher's energy level is high. If this form of self-evaluation can been inculcated into the teacher's daily lesson planning, then evaluation would happen every day or every period of the day rather than the twice-yearly ritual of principal observation. One technique for self-evaluation is videotaping the teacher and the students during a lesson. Videotaping allows the teacher to see not only an accurate picture of the activities of the classroom, but also can be played over when the time is beneficial for teacher's learning. It is also common practice for the teacher to view the tape with a supervisor, colleague, or evaluator (Haetel, 1993). Figures 6.9 and 6.10

list the criteria and critical elements categories that the Vancouver (WA) School District has developed to assist the teacher in the self-evaluation process. Each of the criteria contains categories and critical elements (benchmarks) for proficiency and distinguished levels of performance.

Portfolios: It is common for members of professions other that education to use a portfolio and to present that portfolio to be judged by others. The artist seeking commission of a work, an architect, seeking to design a new building, a consultant, seeking to obtain new work are all examples of use of the portfolio by others. The portfolio is the collection of thoughtfully selected exhibits or artifacts and reflections indicative of the teacher's ability or progress toward goals or established criteria. Portfolios are now a central component of the certification process by the National Board for Professional Teaching Standards (1991). Colorado requires all teachers and administrators to prepare portfolios in order to renew their licenses (Wolf, 1996). Teachers and administrators in Connecticut are developing portfolios that are not only powerful professional development tools, but also serve as substitutes for formal observation (Van Wagenen and Hibbard, 1998).

The process of development of a portfolio is: the selection of artifacts relating to the criteria; the writing of reflections that describe, analyze and assess the experiences illustrated by the artifacts; and a written plan for future actions. Such a plan is review by a small (2 or 3 member) peer team and then by the administrator who adds a written endorsement or send the portfolio back for refinement. Figure 6.11 presents expanded self-assessment criteria. Figure 6.12 displays the characteristics of an evaluation portfolio for teachers and Figure 6.13 is a sample table of contents of a teacher portfolio.

Figure 6.10 Self Assessment Summary Sheet—Criteria and Critical Element Categories

Criterion No. 1 *Knowledge and Curriculum*: Knowledge of Subject Matter, Professional Preparation, Efforts Toward Improvement, State & District Essential Learnings and Learning Objectives

Criterion No. 2 *Student Learning*: Instructional Skill, Interest in Teaching Students, District Instructional Practices, and Use of Total Learning Resources

Criterion No. 3 *Classroom Management*: Classroom Organization and Management, Student Discipline, Professional Classroom Practices, and a Quality Learning Environment

Criterion No. 4 *Educational Leadership and Professionalism*: General School Service, Leadership, Professionalism

Criterion No. 5 *Assessment & Technology*: Life-Long Learning, Conducting and Applying Research, New Approaches to Student Learning, Use of Data, Use of Technology

Criterion #1	Criterion #2	Criterion #3	Criterion #4	Criterion #5
1.1 Subject Matter	2.1 Lesson Structure	3.1 Interactions	4.1 Parent Communications	5.1 Prof. Development
1.2 Prior Knowledge	2.2 Meaning	3.2 Value of Subject	4.2 Student Progress	5.2 Assessment of Lesson
1.3 Pedagogy	2.3 Activities	3.3 Quality of Work	4.3 Collegial Relationships	5.3 Student Information
1.4 Developmental Characteristics	2.4 Presentation of Content	3.4 Engagement of Learning	4.4 Volunteering	5.4 Student Data
1.5 Student Skills	2.5 Instructional Grouping	3.5 Transitions	4.5 Student Success	5.5 Standards
1.6 Cultural Heritage	2.6 Directions	3.6 Non-Instructional Duties		5.6 Instructional Use of Technology
1.7 Instructional Goals	2.7 Verbal and Written Language	3.7 Student Behavior		5.7 Use of Technology in Assessment
1.8 Materials and Resources	2.8 Questions	3.8 Response to Behavior		
1.9 Instructional Goals	2.9 Strategies	3.9 Environment		

Figure 6.11 Self-Assessment Criteria Expanded

Criterion No. 1 Knowledge and Curriculum: Knowledge of Subject Matter, Professional Preparation, Efforts Toward Improvement, State & District Essential Learnings and Learning Objectives.

	Critical Elements Proficient	Category	*Critical Elements* Distinguished
1.1	Teacher displays solid subject matter knowledge.	**Subject Matter**	Teacher displays extensive knowledge of the subject matter and relationships to other parts of the curricula.
1.2	Teacher's plans and practices demonstrate understanding of students' prior knowledge of relationships among topics and concepts, and are at the correct level of difficulty.	**Prior Knowledge**	Teacher actively builds on understanding of students' prior knowledge of prerequisite relationships when describing instruction or seeking causes for student misunderstanding.
1.3	Pedagogical practices reflect current research.	**Pedagogy**	Teacher displays continuing search for best pedagogical practices and anticipates student misconceptions.
1.4	Teacher displays understanding of typical developmental characteristics of age group, exceptions to general patterns, and learning styles.	**Developmental Characteristics**	Teacher displays knowledge of developmental characteristics of age group, exceptions to the patterns, the extent to which each student follows patterns, and uses varied approaches to learning.
1.5	Teacher displays knowledge and application of students' skills and learning styles for groups of students.	**Student Skills**	Teacher displays knowledge of each individual student's skills and knowledge, including those with special needs.
1.6	Teacher displays knowledge of the interests or cultural heritage of groups of students.	**Cultural Heritage**	Teacher recognizes the value of the cultural heritage of each student and integrates it into the curriculum.
1.7	Instructional goals are suitable for most	**Instructional Goals**	Instructional goals account for varying learning needs of individual students.
1.8	Teacher applies instructional materials and student resources adopted by the school or district.	**Materials and Resources**	Teacher seeks out and utilizes materials and resources that complement and enhance those of the district.
1.9	Lessons are based on sound instructional practices, align with essential learnings, and are at the correct level of difficulty.	**Instructional Goals**	Lessons, learning activities, and materials align with essential learnings, are highly relevant to students and instructional goals, and meet individual student needs.

Criterion No. 2 Student Learning: Instructional Skill, Interest in Teaching Students, District Instructional Practices, and Use of Total Learning Resources.

	Critical Elements Proficient	Category	Critical Elements Distinguished
2.1	Instructional objectives clearly define the planned learning, match student behavior with the learning, recognize conditions affecting the learning, and define acceptable performance.	Lesson Structure	The lesson's structure is appropriate for all students to achieve the learning and accommodate individual differences in learning.
2.2	Materials, exercise, and instructional practice allow for reinforcement and retention of the learning. Teacher uses closure to assess student learning and decide whether to reteach, practice, or move on.	Meaning	In addition to materials and instruction, the lesson has sufficient meaning to increase the motivation to learn and speed up learning. The teacher uses closure at all strategic points and is able to assess each student's learning.
2.3	Activities, materials, and assignments are appropriate to the instructional objective and to students. Students are actively engaged in the lesson.	Activities	All students are actively engaged in the activities and assignments in their exploration of content. Students initiate or adapt activities and projects to enhance understanding.
2.4	Presentation of content is appropriate and links well with students' previous knowledge and experience. Lessons are monitored and adjusted as necessary.	Presentation of Content	Students are able to use examples and analogies to contribute to representation of context.
2.5	Instructional groups are productive and fully appropriate to the students and to the instructional goals of a lesson.	Instructional Grouping	Teacher facilitates the influence of students with instructional groups to advance group understanding.
2.6	Teacher directions and procedures are understood as demonstrated by student performance.	Directions	Teacher directions and procedures anticipate possible student misunderstanding.
2.7	Teacher's spoken and written language is clear and correct. Vocabulary is appropriate to students' age and interest.	Verbal and Written Language	Teacher's spoken and written language is correct and expressive, with well-chosen vocabulary that enriches the lesson.
2.8	Most of teacher's questions probe for depth of understanding and elicit information from all students. Adequate time is available for students to respond.	Questions	Teacher's questions are uniformly high quality, probe for depth of individual student understanding, and contribute to higher order thinking.
2.9	Teacher persists in seeking approaches for students who have difficulty learning, and applies a moderate repertoire of intervention strategies.	Strategies	Teacher possesses and uses an extensive repertoire of strategies and additional resources to assist students who need help.

Criterion No. 3 *Classroom Management:* Classroom Organization and Management, Student Discipline, Professional Classroom Practices, and a Quality Learning Environment

	Critical Elements — Proficient	Category	Critical Elements — Distinguished
3.1	Teacher-student and student-student interactions are mutually respectful and free of abusive or demeaning behavior.	**Interactions**	Teacher demonstrates genuine caring and respect for individual students and elicits student respect for teacher and other students as individuals.
3.2	Teacher conveys enthusiasm for the subject, and students demonstrate consistent commitment to its value.	**Value of Subject**	Teacher provides the opportunity for students to demonstrate through their active participation, curiosity, and attention to detail that values the subject's importance.
3.3	Teacher insists upon and positively motivates students to strive for high quality.	**Quality of Work**	Teacher provides the opportunity for students to take obvious pride in their work and initiate improvements on their own.
3.4	Instructional goals and activities, interactions, and the classroom environment convey high expectations for student achievement.	**Engagement of Learning**	Teacher involves students in the planning and the assessment of learning, thereby gaining student ownership and motivation.
3.5	Transitions occur smoothly with little loss of instructional time.	**Transitions**	Transitions are seamless with students assuming some responsibility for efficient operation.
3.6	Efficient systems for performing non-instructional duties are in place resulting in minimal loss of instructional time.	**Non-Instructional Duties**	Systems for performing non-instructional duties are well established with students assuming considerable responsibility for efficient operation.
3.7	Teacher has clearly conveyed standards of conduct to all students. Teacher is alert to student behavior at all times.	**Student Behavior**	Students are encouraged to monitor personal and peer behavior, correcting one another respectfully.
3.8	Teacher response to misbehavior is appropriate and successful and respects the student's dignity. Student behavior is generally appropriate.	**Response to Behavior**	Teacher response to misbehavior is highly effective and sensitive to students' individual needs. Student behavior is entirely appropriate.
3.9	The classroom presents a safe environment, and furniture and resource arrangement does not inhibit or distract from learning.	**Environment**	The classroom is orderly, well maintained, and safe. Classroom furniture and resources are arranged skillfully to promote student learning.

Criterion No. 4 *Educational Leadership and Professionalism*: General School Service, Leadership, Professionalism

	Critical Elements	Category	Critical Elements
	Proficient		Distinguished
4.1	Teacher provides information to parents about the instructional programs and makes reasonable efforts to engage families in student learning.	**Parent Communications**	Teacher provides frequent information to parents and uses frequent and creative strategies to engage parents in the instructional program.
4.2	Teacher communicates with parents about students' progress on a regular basis and is available as needed to respond to parent concerns.	**Student Progress**	Teacher provides information to parents frequently on both positive and negative aspects of student progress. Response to parent concerns is handled with sensitivity.
4.3	Support and cooperation characterize professional relationships with colleagues.	**Collegial Relationships**	Support and cooperation fosters professional relationships with colleagues. Teacher takes initiative in assuming leadership responsibilities.
4.4	Teacher volunteers to participate and contribute in school and district projects and/or events.	**Volunteering**	Teacher volunteers to participate in school and district projects and/or events, making a substantial contribution, and assumes a leadership role in some aspect of school life or district project.
4.5	Teacher works within the context of a particular team or department to ensure that all students receive a fair opportunity to succeed.	**Student Success**	Teacher makes a particular effort to challenge negative attitudes and helps ensure that all students, particularly those traditionally under served, are honored in the school.

	Critical Elements	Category	Critical Elements
	Proficient		Distinguished
5.1	Teacher seeks out opportunities for professional development to enhance content knowledge and pedagogical skill.	**Professional Development**	Teacher seeks out opportunities for professional development and makes a systematic attempt to implement new strategies to enhance learning.
5.2	Teacher makes an accurate assessment of a lesson's effectiveness and the extent to which it achieved its goals.	**Assessment of Lesson**	Teacher's assessment of a lesson's effectiveness is demonstrated by specific examples from the lesson, weighing the relative strength of each, and making appropriate adjustments.
5.3	Teacher's system for maintaining information on student completion of assignments, student progress , and non-instructional activities is accurate and well maintained.	**Student Information**	Teacher's system for maintaining student information allows an accurate representation of individual student progress and improved planning of individual student needs.
5.4	Multiple forms of student data are used to assess instructional goals.	**Student Data**	Assessment results are used to support continuous improvement of the instructional processes and meeting of all group and individual student needs.
5.5	Assessment criteria and standards are clear, have been clearly communicated to students, and are used to plan for individuals and groups of students.	**Standards**	Teacher creates continuous awareness and understanding on the part of students as to how well they are meeting the established standards. Students contribute to the development of the criteria and standards.
5.6	Teacher is adept in the use of technology for instructional purposes as provided by the district and uses it effectively.	**Instructional Use of Technology**	Teacher stays abreast of the evolving use of technology in the instructional process and takes the initiative to design learning experiences around available technology.
5.7	Teacher uses technology for student assessment as provided by the district.	**Use of Technology in Assessment**	Teacher optimizes the use of available technology for student assessment, record keeping, and communication purposes.

Figure 6.12 Characteristics of an Evaluation Portfolio for Teachers

- Positive and personal
- Both *formative* and *summative*
- Authentic" documentation
- Creates ownership and commitment
- Promotes dialogue among teachers as well as between teacher and principal
- Allows teachers to use and understand it before encouraging students
- A more holistic view of evaluation

Figure 6.13 Sample Teacher Portfolio Table of Contents

Introduction

Résumé

Beliefs and Values about Teaching and Learning

Teaching Goals and Artifacts

Short (1 year)

1. Learner-centered Instruction (Achievement of Students)
2. Teaching and Learning (Curriculum Development)
3. Communication with Others
   - Peers
   - Principal
   - Parents
   - Students

Long (5 years)

1. Professional Development Plan
2. Mentor to Others
3. District Level Responsibilities
4. Other Professional Responsibilities

Accolades

A Special Case of Evaluation: Coaches

It is important for the principal to be very involved in the evaluation of coaches who are assigned to his building whether or not they are on the teaching staff. Often this task is delegated to the athletic director or assistant principal. Nevertheless, the principal should be responsible for, and very conversant with the evaluation procedures. In addition the principal should review, and sign off on all coaching evaluations. In addition, the principal should evaluate the athletic director in that role. The head coach should evaluate the assistants and discuss these evaluations with the athletic director prior to having these evaluations signed by the principal.

The performance appraisal of coaches is intended to provide feedback to coaches regarding their performance. Such appraisal is intended to help the coach improve their performance, and in turn, the performance of their student athletes. The evaluation should be based on criteria established at the time of hire and reviewed/revised annually. Data regarding the appraisal of the coaches should be based on both game and practice observations.

Areas for assessment include:

Coaching

Professional Relationships with players

Discipline

Professional Relationships with Colleagues

Public and Parent Relations

Management Responsibilities

Professional Growth

Overall Performance.

If the coach receives evaluation in the range of needs improvement, then the evaluator must provide specific data and sources of information and suggest ways to improve. The performance of coaches must be considered by the principal and other evaluators as very important and done with care.

Key Idea
Coaching is teaching where there are many evaluators present.

There are uncommon but extreme cases of unfit coaches. The coaching profession has one of the highest rates of sexual-misconduct complaints. A Seattle Times newspaper analysis of the Washington State of the Superintendent of Public Instruction data shows that teachers who coach are three times more likely to be accused of and investigated for sexual misconduct by the state than noncoaching teachers (Willmsen and O'Hagan, 2003).

Evaluation of Classified Personnel

It is not uncommon that the number of classified staff members that the principal must evaluate will exceed the number of teachers. The National Center on Educational Statistics reported a 49% increase in instructional paraeducator employment compared to a 13% increase in student enrollment and an 18% increase in teacher employment between 1990 and 1998 (NCES). In many cases the classified staff may work under the day-to-day supervision of the teacher as is the case with paraeducators. This however, does not change the principal's responsibility for the summative evaluation. Gerlach (2003) emphasizes the principal's role. "Even though teachers are responsibility for the day-to-day instructional supervision of paraeducators, principals are responsible for the administrative supervision that includes the hiring, preparation, evaluation and dismissal of paraeducators." Gerlach (2003) lists the principal's major responsibilities in working with paraeducators:

+ Recruiting, interviewing and hiring
+ Assigning paraeducators to specific programs, teachers, classroom, or teacher teams
+ Developing appropriate job descriptions
+ Developing appropriate policies for the employment, training, and supervision of paraeducators
+ Evaluating paraeducators and their supervising teachers
+ Promoting effective teamwork in the building and within paraeducator teams
+ Providing professional development opportunities for paraeducatiors and those who supervise them
+ Providing leadership in support of effective teamwork
+ Document the training requirement of paraeducators.

These responsibilities could easily be extended to other classified staff members that are assigned to the building: custodians, secretaries, and clerical assistants. If the principal is to be held accountable for the staff and results in the building, all personnel must report to the principal. Of course, while the day-to-day supervision may fall to others: office manager, head custodian, teachers or assistant principals, the principal must provide general oversight. In particular, the principal should enlist the support and advice from others who might have technical expertise without relinquishing the evaluative role. In many cases the principal will want to cooperatively evaluate the classified staff with those who have technical expertise in order to create a cooperative climate in the building. It will be increasingly important for the principal to understand and comply with the provisions paraeducators must meet regarding assessment within the provisions of the No Child Left Behind (NCLB) federal legislation enacted on January 8, 2000.

Principal Evaluation in a Performance-Based School

The evaluation of teachers, coaches, and the classified staff are very important to the performance-based school. There is no question that student achievement in a performance-based school is a shared responsibility involving the student, family, educators, and the community. However, as the leader, the principal is accountable for the continuous growth of individual students and increased school performance (AWSP, 2002).

In addition, the association (AWSP, 2002) advocates for authentic assessment for principals which has these *elements*:

- ◆ Clear standards for principal performance
- ◆ Specific and measurable goals
- ◆ The use of measure/data for assessment
- ◆ Provisions for developmental and expertise ability levels
- ◆ Ongoing meeting and dialogue to track, assist and encourage progress
- ◆ Training, support, and authority provided for the principals
- ◆ Expectations of self-evaluation and personal growth planning
- ◆ Use of assessment data to plan next steps in professional growth and development

Further, the association holds that principal assessment is designed to assist leadership growth and hold the principal accountable for student achievement by using the following *process*:

- ◆ Providing support, encouragement, assistance, and timely intervention to meet standards appropriate to the developmental level of the principal
- ◆ Assist the principal in self-evaluation and planning for continued professional development
- ◆ Recognizing and rewarding excellence in performance
- ◆ Assisting and holding accountable principals whose performance does not meet identified standards, including taking ac-

tion with principals whose unsatisfactory performance does not improve over time.

The Context for Principal Evaluation

Authentic assessment of principal performance requires the evaluation to be embedded in the leadership tasks of the principal. Both district practice and the state legislation require schools to collaboratively develop, implement, and monitor annual School Improvement Plans (SIP). The SIP is a driver for the school's self-assessment, as well as helping identify the principal' leadership tasks, goals, monitoring, and evaluation.

Both the SIP and the principal goal setting begin with data collection and short- and long-term analyses of student achievement and school environmental information, measured over one-year, three-year, and six-year increments. Conditions that enhance or block learning assist in prioritizing critical next steps to increase student achievement and teacher efficacy. This data forms the basis for the SIP and the goals for the principal's performance evaluation.

Implementation of Principal Evaluation

Using the data, the SIP, and self-evaluation, each principal, in collaboration with the supervisor, determines the two or three Principal Leadership Priorities that are keys for addressing the current needs of the school.

> **Example:** Data indicates need for a goal focusing upon increasing student performance in reading. Data also indicates two essential elements necessary for accomplishing the reading goal: increased student daily attendance and the training of all staff in the use of reading skills. These three Principal Leadership Priorities are the most important needs to accomplish in the SIP and, thus, determine the principal's performance focus both during the immediate year as well as the longer three to six-year time period.

In many cases Principal Leadership Priorities will include key district goals. However, in no case should there be more than a total of three principal priorities.

Once the Principal Leadership Priorities are established, they are linked with the appropriate ISLLC standards and their related Performance Indicators to identify principal leadership activities and professional growth focus. Collaboratively, the principal and supervisor plan and implement strategies to accomplish the priorities. Together, they also identify and agree upon measures and indicators to track progress and the knowledge/skills, support and authority necessary for goal accomplishment.

Ongoing dialogue and collaboration: Data are collected by both principal and supervisor, progress tracked, mid-course corrections made, and sequenced steps developed. Continuous feedback, coupled with evaluation conferences to share data prior to the final written evaluation ensures no surprises when the summary evaluation is completed.

Implementation Options: The evaluation process must have a stable core of authenticity that enables principals to have the meaningful dialogue about their leadership work. However, district uniqueness requires that process be flexible and adaptable to local culture. Thus, a principal and supervisor dialogue will likely develop about the local particulars of the new principal evaluation in a performance-based school.

Technology in the Evaluation and Supervision Process

The principal would be well advised to develop word processing skills to the level of being able to take data observed in the classroom directly onto the laptop and down load it to the computer for editing and refinement. This could be a major time saving procedure. Some excellent internet sites are:

- ◆ www.teachersevaluation.net/NewPractices
- ◆ info@creatingchange.com

    This is the site for Supervision Assistant®, which claims to dramatically increase the effectiveness of the supervision and evaluation process with this revolutionary internet-base employee evaluation software.

- ◆ www.nrcpara.org/bibliography/index.html

    This is an annotated bibliography highlighting paraeducator training resources, administrative guidelines, and personnel preparation models.

- ◆ www.para.inl.edu

    This site offers training that is comprehensive, easily accessible, and beneficial to both the paraeducators and the teachers who supervise them.

- ◆ www.aasa.org/issues and insights/ESEA/

    This site is a highly useful gateway to resources and best practices to assist school personnel implement the No Child Left Behind Act.

Conclusion

A great deal of material has been covered in this chapter relating to the supervision and evaluation process and certain ideas have surfaced that seem to be the keys to success for the whole process:

♦ Attention is paid to teacher input into the process.

♦ Collegial observation and self-observation are allowed (using videotaping, for example).

♦ Feedback is frequent and observations are followed up with goal setting.

♦ The performance criteria are specific and subject to teachers' input when they are formed.

♦ Evaluators give detailed suggestions rather than vague criticism or irrelevant observations about teaching (Weber, 1987).

♦ The evaluation of coaches and classified staff are areas that deserve the principal's close attention.

The following quote from Weber (1987) offers what I feel is a fitting conclusion to the material we have been studying in this chapter:

> "For observations to be worthwhile, the experience of practitioners and researchers indicates that they must be carried out by knowledgeable observers using a well-planned, well-recorded set of teaching criteria. Moreover, the results should be diplomatically discussed with the teacher and followed up with further observations and opportunities for teacher self-appraisal.
>
> For the evaluation process to pay back the maximum return on the investment of time and energy, that process should be integrated with goal-setting programs and other developmental activities."

Principals should put their best effort into the evaluation process and enjoy the benefits. Remember, as principals help others become successful, they will experience success as instructional leaders and developers of teachers.

Supervision and Evaluation—Case Study

Wayne Olson was in his second year as principal of Arcadia Elementary School. He was an effective principal well regarded by teachers, students, parents, and the superintendent.

He had been an outstanding teacher and his students always scored above the school average on both criteria-referenced and norm-referenced tests. Wayne was promoted to principal after he completed his academic coursework at the local university and his year-long internship at Arcadia Elementary.

Wayne felt that his teachers were doing a very good job of teaching and he was eagerly awaiting the results of the state-wide testing of his fourth grade students. When the results came back, Wayne was shocked to see that the scores were below average for Janet Wodjenski's class. He knew that she was not his best teacher in the fourth grade, but he felt in visiting her classroom that the students and teacher were appropriately on-task.

Wayne decided that he needed more information and talked to some of the students and to the teachers who taught Ms. Wodjenski's students in the third grade. He also talked to the Janet. Nothing seemed to fit a pattern, but he was still concerned and decided to send a survey to the parents regarding their view of instruction in the classroom. Olson did send a copy to Janet on the same day he mailed it to the parents of the students.

Questions for the prospective principal:

1. What reasons would you propose for the decline in test scores?
2. Would you have done what Olson did? What could he have done?
3. What long-range problem could result from Olson's decision to survey the parents?

Comprehensive Questions

1. How can a principal minimize the teacher's stress level in regard to the observation and evaluation process?

It is the principal's job to distinguish between events a teacher should be able to control and uncontrollable situations. How might a principal go about doing this?

3. Assuming a principal is able to recognize "outstanding" instruction, how might he train himself to retain objectivity during an observation?
4. If a teacher comes to you and asks for help with discipline of the class, what would you do to assist the teacher?

Extended Activities

1. Write an evaluation of a strong teacher. Write an evaluation of an average teacher. Compare and contrast the evaluations.
2. Develop your own set of questions for the postobservation conference (short and effective).

3. Practice listening by visiting classrooms often and compliment-ing teachers' efforts. Listen for their feedback.

4. Ask your teachers and classified staff for their expectation of the principal as evaluator. Summarize the data and share it with your staff and superintendent.

5. What role should student achievement plan in the evaluation of a teacher?

References

Acheson, K. A., and M. D. Gall (1987). *Techniques in the clinical supervision of teachers: Preservice and inservice applications,* 2nd ed. New York: Longman.

Association of Washington School Principals (2002). *Principals evaluation in a performance-based school.* Olympia, WA.

Blackburn, R., D. Hare, and W. Kritsonis (1989). Pre-evaluation conference. *National Forum of Applied Educational Research Journal, 1.*

Bolton, D. L. (1973). *Selection and evaluation of teachers.* Berkely, CA: McCutchan.

Brandt, R. (1996). On a new direction for teacher evaluation: A conversation with Tom McGreal. *Educational Leadership, 53,* 6: 30–34.

Cascio, W. F. (1982). *Applied psychology in personnel management.* Reston, VA: Reston Publishing.

Cogan, M. L. (1973). *Clinical supervision.* Boston: Houghton Mifflin.

Darling-Hammond, L. (1986). A proposal for evaluation in the teaching profession. *The Elementary School Journal, 86,* 531–551.

Dunkelberger, G. E. (1987). Making the most of the post-observation conference. *Bulletin, 71,* 503.

Gagawski, R. A. (1980). Collaboration is key: Successful teacher evaluation not a myth. *NASSP Bulletin, 64*(434), 1–7.

Goldhammer, R., R. H. Anderson, and R. J. Krajewski (1993). *Clinical supervision: Special methods for the supervision of teachers,* 3rd ed. New York: Holt, Rinehart and Winston.

Gerlach, K. (2003). *Let's team up! A checklist for paraeduators, teachers, and principals.* Washington, D.C.: National Education Association.

Huddle, G. (1985). Teacher evaluation: How important for effective schools? Eight messages from research. *NASSP Bulletin, 69*(479), 58–63.

Hyman, R. T. (1986). *School administrator's faculty supervision handbook.* Englewood Clifts, NJ: Prentice-Hall.

Iden, D., C. Fisher, and M. Taylor (1979). Consequences of individual feedback on behavior in organizations. *Journal of Applied Psychology, 5.*

Keylin, L. (2000, January) Seminar on Teacher Evaluation in Burlington-Edison School District (WA).

Latham, G. P., and G. A. Yuki (1975). A review of research on the application of goal setting in organizations. *Academy of Management Journal, 18.*

Lieberman, M. (1998). *Teachers evaluating teachers: Peer review and the new unionism.* New Brunswick (USA): Transaction Purblishers.

McGreal, T. L. (1982). Effective teacher evaluation systems. *Educational Leadership, 39*(4), 303–305.

Nemeroff, W. F., and K. N. Wexley (1977). An exploration of the relationships between the performance feedback interview characteristics and interview outcomes as perceived by managers and subordinates. *Journal of Occupational Psvchology, 52.*

Peterson, C. H. (1982). *A century's growth in teacher evaluation in the United States.* New York: Vantage.

Redfern, G. B. (1980). *Evaluating teachers and administrators: A performance objectives approach.* Boulder, CO: Westview.

Sergiovanni, T. J. (Ed.) (1982). *Supervision of teaching.* Alexandria, VA: Association for Supervision and Curriculum Development.

Stiggins, R. J., and Bridgeford, N.J. (1985). Performance assessment for teacher development. *Educational Evaluation and Policy Analysis, 7*(1), 85–97.

Sweeney, J. (1989). The supervisory conference: Being the best you can be. *The Practitioner, 1.*

"Toledo School District Achieves Better 9th Grades Exam Results," *Toledo Blade,* November 1, 1997, p. 9.

Van Wagenen, L. and K.M. Hibbard (1998). Building Teacher Portfolios. *Educational Leadership, 55*(5).

Washington Association of School Administrators (2000). *Supervision and Evaluation for Education Reform: A Toolkit for Administrators.* Olympia, WA.

Weber, J. R. (1987). *Teacher evaluation as a strategy for improving instruction.* Eugene, OR: University of Oregon (ERIC Clearinghouse on Educational Management).

Willmsen, C., and O'Hagan, M. (2003). "Coaches who prey." *The Seattle Times,* December 16, 2003.

Wise, A.E., et al. (1985). Teacher evaluation: A study of effective practices. *The Elementary School Journal, 86*(1), 61–121.

Wolf, K. (1996). Developing an effective teaching portfolio. *Educational Leadership, 53*(6).

7

Assisting
the Marginal Teacher

Reasons for Studying the Marginal Teacher

- The marginal teacher can cause the principal significant problems and cause the expenditure of massive amounts of both time and money.

- The process of working with the marginal teacher can be a challenge to the professional skills of the principal.

- The students deserve a quality teacher, and it is the responsibility of the principal to improve the effectiveness of the teacher.

- Awareness and identification of the marginal teacher, and the willingness to confront the teacher and the behavior, will relate to the effectiveness of the principal. If you cannot improve the teacher's effectiveness then the focus of the problem is on the principal, not the teacher.

- The marginal teacher can create a morale issue for other teachers. Principals who have the courage to put teachers on a plan of assistance raise the bar for other teachers as well as honoring their own work.

> *It is critical to understand that even if you do not have a marginal teacher, you always have a weakest teacher.*
>
> David Peterson, Student in Class

ISLLC Standards Covered in this Chapter

Standard 2:

- A school administrator is an educational leader who promotes the success of all students by advocating, nurturing, and sustaining a school culture and instructional program conducive to student learning and staff professional growth.

Standard 3:

- ◆ A school administrator is an educational leader who promotes the success of all students by ensuring management of the organization, operations, and resources for a safe, efficient, and effective learning environment.

Standard 5:

- ◆ A school administrator is an education leader who promotes the success of all students by acting with integrity, fairness and in an ethical manner.

Introduction

This chapter provides the necessary framework for school principals in two areas: (1) increasing student learning by improving instruction, and (2) increasing their skills to work effectively with teachers identified as having professional deficiencies. While the scope of these areas is broad, principals must maintain a clear vision of their goals for instruction, and what expectations they set for teachers to continually meet those goals.

Sections in this chapter are designed to address specifically, programs that identify the marginal teacher, effectively assist teachers in professional improvement, and to provide remediation for teachers found in need of improvement. Also, the steps involved in the probationary process for teachers who fail to meet improvement requirements are shown in detail. The materials included in this chapter range from sample documents and model programs, to suggested procedures and forms, all for practical use. They are provided so that a practicing principal can have access to materials which would be used in the procedures described.

The Marginal Teacher

> **Key Idea**
>
> *Nobody likes to deal with the most frustrating, resistant, ineffective, and negative staff members in the school—but principals must—and good principal must do so effectively.*
>
> T. Whitaker, *Seizing Power from Difficult Teachers*

Most teachers in our nation's schools are competent, conscientious, and hardworking individuals. All too often their efforts are overshadowed by the poor performance of a relatively small number of incompetent classroom teachers. These incompetent teachers must be identified and assisted by the principal, and if they fail to improve, they must be dismissed. Rogus and Nuzzi (1993) identify these common behaviors of marginal teachers that have a "negative or questionable impact on student learning": (1) Failure to create an appropriate classroom atmosphere; (2) Lack of personal insight and motivation; and (3) unwillingness to accept responsibility for problems. Figure 7.1 lists 10 characteristics that often indicate a marginal teacher. Principals need to be alert to these characteristics and, when present, intercede in a very timely fashion in order to keep the problem from becoming more serious.

Figure 7.1 Ten Characteristics of a Marginal Teacher

- Lacks "bell to bell" planning.
- Does not teach to the curriculum in general and to specific objectives in particular.
- Students become easily distracted and are off-task.
- Lacks enthusiasm for students and teaching.
- Doesn't provide meaningful and timely feedback to students.
- Has poor personal relations with students.
- Exhibits poor teaching skills.
- Unorganized classroom and lessons.
- Does not establish expectations for student behavior and thus, discipline is usually a major problem.
- Lacks knowledge of the subject matter.

School districts that wish to confront this challenge face a formidable array of legal, technical, and human problems. These problems can be overcome if school districts are willing to adopt an organizational approach to deal with incompetent teachers in an integrated, comprehensive fashion. The eight elements comprising a useful approach are:

- Establish "improvement in teaching" as a high priority for the district.
- Adopt and publish reasonable criteria for evaluating teachers.
- Adopt sound procedures for determining whether teachers satisfy these criteria and apply these procedures uniformly to teachers in the district.
- Provide unsatisfactory teachers with remediation (assistance) and a reasonable period of time to improve.

- Establish and implement procedures for ensuring that principals have current competencies in the areas of supervision, evaluation, and in providing assistance.

- Provide principals with the resources needed to carry out their responsibilities.

- Hold principals accountable for evaluating and dealing with incompetent teachers.

- Provide incompetent teachers with a fair hearing prior to making the dismissal decision. (Bridges, 1990)

Principals who follow this systematic approach reap several noteworthy benefits. In districts that use this approach, principals are much more likely to confront the poor performers and to induce improvement, resignations, or early retirements if they fail to improve (Groves, 1985). Moreover, in those schools where principals are issuing formal notices of incompetence and inducing incompetents to leave, the students' achievement tends to be higher than in those schools where principals ignore the problem of poor performance (Groves, 1985; McLaughlin, 1984). Finally, the administration is much more likely to have its dismissal decisions upheld if the teacher chooses to contest the decision, rather than to resign or retire early (Bridges, 1990).

The success of any organizational program is based on the level of priority that the program holds in the school district. This is true for educational programs designed to improve teacher instruction, or provide remediation for teachers found to be marginal. The task of a school district's leadership, both at the superintendent and principal levels, is to ensure that "improvement in teaching" becomes and remains the centerpiece of the district's agenda. This idea is paramount since the improvement of instruction leads to improvement in learning.

When a teacher is performing in a marginally effective manner and the principal does not confront the teacher with the problem, then the principal is also performing in a very marginal manner. So just what can the principal do?

First, take time during the recruiting and selection process to make reasonably certain that you have selected a competent teacher. Looking at potential candidates from an ecological perspective can help predict success or failure. Parker Palmer, (2000) noted teacher of teachers, asks an ecology question when he queries: "Are you well suited to the job?" Palmer points out that the vocational question is not then, "What should I do with my life?" It is a much more elemental and demanding question: "Who am I?" Or perhaps even "what is my nature?" He further maintains that good teaching cannot be reduced to technique, but comes rather from the very identity and integrity of the teacher. When a teacher achieves an integration of self and job, the results are very positive. Therefore, the principal must pay attention to both the person and personality of the prospective teacher to understand how they might operate in the classroom.

Key Idea

Do not be overly persuaded by special courses taken during the college experience. Instructional Theory into Practice (ITIP), whole language approaches, Math Their Way, and others can be learned later if need be. Select a teacher who cares about students and was very successful in student teaching or in previous classroom teaching.

Second, during the orientation and induction programs make sure you discuss the job description with the teacher, answer any questions regarding it, and obtain the signature of the teacher on the job description. (See chapters covering Recruiting, Selection, and Induction.)

Third, introduce teachers to the evaluation form and procedures so that they know what they are being evaluated on and what form it will take (see Figure 6.1). In addition, introduce and explain the National Education Association's Code of Ethics of the Education Profession (www.nea.org) or your state's Code of Professional Conduct.

Fourth, even though principals will be very busy during the first two weeks of school, they must find the time to visit the classrooms of all teachers new to their building. There are two main reasons for doing this: (1) to validate the selection process; and (2) to identify any potential problems, which, if corrected early, will save substantial time and effort later. Consider Figure 7.2, which illustrates the problem that is created if the teaching deficiency is not noted early.

Fifth, check weekly with the new teachers' mentors for the first three months and periodically throughout the year. If there are any early signs of problems, then the principal should intervene to assist or provide external assistance in a timely manner.

Key Idea

When you make an early visit (within the first two weeks of the school year) to the classroom of a teacher there are generally two things that can happen: things are going fine or they are not. If they are going fine, you need to reinforce and affirm the teacher; if they are not going fine, then you need to provide assistance. Either way, you, the teacher, and the students will benefit.

Sixth, meet individually with each teacher new to your building, ask questions regarding how things are going and provide assistance if needed.

Figure 7.2 Teacher Performance and Principal Intervention

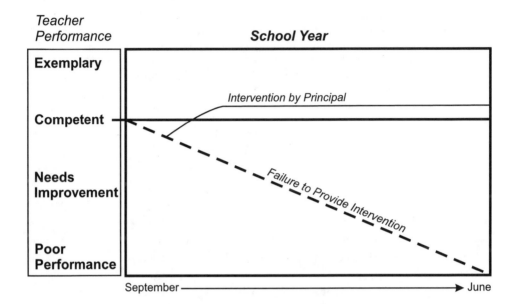

Types of Remediation

Once a teacher is having serious problems regarding teaching, it is incumbent on the principal to provide timely assistance to make the year instructionally successful for both the teacher and the students.

The principal can do the following:

- ♦ Work with the teacher to set short-term goals that relate directly to the district's established criteria of successful teaching. Reference should be made to the district's evaluation form.

- ♦ Provide release time for the teacher to observe successful teachers, preferably out of the building, and provide time to assist the teacher with reflections on the observation. It is best for the beginning teachers to observe a good teacher but not a great one lest they become discouraged and feel that they "could never teach like that."

- ♦ Examine the class in terms of its composition of difficult students. Perhaps the transfer of a couple of students could assist in making the classroom more manageable.

- Provide help and support in the acquisition of teaching materials.
- Provide extra time for the mentor and the teacher to discuss the lessons, curriculum, and classroom procedures.
- Provide assistance through the Employee Assistance Program (EAP). A detailed explanation of the program is included later in this chapter.

Planning

Planning is one area in which principals can assist the marginal teacher. If the teacher is well-planned, then the problem shifts to the more complex phase of the lesson: implementing the plans. Figures 7.3, 7.4, and 7.5 are examples of daily, unit, and year-long plans. These provide the format to enable the principal to assist the teacher with phases of the planning process.

Figure 7.3 Daily Plan

Objective:

Be able to distinguish between solids, liquids, and gases.
Be able to determine melting point, boiling point, freezing point, and point of condensation of water; sublimation

Materials Needed:

2 flasks, watch glass, thermometer, beakers, mercury, water, salt, iodine, dry ice, regular ice chips, paper, pencil

Activities:

5 minutes	Define and show examples of solids, liquids, gases
10 minutes	Define and demonstrate mp, bp, fp, pt. of condensation
20 minutes	Students work in groups of two Starting with ice in a beaker, heat and measure the temperature at which it changes to liquid, then a gas (Record data)
10 minutes	Demonstrate heating iodine Sublimation (gas to solid with no liquid state between)
5 minutes	Students measure dry ice and observe sublimation (record data) Lab write-ups due tomorrow
5 minutes	Discuss results

Evaluation:

Questioning
Lab write-up

Figure 7.4 Unit Plan—Chemistry Outline

September 14–
September 25 (2 weeks)

Properties of Elements

1. LAB, Behaviors of elements
2. LAB, Categorizing the elements—metals/nonmetals
3. LAB, Behaviors within the categories and He

September 28–
October 9 (2 weeks)

Organization of the Elements

4. Periodical behaviors, Mendeleev's theory
5. Periodical chart

October 12–30
(3 weeks)

Acids and Bases

6. PH levels—So what!
7. LAB, Testing for acid and base
8. LAB, Does Rolaids really spell relief?
9. What causes cars to rust?

November 2–6
(1 Week)

Chemistry at Home

10. Carbon units
11. Putting strings of chemicals together, Polymers
12. Making it go faster and cheaper
13. Making alcohol—is it safe to drink?

Figure 7.5 Year-Long Plan—Physical Science Outline

September 1–11
(2 weeks)

Introduction, Chapter 1

September 14–
November 6 (8 weeks)

Chemistry Chapters 5, 8, 9, 6, 7, 13, 14, 10, 11

Properties of Elements

Organization of the Elements

Acids and Bases

Chemistry at Home

November 9–
December 11 (5 weeks)

Light and Sound Chapters 15, 16, 17, 18

Waves and Electromagnetic Radiation

Reflection and Refraction

Optics

Sound

December 14–
January 22 (4 weeks)

Electricity Chapters 21 and 22

Static Electricity

Magnetism and Currents

Circuits

January 25–
March 25 (8 weeks)

Physics Chapters 2, 3, 4

Work's Effort

Simple Machines

Laws of Motion

March 28–
April 29 (4 weeks)

Heat Chapters 19, 20, 23, 24

Specific Heat and Heat Transfer

Heating and Cooling

Alternate Energies

May 2–May 27
(4 weeks)

Earth Science

May 30–June 8
(1 week)

Testing and School Closing

Implementing the Plans

Once the teacher is well-planned their implementation becomes critical. The following are implementation techniques with weak and strong examples of each. The principal should assist the teacher to internalize these techniques through modeling and discussions.

- Stating Concepts of Processes

    Set concepts or processes and general overview for the day. Tell students what you want them to do or learn.

    - *Weak example:* "We're going to work on a couple of things today."

    - *Strong example*: "We're going to work in a large group for 30 minutes generating advertising ideas for 5 products. Then we will work in small groups for 25 minutes, where each group will write product advertising."

- Classroom Routine

    Teach routines for all classroom activities including turning in and receiving back work, notebook organization, transitions to different-sized groups, cleanup, listening, and lecture skills, etc.

    - *Weak example*: "Let's count off again today in fours so we can work in small groups again."

    - *Strong example*: "Move to your previously established small groups for group work."

- Directions

    Keep lesson directions separate from other classroom business. Club announcements, money collecting, and so on, should be first or last. Give complete directions for each activity, so the activity doesn't have to be interrupted for additional or clarifying directions.

    If the activity is long and involved, work it section by section: Give directions for Section I, then have students complete Section I; give directions for Section I, then have students complete Section II; and so on.

- Directions and Planning

    Plan ahead to help students behave appropriately and remain on-task.

    - *Weak example*: "We're all going to the library today to work on projects, so let's go."

- *Strong example*: "Because we're going to the library today, I'll take attendance twice, at the beginning and end of the period. If you have seven or more file cards completed for your report at the end of the period, you will receive the participation points."

♦ Directions and Planning

Break down assignments into steps to ensure students' learning and time-on-task. For example, a term paper will require a topic, an outline, note cards, and a rough draft before the finished product can be completed. Each of these steps can have due dates and/or amounts of time in which each one can be completed, checked, and given participation points. Checking all the steps along the way will greatly aid the weaker student to get the finished product completed well.

♦ Directions for Explicit Outcomes

State high expectations and make the desired outcome(s) very clear.

- *Weak example*: "Turn in a good business letter."

- *Strong example*: "Complete a business letter of three paragraphs on unlined white paper, written in black ink. It should have no mistakes and be of a quality that you would send on the job. Follow the correct form in the sample I gave you."

♦ Planning for Higher Level Thinking Skills Instead of Rote Repetition

When planning lessons, always think of ways students can demonstrate thinking instead of memorization.

- *Weak example*: "What should you wear to an interview?" Students: "Conservative clothes."

- *Strong example*: "Here are some cards where each describes an outfit a person wore to a job interview for an office job. Read the cards and be prepared to describe what is good and what ought to be improved about each of the outfits." Student: "The black suit and white blouse are fine, but the woman should not have been wearing patterned stockings and sling-back shoes."

♦ Judging Time Allotments for New Lessons

To determine how much time a new activity should take, compare it with a similar one you've already taught. If you think students may finish quickly, or you're unsure of time, plan an additional short activity that can be adjusted to use 5–15 minutes of extra time. It is always better to plan too much, than to feel anxious because you're out of material.

♦ Preparing Materials and Classroom Setting

See your materials and setting through your students' eyes and adjust accordingly. In the empty room, sit in several of the least desirable seats. Can you see the chalkboard, the overhead, and the teacher? Sit in the very back seat in the room, can you read the materials on the overhead easily? Do they look clear, attractive, and interesting, or are they poorly written, or just copies of dittos the students already have? Use colors, appropriate cartoons, and graphics as attention-getters!

Look at the materials used as handouts. Do they reflect concern about quality, or do they have typing errors, and poor quality printing? If students are to write on them, do they have adequate space for neatly written answers? Are the directions explicit?

♦ Positive Attitude

Always demonstrate a positive attitude. Praise twice as much as you correct or discipline. After each class, mentally review things you liked about the class, or about the performance of individuals. Think of ways it could be improved and resolve to do it at the very next opportunity! (The formula, praise twice as much as you discipline or correct, is used very successfully in dropout programs, juvenile detention, etc.)

Remediation Program

Hopefully, the principal has been successful with informal procedures to assist the marginal teacher. However, there are times when the principal must formally confront the problem and develop a Plan of Assistance for the teacher. A sample program follows. The five items that are unsatisfactory come from the teacher evaluation form.

Plan of Assistance for John Doe, Music Teacher

The following is designed to assist you in improving your performance as a classroom teacher. My observation of your teaching indicates the following areas of performance to be unsatisfactory and in need of improvement:

I.   Professional Preparation and Scholarship

II. Instructional Skill

III. Classroom Management

IV. Handling of Student Discipline and attendance problems

V. Effort toward improvement when needed

Specifically, it is recommended that immediate attention be given to the following:

I. **Professional Preparation and Scholarship**
   A. Your performance reflects the following deficiencies:
      1. Inability to consistently establish immediate and long-range objectives and prepare effective plans to meet objectives;
      2. Inability to plan appropriately and in a timely manner for nonclassroom activities;
      3. Inability to consistently start class in a timely manner.
   B. We recommend that your preparation skills be improved during the probationary period to include:
      1. Ability to consistently establish immediate and long-range objectives and prepare effective plans to meet objectives;
      2. Ability to plan appropriately and in a timely manner for nonclassroom activities;
      3. Ability to consistently start class in a timely manner.
   C. Suggestions that would assist you in correcting the above deficiencies include:
      1. Outline your curricular objectives in each subject area for the remainder of the second semester with the time allotted for each objective;
      2. Complete daily lesson plans by Friday for the following week. Components of the daily lesson plan would include:
         a. statement of objectives
         b. text pages to be covered
         c. supplementary materials/handouts to be used
         d. assignments
         e. method of evaluation of the learning
         f. schedule of class time use
            Following the conclusion of each school day, adjust your lesson plans for the next day and the remainder of the week, based upon the progress actually made.
      3. Begin each class by communicating to students your learning objective for the period. Write the objective on the board prior to class.

4. One month prior to the spring concert, submit an outline of planning procedures with timelines based upon criteria outlined by the principal.

5. Begin class promptly at the scheduled time, which requires the timely pick-up of elementary music students from their classroom.

6. Maintain an extra set of Elementary Band Method books to be available for class use only, for students who have not brought their music to class. This music should be readily available to hand out and should be retrieved at the end of the period. Appropriate measures should be taken to ensure that students bring their music.

II. Instructional Skill

A. Your performance reflects the following deficiencies:
1. Inability to teach each lesson with observable objective(s);
2. Inability to adequately monitor student participation and progress and make provisions for differences in ability and interest among students;
3. Inability to implement effective home practice program for elementary band students;
4. Inability to consistently require students to properly handle music instruments.

B. I recommend that your instructional skills be improved during the probationary period to include:
1. Ability to teach each lesson with observable objective(s);
2. Ability to adequately monitor student participation and progress and then, make provisions for differences in ability and interest among students;
3. Ability to implement effective home practice program for elementary band students;
4. Ability to consistently require students to properly handle music instruments.

C. Suggestions which would assist you in correcting the above deficiencies include:
1. Circulate among students during the class period. Monitor individual student progress periodically during class. Provide additional instruction for students requiring additional help and initiate parental cooperation and assistance.

2. Provide elementary band students with a home practice assignment sheet after each band period. Assignment sheets would be prepared prior to class and given to students at the end of the period. Assignment sheet changes would be made after class and brought to the homeroom teacher. Parent signature would be required verifying practice, and students not returning a signed assignment sheet would be assigned a 20-minute practice session with you within one day during an optional time period, that is, P.E., student lunch time, after school.

3. Instruct and demonstrate to students how to appropriately hold and handle instruments.

III. Classroom Management

A. Your performance reflects the following deficiencies:

1. Inability to keep classroom and storage area neat and tidy;

2. Inability to consistently prepare materials for class in advance of lesson.

B. I recommend that your classroom management skills be improved during your probationary period to include:

1. Ability to keep classroom and storage area neat tidy;

2. Ability to consistently prepare materials for class in advance of lesson.

C. Suggestions which would assist you in correcting the above deficiencies include:

1. Keep classroom floor free of music and litter. Keep sheet music organized and appropriately stacked and stored. Assign area on shelves for drumsticks. Keep desks, chairs, and music stands arranged in orderly manner. Keep piano and desk area neat and tidy. Keep instruments in their cases and on the storage shelves if possible. Keep storage shelves tidy and free of litter.

2. All sheet music, handouts, and other instructional materials should be prepared and laid out in a sequential and orderly manner in advance of a lesson for immediate distribution.

3. All audio-visual equipment and materials needed for a lesson should be obtained and ready for use prior to the start of the class.

IV. Handling of Student Discipline and Attendant Problems

A. Your performance reflects an inability to consistently establish order and discipline in the classroom.

B. I recommend that your handling of student discipline be improved during the probationary period to reflect an ability to consistently establish order and discipline in the classroom.

C. Suggestions which would assist you in correcting the above deficiencies include:

1. Communicate to students appropriate expectations for conduct and behavior. These would include the following:
   (a) students will arrive at class punctually
   (b) students will take their seats in a timely and orderly fashion
   (c) students will sit in their seats properly and remain in their seat unless otherwise instructed
   (d) students will be quiet and attentive when you are instructing
   (e) students will not be loud, disrespectful, or engage in rough housing

2. Misbehavior should result in appropriate and *consistent* consequences. This is best accomplished through a process of progressive discipline depending on the nature of the offense. Follow the adopted school sequence for dealing with discipline:
   (a) student reprimand
   (b) conference with student
   (c) detention—give notice; maximum 30 minutes
   (d) parent contact
   (e) parent conference
   (f) referral to principal

3. Maintain a current log on each student you have disciplined. Each entry should state the date of misconduct, the nature of the misconduct, and action taken.

V. Effort Towards Improvement When Needed

A. Your performance reflects an inability to consistently implement suggestions in a timely and consistent manner.

B. I recommend that you accelerate your effort toward improvement during the probationary period to reflect your ability to consistently implement and sustain the suggestions for improvement.

C. Suggestions which would assist you in correcting the above deficiencies include:

1. Maintain an ongoing written log of ideas and suggestions for improvement for periodic reference; and

2. Establish and meet timelines for implementing suggestions.

Assistance Provided

A probationary team composed of the high school principal, a music teacher from the middle school, and a teacher of your choice will observe and assist you in improving your performance. In addition to the personal observations and evaluation conferences, the following assistance will be made available to you:

A. Probationary Team Assistance. The team will work with you on improving your performance as outlined in this program.

B. Visitation to other classrooms both in our school and others.

C. Consultant help. The probationary team will work with you to determine if appropriate personnel is available to assist and implement probationary plan.

D. Release time to attend workshops that might assist you in your program for improvement.

E. Additional resources shall be utilized that you and the probationary team might both deem appropriate.

Principal: _____

Date: _____

I have reviewed and understand the above and agree that it represents a reasonable program to aid in the improvement of my performance.

Teacher: _____

Date: _____

Meetings with the Marginal Teacher

There is no question that after the development of a program of assistance, that things are very serious. The principal would be well advised to follow these guidelines when meeting with the marginal teacher:

♦ Never deal alone with a teacher who has a Union Representative. Have your own witness—preferably not another teacher, however.

♦ Take careful notes and have your witness take notes.

♦ Document everything—incidences around the building, parent conferences, and observations.

♦ If you request to see plan books or correspondence, make copies.

♦ Review strategy of other administrators for feedback.

♦ Keep central office personnel and superintendent informed.

♦ *Know* the contract between the Teachers' Association and District.

- Know and use correct terminology. Know the law.
- Contact your attorney to review all legal procedures and documents. You cannot do this too early.
- If written documentation is given to teacher, have the teacher sign.
- You set meeting times and determine length.
- Avoid debate.
- If nonrenewal is evident—don't reveal decision until after the legal end of probation.
- They may resort to attacking you. Any skeletons in your closet?
- Be up front—no hidden agendas.

Employee Assistance Program

At some time in the personal or work life of school employees, every person faces problems that are solved individually or with help from others. Some problems, however, require professional help and guidance. Approximately 5% to 8% of the nation's workers have problems that affect their job performance. These problems become even worse without assistance.

Because so much of our lives revolves around the work environment, a key to assistance for problems is often found in this setting. It is not only possible and humanitarian to help, but also it is essential for the protection, growth, and development of an important national resource, our working school employees (Melgram, 1986).

Definition

The Employee Assistance Program (EAP) is a practical but responsive attempt to improve performance by constructing therapeutic strategies to help employees deal with their personal problems and thus improve their work performance (Melgram,1986). The EAP enables principals to identify employees who are having difficulties performing their jobs and refer them to the EAP if it applies. Many school districts offer confidential professional help to employees who have substance abuse, psychological, marital, family, financial, legal, or other problems (Balzer & Pargament, 1987).

History

In the late 1930s, Alcoholics Anonymous (A.A.) was founded and demonstrated that it could help alcoholics recover from their addiction. At the time, the Du Pont Corporation met with the founder of A.A. to discuss rehabilitation for alcoholic employees as an alternative to dismissal (MBA, 1993). The Eastman Kodak Company also provided assistance for their alcoholic employees through their Medical Department. Mental health programs were developed in the 1940s by the Caterpillar Tractor Company, American Cyanamid Company, and others (Melgram, 1986).

Some companies' attempts to develop employee programs were short-lived. Even though alcoholism was regarded as an occupational health problem, by the late 1950s, only 35 companies had occupational alcoholism programs. By 1973 the number of programs in the United States had expanded to 500. The number of programs increased to nearly 2,400 by 1977 and 4,000 by 1979. In 1986, 57% of the Fortune 500 companies had some type of program for their employees (Melgram, 1986).

In the early 1970s, programs began to offer assistance for a broad range of employee problems. These comprehensive programs dealt with a variety of problems and decreased the chance of participants being labeled. Currently, this kind of "broad brush" program is designed to "identify people needing assistance (for all types of problems), refer them to appropriate sources of treatment, and provide supportive services during and after the treatment period" (Melgram, 1986).

Structure of Employee Assistance Programs

The goals of an EAP are to:

- Assist employees with personal problems
- Provide an alternative to disciplinary action for employees who are having job performance problems
- Help company maintain a stable, well-functioning work force
- Decrease company expenses caused by the loss of well-trained employees (Melgram, 1986)

In resolving any human problem, it is essential to accurately assess the nature of the problem, provide treatment, and maintain a continuing improvement program. Teachers and school leaders should be supportive of the EAP in assisting the employee with a problem as it directly affects the school and district. They should be partners in the design and implementation of the EAP.

When an employee is identified, it is vital that the principal arrange a private meeting to relate the issues and specific concerns of job performance. At that time, a suggestion is made that the employee utilize the services of the EAP. The employee may reject or accept the offer. If the employee accepts, he or she is put in contact with an EAP counselor who assesses the problem and plans a course of action.

Program Framework

Without altering or amending any of the rights or responsibilities of the employee of the Sample School District, it is the policy of the Employee Assistance Program to handle such problems within the following framework:

◆ **We recognize that almost any human problem can be successfully treated** provided it has been identified in its early stages and referral is made to appropriate care. This applies whether the problem is one of alcoholism, other forms of chemical dependency, or other personal problems. Therefore, employees having a problem, which they feel could adversely affect their job performance or personal well-being are encouraged to voluntarily seek assistance on a *confidential* basis by utilizing the professional assistance of the Employee Assistance Counselor.

◆ **When an employee's job performance or attendance is unsatisfactory** and the employee is unable or unwilling to correct the situation either alone or with normal supervisory assistance, a personal problem may be the cause of the job performance difficulties. In such instances the employee's immediate supervisor has a responsibility to recommend that the employee utilize the Employee Assistance Program. Employees referred to the program by their principals will receive recommendations appropriate to their needs to secure services necessary to resolve the problem.

◆ **It is the responsibility of the employee** to comply with the referral for assistance and follow the recommendation of the Employee Assistance Program.

◆ Under the provisions of this policy, employees are assured that if personal problems are the cause of unsatisfactory job performance, they will receive careful consideration and an offer of appropriate assistance to help resolve such problems in an effective and confidential manner. Employees are assured that program records will be reserved in the highest degree of confidence.

◆ **In instances where it is necessary, time off** may be granted for treatment or rehabilitation consistent with the applicable benefit package.

◆ **Because employee work performance and attendance** can be adversely affected by the problem of an employee's spouse or other dependents, the employee can receive consultation from the Employee Assistance Counselor regarding problems of family members as well.

♦ **It should be emphasized that the Employee Assistance Program** and the disciplinary system each has its appropriate use. An employee's refusal to use the Employee Assistance Program is not in itself a cause for disciplinary action. The Employee Assistance Program is to be used in conjunction with applicable district policies and procedures.

Figure 7.6 graphically describes how to access and use the Employee Assistance Program.

When employees are experiencing personal problems, there are usually indications of these concerns in their interaction and functioning within the school environment.

Documentation of problems and concerns is essential to identify and intervene with the employee. Outlined below are areas of concern, which can be identified and observed in the workplace. Very often, job performance problems are only "the tip of the iceberg" of underlying personal or emotional problems. Principals should be alert to *early indicators of possible problems.*

♦ **Absenteeism**

- Unauthorized leave

- Excessive sick leave

- Monday or Friday absences

- Repeated absences of two to four days

- Repeated absences of one to two weeks (five to ten days)

- Excessive tardiness, (especially on Monday morning or in returning from lunch)

- Leaving work early

- Peculiar and increasingly improbable excuses for absences

- Higher absenteeism rate than other employees for colds, flu, etc.

- Frequent, unscheduled short-term absences (with/without medical explanation)

♦ **"On-the-job" absenteeism**

- Continued absences from worksite (more than job requires)

- Frequent trips to water fountain or restroom

- Long coffee breaks

- Physical illness on job

- **High accident or mistake rate**
  - Accidents on the job (whether serious enough for workman's compensation claim or not)
  - Frequent trips to nurse's office
  - Accidents off the job (but affecting job performance)
- **Difficulty in concentration**
  - Work appears to require great effort
  - Jobs take more time than normal
  - Hand tremor when concentrating
  - Frequently seems to stare off into space
- **Confusion**
  - Difficulty in recalling instructions, details, etc.
  - Increasing difficulty in handling complex assignments
  - Difficulty in recalling own mistakes
- **Alternating work patterns**
  - Alternating periods of very high and very low productivity
- **Resistance to change**
  - Doesn't change easily
  - Rigidly maintains current behavior, despite instructions to change
- **Change in employee's physical condition/appearance**
  - Comes to work impaired
  - Returns from lunch impaired
- **Lower job efficiency**
  - Takes more time to complete task
  - Increased waste
  - Damaged products
  - Lower production
- **Problems with other employees**
  - Arguments
  - Threats
  - Violence
  - Can't get along

There are numerous other concerns and problems, which may be observed. It is important to document the performance problems and to discuss the behavior with the employee. Please remember, the EAP is available to discuss the work performance issues and to offer support in changing behaviors.

Principals are in the best position to know the extent of the problems on the performance of the teacher. However, few principals possess the professional capabilities necessary for diagnosing employee problems. Consequently, the principal will be expected to do *only* that for which he has received training: *supervise* and *refer*.

Figure 7.6 Mandatory Employee Referrals to EAP

Confidential

Please complete this referral information and fax it to (xxx) xxx-xxxx along with other documentation and agreements signed by the employee. Thank you.

Company:	Date Referred to EAP:

Employee Name

Supervisor/contact Person:

Supervisor/contact Phone:

Job Performance Affected: Job in Jeopardy:
☐ Yes ☐ No   ☐ Yes ☐ No

Date Employee must Contact EAP By:

Date of Employee's Return to Work:

Presenting Problem/issues:

Check One: ☐ Drug/Alcohol Issues ☐ Anger Management ☐ Mediation Emotional ☐ Other, Please Explain:

Drug Screen Performed: ☐ Yes ☐ No Results: ☐ Positive ☐ Negative

Previous Incidents:

Additional Comments:

Principals should follow the steps below to assist the employee and provide appropriate assistance:

- Document what you *see—not* what you suspect (or what you are led to believe)
- Diagnose unacceptable job performance—*nothing else*
- Delegate the diagnosis of complex causes to the EAP professionals

Documentation

When an employee's job performance deteriorates, it is essential that the supervisor document behavior before taking action. These records allow the supervisor to approach the employee in a constructive manner. Documentation should be as specific as possible. Be sure to include the dates, times and place where you observed the performance problems.

Job performance, *not* personal problems, should be the focus for documentation and feedback. Avoid labeling or diagnosing the employee's problem. The EAP is designed to handle the underlying personal and/or emotional issues. These issues may include family/relationship concerns, alcohol/drug problems, job-related adjustments and communication difficulties.

Your documentation is confidential and therefore should not be shared with anyone except the employee or your supervisor.

Consultation and Referral to EAP

The goals of constructive confrontation are:

♦ Confront the behavior, not the person

♦ Encourage a change in behavior

♦ Before confronting the employee, you may want to contact the EAP for some assistance, advice and support.

♦ Select a location and time for your meeting, which affords privacy and is free from any disturbances.

♦ Use your documentation so you can "let the record speak for itself."

♦ Discuss job performance in a caring way without counseling, labeling, and/or diagnosing the employee's problem(s). Make it brief and to the point.

♦ Recognize the employee's value to the organization, but convey clear expectations of change and discuss the consequences should job performance *not* improve.

♦ Remind the employee that the EAP is free, confidential and easy to access.

♦ Encourage the employee to call the EAP and give the telephone number.

Follow-up

♦ Be sure to schedule another meeting with the employee in the near future to review their progress.

- Reinforce improved performance and support the employee's efforts.

- If performance doesn't improve or deteriorates, consult with your human resources department on your school's disciplinary policies.

- Discuss your organization's standard disciplinary procedure with the employee.

Personal problems that interfere with job performance are often too big to solve alone. Employers encourage their employees to maintain their physical and mental health by providing an Employee Assistance Program for the employee and their families. The EAP provides a confidential resource outside the workplace that assists employees with personal problems in a variety of areas. The initial assessment consultations are free for the employee and their immediate family members as they are paid for by the district.

The EAP is a very impressive resource for the employees of school districts who care about more than job performance—the district cares about the well-being of each employee.

Use of Technology with the Marginal Teacher

A Google search of both the marginal teacher and employee assistant programs offer numerous resources for the principal. Here are a few of the results of that search:

- www.opm.gov.ehs.eappage.asp

  This is an excellent source from the Office of Personnel Management in the Federal Government.

- www.wapassn.org

- www.theeap.com

- http://westy.jtwn.k12.pa.us/users/sja/Supervision-3 .html

  This site contains a transcript and a summary of the 1987 video "Supervising the Marginal Teacher."

- http://www/naesp.org

  This article provides an overview of how to deal with marginal teachers from evaluating and observing to mentoring and planning.

Assisting the Marginal Teacher—Case Study

Alison Nutt was a ten-year veteran at Mt. View High School in a school district that had only one high school. She taught home economics and while she was never a candidate for teacher of the year she had never been put on probation or given any particular reason to think that her evaluation was less than satisfactory. She knew that her program was dropping in enrollment, but she accredited the decline to the emphasis students and their parents were placing on academics rather than on the vocational programs of the high school.

In the spring of the year the enrollment data was even more a problem for the Nancy Conard, the principal. Students were signing up for classes for the following year and there was a major problem in the home economics department: There were not enough students for a half-time teacher let alone a full-time teacher with tenure. At about the same time, the assistant principal, who had been conducting the evaluations of Alison for the past five years met with the Nancy over the enrollment problem and said he was not surprised. Alison seemed to lack interest in the program and in teaching students. She wasn't doing anything particularly wrong but the lack of excitement for both program and students was increasingly more apparent to the assistant principal. Conard made an announced visit to Alison's classroom and concurred with the evaluation of the assistant principal. In the postobservation conference with Alison, Nancy did not expect the turn of events.

Alison was very anxious as she waited for the conference to be held in Conard's office. Conard did not know exactly how she would proceed other than sharing the data that she gathered during her visit to the classroom and offering to help Alison reflect on the data. Hopefully, she could get Alison to come up with some reasons for the low enrollment and her apparent lack of enthusiasm. After some normal chitchat, Nancy launched into revealing the data from her observation. Almost immediately Alison interrupted and said that she did not like teaching at the high school level and never really did. Tears followed. She explained to Nancy that she really liked the child growth and development classes in her college course work and felt that she would be much better in the elementary school. That was her interest and true love in the teaching field.

Conard met with the superintendent and they agreed that maybe a good transfer would be best for everyone. One of the elementary principals, who had a vacancy at the third grade level, was contacted and asked if he would interview Alison and see if there was a match between her skills and the needs in the third grade. He concluded that she needed to visit some third grade classrooms and make sure that this is what she wanted. She did and showed sparks of enthusiasm about the possibility of teaching at that level. The elementary principal outline his requirements that included college courses in the teaching of reading and math, and a general course in teaching at the elementary level. Alison was very agreeable because the district also agreed to pay for the classes. The elementary principal went over the job description with Alison, explained it to her and when she agreed with it, had her sign it.

School started and it wasn't long before there were complaints about Alison and her lack of understanding of third graders and the curriculum. Alison was given feedback and more time to improve. Things were not working and in fact, were getting worse. The superintendent, principal, and Alison had a conference wherein she broke down and cried. She thought the district had been very good to her and tried to accommodate her transfer but that she did not like teaching and wanted to quit but her husband wouldn't let her because the family had become dependent on the two incomes.

Questions for the prospective principal:

1. If you were the elementary principal, what would you do in the short term and in the long term?
2. How could this have been avoided?
3. Was the district wrong in granting such a transfer?

Comprehensive Questions

1. How can a principal distinguish between a marginal teacher and an inexperienced new teacher?
2. As a principal who is dealing with a marginal teacher, what support or assistance would you need?
3. The personal and professional problems of a marginal teacher are often intertwined. What responsibility does the principal have in each area?
4. At what juncture in the process would you involve the central office staff and/or the school's attorney?

Extended Activities

1. Interview a principal and district personnel with regard to procedures used with a marginal teacher.
2. Contact your local Employee Assistance Program representative to review services offered to marginal teachers.
3. Interview the local teachers' association leadership regarding their role in working with the marginal teacher.

References

Balzer, W., and K. Pargament (1987). The key to designing a successful employee assistance program. *Personnel*, 48–54.

Blai, B. (1985). Staying well at work. *Viewpoint, 120*, 1–8.

Bridges, E. M. (1990). *Managing the incompetent teacher*. Eugene, OR: University of Oregon (ERIC Clearinghouse on Educational Management).

Bridges, E. M. (1986). *The incompetent teacher. The Stanford series on education and public policy*. Philadelphia: The Falmer Press.

Costa, A., and R. Garmston (1987). *The art of cognitive coaching: Supervision for intelligent teaching*. Sacramento, CA: The Institute for Intelligent Behavior.

Galleti, S. (n.d.). *Working with the marginal teacher*. Lake Stevens, WA: Lake Stevens School District.

Glickman, C. D. (1981). *Developmental supervision*. Alexandria, VA: Association for Supervision and Curriculum Development.

Glickman, C. D. (Ed.) (1992). *Supervision in transition: The 1992 yearbook*. Alexandria, VA: Association for Supervision and Curriculum Development.

Goldhammer, R., R. Anderson, and R. Krajewski (1993*). Clinical supervision: Special methods for the supervision of teachers*. Forth Worth, TX: Harcourt Brace Jovanovich.

Groves, B. (1985). An organizational approach to teacher evaluation. Doctoral dissertation, Stanford University.

Health Venture (HV) (1987). *Summary of services of Employee Assistance Program for Shelton School District*. Sponsored by St. Joseph Health Services.

Jackson, C. M. (1991). Assisting marginal teachers: a training model. *Principal*, September.

Maschhoff, Barr, and Associates (MBA) (1993). *Employee Assistance Program Supervisor Manual*.

McLaughlin, M. W. (1984). *The Lake Washington School District No. 414 teacher evaluation: A study of effective practices*, edited by A. Wise, L. Darling-Hammond, M. McLaughlin, and H. Bernstein. Santa Monica, CA: The Rand Corporation.

Meilleur, C. C. (n.d.). *Teacher probation*. Kirkland, WA: Lake Washington School District.

Melgram, G. (1986). Employee assistance: Policies and programs. *Rutgers Center for Alcohol Studies Pamphlet Series*, 1–22.

Palmer, P. (2000). *Let your life speak*. San Francisco: Jossey-Bass.

Parker, M. R., and M. S. Adams (n.d.). *Remediation of the marginal teacher*. Meeting Vernon, WA: Educational Service District No. 189.

Rogus, J. F. and Nuzzi, R. J. (1993). Helping the Marginal Teacher. *NASSP Practitioner* 20:1.

Whitaker, T. (1999). Seizing power from difficult teachers. *High School Magazine*. (7), 36–39.

8
Staff Development

Reasons for Studying Staff Development

♦ The teacher's responsibility is developing students; developing teachers is a major responsibility of the principal.

♦ Education is changing rapidly. To keep up with those changes, school personnel must learn new techniques, methods, and procedures.

♦ If the mission of the school district contains the phrase "lifelong learners" and if school personnel expect that of the students, then they should expect it of themselves.

♦ With the advent of school-based leadership, many of the previous central office responsibilities will be shifted to the principal. Staff development is one such area.

Staff development takes curriculum off the shelf.

ISLLC Standards Covered in this Chapter

Standard 2:

♦ A school administrator is an educational leader who promotes the success of all students by advocating, nurturing, and sustaining a school culture and an instructional program conducive to student learning and staff professional growth.

Standard 5:

♦ A school administrator is an education leader who promotes the success of all students by acting with integrity, fairness, and in an ethical manner.

Introduction

One way to assess the quality of a school is to look at the students who are products of that district. To ensure that those students are of high quality, the principal needs to attend to the growth and development of the staff. The certified, classified, and support staff members must all be involved in an ongoing staff development process. This process must provide educational opportunities in order to cultivate both meaningful change and continuous growth toward excellence.

Key Idea

The mission of every school is the growth and development of students through the growth and development of staff.

The primary job of educators is to teach students and to help them reach their academic potential. The better our teachers are equipped to teach, the better they will be able to provide exciting educational experiences and thus, improve academic achievement of their students. The education profession is always changing and there is a need to remain current. In other words, educators must continue to learn.

Mission statements in many school districts call for students to be "lifelong learners." Educators should not expect anything less of themselves. Within the schools, staff development is the vehicle by which our lifelong learning takes place. It is only through the continual expanding and enhancing of skills that educational personnel can maximize their ability to teach children. When you are talking about school improvement, you are talking about people improvement.

The Case for Staff Development

Key Idea

The money spend on staff development should be considered an investment, not an expenditure.

Never before has there been a greater recognition of the importance of professional development for teachers. Every proposal to reform, restructure, or transform schools emphasizes professional development as the primary vehicle in efforts to bring about needed change (Guskey, 1994). This critical role played by professional development in any effort to attain the goals of educational reform has been recognized and advocated at the national level. President Bush and the nation's governors cited professional development for teachers as one of the original six national education goals adopted in 1989 (Northwest Regional Educational Laboratory, 1994). Goal four states that, "By the year 2000, the nation's teaching force will have access to program for the continuous improvement of their professional skills and the opportunity to acquire knowledge and skills needed to instruct and prepare all American students for the next century."

At the state level, Bergeson (2003), Washington State Superintendent of Public Instruction, identifies Focused Professional Development as one of the Nine Characteristics of High Performing Schools. Bergeson's definition of Focused Professional Development: "[A] strong emphasis is placed on training staff in areas of most need. Feedback from learning and teaching focuses extensive and ongoing professional development. The support is also aligned with the school or district vision and objectives." At the local district and school level professional development has taken on increased emphasis and significance in the school reform efforts.

How to Organize Staff Development

Staff development is an ongoing process that needs to grow and develop over a period of time. The successful staff development program should incorporate these essential elements:

Research—Gathering of information

Training—Making the subject come alive

Modeling—Showing the audience

Practice—Experiencing the reality

Coaching—Feedback for perfection

Evaluation—Improving the learning

There are five steps in providing effective staff development:

- Getting Started
- Collecting Data
- Planning
- Implementing
- Evaluation

These steps can be accomplished through the setting of goals, following the philosophy and mission statements of the district, establishing building committees, providing a plan for continuous staff improvement and evaluation, and allowing for budgetary needs. This chapter will focus on how to accomplish these steps. Figure 8.1 outlines the process.

Figure 8.1 Staff Development: The Process

Getting Started
Staff Development Committee
Professional Development
Principal Responsibility
Central Office Responsibility

Collecting Data
Staff Development Steering Committee
Teacher Input
Administrative Input
Faculty Requests
Research
Conversations

Planning
Reviewing Timely Goals
Determining Needs
Brainstorming
Setting Priorities
Assuring Budget:
- Fiscal Year
- Summer
- School Year
- Grants
Setting Timelines
- Immediate
- Short-Term
- Long-Range

Implementing
Selection of Trainers
Training Segment
Selling the Program
Support of Building Principals/Supervisors
Understanding the Adult Learners:
- *want* to be involved
- *will* resist situations suggesting incompetency
- *respond* to climate of trust, respect, and caring
- *enjoy* collegiality

Evaluation
Regular Feedback: Daily, Weekly, Monthly
Individual Activities
Total Program Evaluation
Projections

Getting Started

Key Idea

Staff development that improves the learning of all students organizes adults into learning communities whose goals are aligned with those of the school and district.

National Staff Development Council's Standards for Staff Development

Figure 8.2 is helpful to use to understand and explain the staff development process to others. The goal of the staff development program is to increase student achievement through ongoing staff development. A comprehensive staff development program is for all employees of the school and district: teachers, secretaries, bus drivers, custodians, maintenance workers, instructional assistants, food service workers, substitutes, and administrators.

Further, it is helpful to think of the staff development program as a dynamic one, as represented by the "spinning top." The elements of the "top" illustrate the areas that are part of the program, while the arrows represent the process.

Figure 8.2 Staff Development

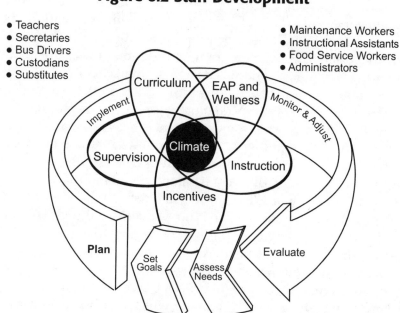

- Teachers
- Secretaries
- Bus Drivers
- Custodians
- Substitutes

- Maintenance Workers
- Instructional Assistants
- Food Service Workers
- Administrators

Increase Student Achievement Through Ongoing Staff Development

Staff Development Committee

Who is responsible for staff development? Traditionally, staff development has been managed at the district level. Central administrators and central offices have been in charge of the entire staff development program in the district. They may organize a staff development steering committee to serve as the in-service training task force and the professional growth planning and review committee. The members can be drawn from the certified staff, counselors, union representatives, and classified staff administrators. Their *goal* will be to oversee continuous professional growth in all staff in accordance with the mission, philosophy, and belief statements of the school district. This *mission* can be accomplished by promoting effective educational changes, supporting and enhancing district goals, providing adequate time and resources to achieve desired goals, representing staff in the determination, planning, and implementation of staff development activities, and encouraging staff

Increasingly, however, school districts are phasing out their central office staff development departments in favor of site-based models or Teachers on Special Assignment (TOSA) who rotate after two years as a TOSA to the classroom. This has promoted interesting changes. Schools can now individualize and specialize their staff development to the needs of their staff. This is effective in that individual schools can do a better job of meeting their own needs. With this new freedom, however, comes the increased responsibility of schools doing their own data collection, planning, implementation, and evaluation of their programs. It also opens up the reality of more than one school in the district doing the same program. This doubles the efforts that would have been made under a centralized model. Interschool collaboration can help to alleviate some of these overlapping efforts. Perhaps a model that is mostly site-based with some central office support would give us the best of both worlds. Under a site-based model, there is heavy demand at the building level. Despite this extra work, research shows that this method does a better job of meeting the needs of the individual staff members as well as meeting special needs of different student populations. Goodlad (1983) found that "the individual school is the most viable unit for educational improvement." Although this assertion is not yet verified through research, the hypothesis that site-based (decentralized) decision making is "better" seems valid. As the practice of site-based management plays itself out, the research will surface to support or negate this movement.

Under this decentralized program, each building within the district also establishes a staff development committee, which would consist of a member of the steering committee or leadership team, an administrator, teachers, and perhaps parents and building or district level specialists. Such a committee would report to the steering committee (leadership team or site council) on a regular basis, submitting plans to ensure continuity and coordination, plan, implement, and monitor building and staff programs, and provide opportunities for development and maintenance of skills acquired.

The staff development committee should focus on the needs of teachers. Effective professional development for increased student learning is best supported in a collaborative environment that includes teachers with a range of experience and the values the contributions of both new and veteran staff members. The specific role of an individual teacher in that collaborative professional environment may vary depending in the teacher's developmental stage.

Beginning teachers generally need to build capacity for effective teaching through content, pedagogy, and classroom management under the guidance of experienced teachers. Their ability to impact students is enhanced if they are working in a collaborative environment that encourages professional learning and improvement.

The needs of experienced teachers center on deepening their knowledge, sharing a common vision of student learning, and engaging in collective inquiry.

Accomplished teachers need to continue to build capacity and find way to contribute their knowledge and experience to the learning community while developing their leadership skills (Bergeson et al. 2003).

Regardless of who is responsible, staff development is a vital aspect of a successful educational program and the committee should hold to certain standards and beliefs such as:

- Promote continued professional growth.
- Believe that adults can learn and want to improve.
- Uphold administrators as models of educational excellence.
- Renew interest in a dynamic and improving profession.
- Provide a needs-based, continuous, growth-oriented program.
- Accept and provide for the difficulty and fear of change.
- Communicate and provide a feeling of togetherness to make change less threatening.
- Develop an atmosphere of trust to encourage risk taking.
- Focus on reward, recognition, and reinforcement of excellence.

Personal Development of Teachers

There are many suggestions to improve the knowledge and the morale of teachers. Here are several of these suggestions as a beginning:

- Professional Growth Plan (PGP)—a plan developed by each teacher/staff member to guide individual and group growth

- In-services led by colleagues or outside speaker—provide in-service credit
- Staff meetings—teachers share information from summer school, conferences, or workshops attended
- Interest sessions—only those who have an interest attend
- Committee meetings—only those who have an interest volunteer and bring findings to whole group
- Informal gatherings—monthly celebration or get-together
- Professional day used to visit other schools, teachers, and programs
- Portfolio for teacher's personal papers, records, goals, etc.

The Principal's Responsibility

The principal plays a vital role throughout all of the stages of staff development. The principal must show a positive attitude. The administrator's attitudes and reactions will have a profound effect upon the success of a staff development program. DuFour and Berkey (1995) state that "if the premise is that people are the key to school improvement, then it follows that the fundamental role of the principal is to help create the conditions that enable a staff to develop so that the school can achieve its goals more effectively." Michigan State University Center on Teacher Learning reinforces the critical role of the principal. "[Teachers] need the support and advice of a principal who understands the demands that reform places on teachers and what it takes to change teachers' roles and practice." (Floden and McDiarmid, 1995). The following are some items that administrators should consider when planning staff development programs:

- Believe in people from the beginning, that they have the potential and desire to succeed; then support them.
- Build on a person's strengths; you hired the teacher for a reason and are investing in him or her.
- Provide your staff with feedback; encouragement, praise, and positive criticism will help them grow.
- Build team spirit through retreats, encouraging cooperative efforts, and brainstorming sessions.
- Inspire commitment to the students, the school, the goals, and the mission.
- Set high standards and praise both the positive direction and the results; teachers will be proud of their organization.

- Remove obstacles to teacher's success by providing the necessary resources needed and clear communication.
- Encourage teachers to ask for staff development and to take risks, to step out and try something new.
- Make work exciting with a relaxed, positive attitude.
- Let people see the results of their work being praised.
- Listen carefully to what the staff verbalizes and omits.

The Central Office Responsibilities

> *One thing is clear: Expectations influence accomplishment. And high expectations start at the top with school board(s) that demonstrate through their example, the importance of continuous improvement.*
>
> Sparks and Vaughn, 1994

Central office administrators should consider the following as they develop policies to recommend to the school board for staff development:

- Promote both the learning of individual school employees and changes in structures and processes within the district and within schools.
- Apply "systems thinking" to improvement efforts and be prepared for the effect of change.
- Heed the advice of those involved in "total quality" efforts in business and education.
- Have a strategic plan for the district.
- Recognize that the school ought to be the key decision-making unit when planning for improvement.
- Invest in improvement and use private and governmental resources effectively.
- Recognize that the most powerful forms of learning are likely to be job-embedded and that employees need at least 5% of their on-the-job time devoted to learning with additional professional days allowed.
- Be models of what you expect from others including special trading, risk taking, and experimentation.
- Remember that staff development is for everyone, not just for teachers.

Collecting Data

> *If you don't know what you're looking for, you won't know it when you find it.*

The collection of data is the next step in providing for effective staff development. To do this, three questions should be considered:

♦ What are our objectives?

Our objective is the education of children. All staff development decisions would be based on the goals and mission of the district. Our schools use, and will continue to use standardized tests to measure student achievement. We are able to assess our children's academic ability. These assessments should provide one source of information for our staff development priorities. When these priorities are matched with educational objectives, we will realize the direction for our staff development program.

♦ What objectives should we help to achieve?

Once the objectives have been reviewed and we have looked at how well our students have done in meeting those objectives, we can generate a list of our students' weaknesses. Of course, we should not place our total faith in the ability of standardized tests to give us all of the information we need to analyze student achievement. In schools, the standardized test is the primary method by which academic achievement is measured, so whether we personally appreciate them or not, we should be able to place a fair amount of validity in their use. Once areas of need have been identified, we can begin to prioritize them and to make decisions about how and when they will be achieved.

♦ What is the best way for us to develop our staff?

There are very strong indications that teachers must see the need for the staff development training if they are going to "buy in" to its need. They also need to arrive at the realization that they must bear at least some of the responsibility for their students' achievement. We also know that successful staff development necessitates the commitment of all staff with a sense of ownership and representation. Seeing the need and "buying in" are vital.

Research by Porter (1981) supported the idea that teachers are willing to change their curriculum when confronted with evidence of its benefit to students, such as:

- Standardized tests results
- Principals' encouragement
- Parents' acceptance
- Other teachers' endorsement

All staff development programs should be rooted in research and should be carried out in moderation. There is no utopia, and no one program should be viewed as such. Teacher interests and needs along with student needs should be the focus. If teachers are motivated for staff development, then staff development will be successful. Similarly, Corcoran (1995) and Guskey (1997) conclude that if teachers don't apply their new knowledge and skills when they return to the classroom, then staff development is "virtually a waste of time."

The classification scheme (Figure 8.3) points out the necessity of teacher involvement in the staff development. The interest level of the individual and the interest level of the institution, be it the central office or building site, are graphed accordingly. A successful staff development presentation will have high institutional emphasis and high individual emphasis. The teacher will have "bought into" the importance of the program, and the institution will be so involved in the program that it will be pressing it with enthusiasm. Likewise, teachers will get involved when they see that something works and that others are interested. When they do, they will praise the program, be involved in its presentation, and will encourage others to do the same.

Figure 8.3 Staff Development Classification System

Teacher Emphasis		Teacher Focused	School Focused
	High	• Low District • High Teacher	• High District • High Teacher
	Low	Unfocused • Low District • Low Teacher	District Focused • High District • Low Teacher
District Emphasis		Low	High

Planning

> *Staff development programs should be established by using a set of assumptions grounded in research and best practice.*
>
> Wood and Thompson, 1993

The planning stage is a necessity for effective and successful staff development. At least in site-based models, the focus of planning staff development lies within inservice training. This type of training is usually best accomplished at the building site. When engaged in staff development planning, it is wise to have your district objectives, including mission and goals, as well as your research data readily available. In-service planning is generally done one school year at a time; however, the recommendation is for a multiyear approach. Such short-term planning can lose focus if long-range planning is not done as well. It is important to make sure that all of your short-range planning fits into your long-range plan. When things become too fragmented, they become confusing and less useful to the staff.

After analyzing research about best staff development practices, the U.S. Department of Education (1997) has identified ten principles of effective professional development and uses them as the basis for recognizing model programs.

Elements of Effective Staff Development Programs

- Focuses on teachers as central to student learning, yet includes all other members of the school community.
- Focuses on individual, collegial, and organizational improvement.
- Respects and nurtures the intellectual and leadership capacity of teachers, principals, and others in the school community.
- Reflects best available research and practice in teaching, learning, and leadership.
- Enables teachers to develop further experience in subject content, teaching strategies, uses of technologies, and other essential elements in teaching to high standards.
- Promotes continuous inquiry and improvement embedded in the daily life of schools.
- Is planned collaboratively by those who will participate in and facilitate that development.
- Requires substantial time and other resources.

- Is driven by a coherent, long-term plan
- Is evaluated ultimately on its impact on teacher effectiveness and student learning, and this assessment guides subsequent professional development efforts.

Some balance should be maintained with regard to the natural overlap of different subjects. We need to realize that, if implemented, an in-service on classroom management, while not directly related to the basic skills, will have the effect of improving basic skill competency by leading to greater instructional time and a higher degree of time on task. Below are several points that should be kept in mind when planning staff development:

- Lawrence and Harrison (1980) suggested weekends, summer, and evenings are more acceptable times to teachers. One school uses the week immediately after school is out for the summer to train. The teachers are very pleased with this time block.
- The best staff development is designed as a collaborative effort by the school staff in cooperation with the principal.
- The single most important factor determining the value teachers place on an inservice education activity is its personal relevance (Holly, 1982).
- Regularly scheduled staff development time should be allocated to protect classroom instruction and preparation time (Ankeny, 1989).
- Budgetary allocations and constraints need to be taken into consideration before starting any project. "If school districts want improved practice, they must provide the personnel, time, materials, and dollars to support the implementation of those changes." (Wood and Thompson, 1993)
- All district employees need a sense of ownership and representation in the staff development goal-setting and decision-making process at the building and district level (Ankeny, 1989).
- Flexibility is necessary when planning district goals and staff development programs. (Ankeny, 1989)
- All staff development decisions should be based on the premise of "what's best for kids." (Ankeny, 1989)
- McDiarmid (1994) describes five principles that are at the core of Kentucky's ambitious and successful staff development program:
  - All staff training is centered on the goal of helping all students learn;

- Teachers are involved in designing their staff development;
- Staff development programs are designed and adapted according to the needs of individual schools;
- Staff development includes both theory and practice; and
- Teachers are given follow-up training and classroom support.

Often staff development programs require that staff members give up time beyond their contracted time for such programs. Although most teachers are interested in improving themselves as educators in order to help students, they are often resistant to giving up their free time to receive training. Following are some ideas for incentives that may help overcome this hurdle:

- Provide activities that equip teachers with the skills to increase their teaching effectiveness or gain increased feelings of empowerment.
- Administrators should participate in staff development activities with teachers. This is an excellent model of what is important.
- Provide opportunities for exchange visits between schools for sharing and discussing problems of mutual concern.
- Delegate responsibility for planning and presenting a workshop on a topic of interest to a group of teachers.
- Pay stipends to teachers who spend their own time planning, presenting, or participating in programs.
- Arrange staff development sessions in comfortable, attractive locations and provide refreshments for those who take part.
- Grant recognition in the form of certificates, plaques, and trophies to teachers who perform leadership roles in staff development projects.

Fred Wood and Steven Thompson (1993) discuss fourteen assumptions that staff development planners need to make when organizing staff development. A synopsis of them follows:

- The school, not the district, is the primary focus of improved practice and staff development.
- Significant change in educational practice takes considerable time and is the result of staff development that is conducted over several years.
- A school culture supportive of improved practice and professional growth is essential to successful staff development.
- All educators should be involved in staff development throughout their careers.

- The principal is key in any staff development effort to improve professional practice.
- Selection of the improvement goals that guide staff development should involve those who have a stake in the future of the students in that school (e.g., teachers, administrators, parents, community leaders, school staff, and the students themselves).
- Those who are changing their professional behavior must make an individual and collective commitment to, and feel ownership for the new programs and practices before they will want to participate in staff development activities.
- Staff development programs should support opportunities for both school improvement and individual professional growth.
- Staff development should enable school personnel to improve professional practice in ways that increase student learning.
- Knowledge about adult learners should serve as the basis for planning and implementation of staff development.
- Change in professional practice is difficult and requires systematic support to implement and sustain it over time.
- School districts have the primary responsibility for providing the resources and staff development necessary for a school faculty to implement new programs and instructional practices.
- Staff development should support instructional and program improvement and should be closely linked to instructional supervision, teacher evaluation, and curriculum implementation.
- School-based staff development, site-based leadership, and site-based budgeting are all important components of school-based improvement.

Wood and Thompson (1993) record the implications and conclusions they've made with regard to their fourteen assumptions, and it seems appropriate to conclude with their findings.

These assumptions will result in staff development that is characterized by (a) school improvement goals serving as the focus for staff development; (b) long-range, multiyear planning; (c) development of a school climate and culture supportive of change and staff development; (d) ongoing staff development for all educators in a district; (e) principals actively participating in all aspects of staff development; (f) involvement of all stakeholders in selecting improvement programs for their school; (g) support for both school and individual professional learning goals; (h) selection of research-based programs; (i) staff development based on the principles of adult learning; (j) follow-up support to implement and sustain changes in professional practice; and (k) staff development functioning as a component of instructional, program, and school improvement systems. We cannot continue to practice staff development and school improvement as if we are not aware of the knowledge base in our field. As staff developers, we call on others to change and behave in new and more effective ways. We must "practice what we preach," examine our assumptions, and learn new ways of behavior that are consistent with research and best practice.

Implementation

> *Staff development is the active ingredient in the recipe for school, teacher, and student improvement.*

Implementation is the next step in an effective staff development program. How a staff development program is implemented will vary from school to school, year to year, and audience to audience. Different people have different needs and require a different approach. This important step should be addressed in the planning stage as well as in the implementation stage. When considering the audience, consider the level of expertise of your teachers. Beginning teachers need more structure in presentations and, in general, a more directive approach. On the other hand, teachers with more experience would much rather learn new ways to work together in teams and add variety to their instructional techniques.

A survey study done by McBride, Reed, and Dollar (1994) indicated that teacher attitudes towards staff development are mixed. The teachers agreed with the reasons and needs for staff development but were often dissatisfied with the results. Teachers wanted staff development, but they wanted it to be tailored to their needs. This last aspect is all too often ignored.

Another problem that needs to be addressed is how much is going to be presented to the audience. Principals and staff developers often make the mistake of trying to do too much in one session. With the cost involved and time constraints, leadership often feels pressed to present as much information as possible during each session. They must keep in mind the resources, the time, the caliber of presenters and the presenters' energy before proceeding. A word of caution: If you don't have these necessary resources, don't tackle the project; it will probably not be successful.

One of the more common themes of a staff development program is to show teachers how to use a new instructional technique. Stallings (1985) recommended the following four-step technique:

- Baseline/pretest: Teacher observation seeking target teacher behavior; preparation of profiles, and setting goals.
- Information: Information provided that links research and practice.
- Guided practice: Teachers adapt the new techniques to their own context and style.
- Posttest: Teacher observation; new profile made; set new goals; assess the training for effectiveness.

Using this basic format, or something similar, will help to ensure the success of your staff development program. There are no unimportant elements.

Much has been said about school restructuring and change. It seems most of the focus has been on changes in policies and procedures. While it is true that those changes will have to be made, change is really about people. If authentic change is to take place, then we must invest in people. When attempting to implement change, training is essential for all employees, students, and parents in areas such as group processes, decision making, team building, and leadership in order for site-based human resources to be effective.

Staff development is not a one-time or even a short-term project. Staff development for change must be viewed as a long-term program. The new way of doing things can easily slip back into the old way of doing things. There needs to be a commitment of support for all involved if change is to be sustained. Research by Hall and Loucks (1980) found that "When innovation is complex, major components should be phased in one or a few at a time." A study done by Gersten, Carnine, and Williams (1982) concurs with those findings. This research seems to indicate that staff development programs given in stages are more successful than one-time presentations. Research done by Lawrence and Harrison (1980) adds that staff development programs presented in this manner allow teachers to try things out a little at a time.

Job-Embedded Learning

Job-embedded learning is one of the most promising approaches to professional development. Job-embedded learning is learning by doing, reflecting on the experience and then, generating and sharing new insights and learning with others.

Wood and McQuarrie (1999) identify three of the most common formal structures which have been created to promote job-embedded learning as:

- Study Groups—Groups of teachers and/or administrators meet to learn more about a particular topic such as cooperative learning, student assessments, or curricular programs. The members of the group review and discuss the literature, visit model programs and discuss the viability of the program in their school or classroom.

- Action Research—Action research involves educators in the process of raising questions about how to improve practice, studying the literature and research according to their questions, and then selecting an approach that might result in improved practice. The selected approach is implemented and data is collected, analyzed and shared, first with the study group and then with the school and/or the district.

- Reflective Logs—Reflective logs are used to encourage learning from the successes and problems encountered during the work day. Teachers and administrators record key events, summarizing what happened, reflect on those experiences and report on what they have learned. Keeping a log helps educators learn how to improve professional practice, to discover what is working or not working, uncover personal strengths, and identify areas where improvement is needed.

Staff development must be relevant. "Research and experience have shown that unclear expectations are one way to guarantee nonimplementation. Teachers appreciate clear objectives. They need to know what they are expected to do and how their roles are to change" (Hall and Loucks, 1980).

This methodology supports current research in the area of staff development. Consider the following:

- During their staff development, teachers need time to reflect upon their present way of doing things.

- It is easier for teachers to make gradual changes, one or two aspects at a time, and then move toward full implementation.

- Teachers need to know how to implement change.

- Feedback and follow-up are imperative to successful staff development.

To reiterate and add to what was stated at the beginning of this chapter, it is imperative to note the importance of the role of the principal. What the principal does is critical to the success of an implementation effort. The principal must play that leadership role in staff development. The principal's attitude is being watched! Some recommendations and implications for the principal to heed are:

- ◆ Provide time for sharing ideas and activities. If common planning time is impossible, consider a peer sharing group which meets during lunch or outside of school time.
- ◆ Choose school goals that encourage cross-curricular or cross-grade level planning.
- ◆ Encourage teachers to teach each other. Have teachers share information from conferences and workshops they attend.
- ◆ Provide opportunities for teachers to observe each other. Facilitate the logistics involved to make it easy to occur.
- ◆ Formalize ways for teachers to work together to solve problems. Make asking for help an acceptable practice.
- ◆ Celebrate small successes. Recognize that change occurs slowly and that small steps can lead to a collaborative culture.

All of this takes time and effort and cannot be forced. The ultimate benefits of improved instruction for students and an improved climate for teachers are worth the time it takes (Jakicic, 1994).

Cline (1993), after an extensive review of the literature, states that successful staff development programs include the following levels:

- ◆ training on a topic that includes best practices and models;
- ◆ additional training that includes more in-depth knowledge of a topic and more best practices from teachers in classrooms;
- ◆ training of teachers and administrators together; and
- ◆ training of principals so they can support teachers as they change their practice.

In conclusion, teachers trying new instructional approaches for the first time need staff development experiences that link theory to practice, address the problems associated with change, and give them the opportunity to work with other teachers. Through a workshop process in which teachers acquired new instructional strategies, reflected upon the change process, and experienced collaboration, participants found themselves well prepared for many of the day-to-day difficulties of innovation implementation. Through the preparation provided by the workshop, participants became more empowered teachers (Jakicic, 1994).

Evaluation

Perhaps the most overlooked step in an effective development program is evaluation. All too often staff development ends with the end of the presentation. We all need feedback to know how we are doing. We are very good at giving immediate feedback to our students, but we often fail to do so with each other. Just as our students work toward outcomes and objectives, so must our staff development program. These outcomes are the criteria by which our staff development program should be evaluated.

With all of the research and planning involved in setting up a staff development program, not to mention the time and expense of getting a presenter and your staff together, it is imperative that some time be spent in evaluation.

Without an effective evaluation process there is little chance for you or your staff to know if your program is working. We all want to know if what we did, worked. Waiting for the results of your academic testing is too long a time span and it does not give us all of the answers.

Follow-up is a must. Coaching and feedback must be part of the program. It does take time and money to do follow-up and to do it right. We want to move on, but we need to realize that we are better doing a few things well than lots of things poorly.

As has been stated before, the most important reason for doing staff development is to learn how to better teach students. Unfortunately not a lot of work has been done to help us match student achievement with staff development. Orlich et al. (1993) found that "While the use of some instructional practices have resulted in improved student achievement, the direct link between teacher staff development and student achievement has not been supported by statistical data from several major studies" (Orlich et al., 1993). Orlich also stated, "School practitioners and theoreticians tend to be too simplistic in their assumptions about the scope and influence of teacher staff development on student performance."

School budgets are becoming increasingly tight. With many programs already being squeezed out, increased advocacy for staff development is necessary. Within this advocacy, the "powers that be" at the district level want to know what they are hoping to get for their money. Schools are increasingly coming under the pressure of validating how each dollar is spent. Principals need to find the best way to use their money. There are at least four levels at which the impact of staff development training could be measured. If we are going to evaluate effectively our "return on investment" (ROI) for our staff development program, we must follow through all four levels:

+ Participants' reaction to the staff development—usually done immediately after the program.

+ Participants' implementation of their new skills and knowledge while performing their jobs.

+ Measurement of the organization's results.

+ Measurement of student learning.

In their article, "Using ROI to Assess Staff Development Efforts," Todnem and Warner (1993) offered these conclusions in using the ROI concepts:

> The current climate of accountability requires that staff developers become fully informed about and skilled in several assessment models. ROI provides a valuable tool to demonstrate impact. In order to determine ROI educators must first define what constitutes ROI. We offer the concept of "meaningful change" as a starting place for expressing the units by which ROI is to be calculated. In schools, ROI needs to be expressed in units that relate to the program goals, express the interest areas of planners and stakeholders, and also are quantifiable. Some staff development efforts may not be readily assessed with the ROI concept. It is our experience, however, the concept of ROI opens up a variety of assessment approaches our colleagues and stakeholders will find acceptable. We invite staff developers to explore the concept of ROI with their constituencies and to share their experiences with others. Together, we can show how staff development benefits students and educational organizations. (Todnem and Warner, 1993)

It is very important for the participants in a staff development program to be involved not only in the planning phase, but all the way through including evaluation. Gelareh Asayesh (1994) concurs, "When participants in staff development are involved in the evaluation of their own training, they become involved in shaping their own growth rather than passively submitting to a third party, the staff developer." All vested parties should be involved in all phases of a staff development program. Do not minimize or eliminate the evaluation component. No staff development program is complete without a thorough evaluation.

Figure 8.4 is a sample middle school staff development plan. Features of this plan include goal statements, performance requirements (*who* is going to do *what* for *whom* by *when*), and indicators of success (evaluation). Further, teachers, secretaries, paraeducators, substitutes, and administrators are part of the staff development program. Still further, all bi-weekly staff meetings have 15–20 minutes devoted to staff development topics.

Figure 8.4 A Sample Middle School Staff Development Plan

Goals:

Policy:	to continue to reinforce and support all personnel with implementation of the discipline procedures.
Curriculum:	to study scheduling and elective options to meet the needs of increasing student enrollment.
Climate:	to support staff morale and student motivation.
Quality Teaching:	to continue to provide encouragement and support for Instructional Theory into Practice, Peer Coaching, and Cooperative Learning.

Performance Requirements:

1. What: "Needs Assessment Survey"
   For: All building staff classified, certified, and substitutes
   By: Building Principal and Staff Development Coordinator
   When: Spring

2. What: "Clerical Staff (Secretaries) In-service"—welcome, review goals, expectations, changes, clarify responsibilities, and discuss building climate.
   For: Secretaries
   By: Building Principal
   When: August 20—return to buildings

3. What: "Orientation"—characteristics of Shelton Middel School students, discipline policy, schedule, building procedures, materials, supplies, expectations, etc.
   For: New teachers, Para-educators, substitutes
   By: Building principal, with counselor, librarian, head secretary, and vice principal
   When: August 29 (before school opens)

4. What: "Collaboration & Team Building"—share goals for the year and skills of collaboration.
   For: All building staff (substitutes invited)

	By:	Building principal with vice principal and 2–3 teachers
	When:	August 30 (half day in-service before school opens)
5.	What:	"Preparing for the First Day"—review discipline policy, classroom management, tips for motivating students, and student expectations.
	For:	All building staff
	By:	Staff Development Coordinator or teacher designate with building principal.
	When:	10:00 am to 12 pm, August 31—(following all-district meeting and preceding catered staff lunch)
6.	What:	"Presenting a Positive Image: Handling Parent, Teacher and Student Interactions" (district offering)
	For:	Clerical and classified staff
	By:	District or Educational Service District Trainer
	When:	Mid-September
7.	What:	"Para-educators in-service"—welcome back, clarify duties, responsibilities, legal rights, expectations, discipline policy, etc.
	For:	Building Para-educators
	By:	Building Principal
	When:	Afternoon 1 hour, August 31
8.	What:	"Peer Coaching" (district offering) ten-hour, one-credit class to set up coaching teams in each building to support implementation of effective teaching strategies.
	For:	All certificated staff (administrators also)
	By:	District Trainer
	When:	Late Sept. through early Oct. (Jan., Mar., and May, follow-up)
9.	What:	"Beginning ITIP"—(district offering)
	For:	All teachers, Para-educators and substitutes
	By:	District Trainer
	When:	October
10.	What:	"Scheduling & Electives Appropriate for Middle School Students"
	For:	Middle School Staff
	By:	Consultant

When:	Early October—delayed start (consultant to remain in the building all day to observe classes, students, study physical site, demographics, and later meet with a building study group who will take his recommendations into consideration as they make school visitations, review research and prepare a recommendation for the staff in March.)

11. What: "EA. Follow-up"—check on assignment of duties, address concerns, seek feedback.

> For: E.A.s
>
> By: Building Principal
>
> When: October C Friday morning, before school coffee hour

12. What: "Motivation & Self-Esteem"—(district offering)

> For: All staff
>
> By: District or ESD Trainer
>
> When: November once a week 10 hours, one credit

13. What: "Integrating Curriculum: Writing Across the Curriculum"—An examination of the writing process.

Staff Meeting Component of Staff Development

Bi-weekly staff meetings will devote 15-20 minutes to staff development topics. The following list is a guide to the topics that will be led by various staff members.

Sept: Team Building Skills, follow-up (invite parent advisory)

Sept: Motivating students for success

Oct: Update: Revise/reflect on discipline policy

Oct: Collaboration: Input on scheduling options

Nov: Implementing ITIP: Tips

Nov: Writing across the curriculum: Tips

Dec: Celebrating Our Gifts—Principal acknowledges each staff member for his/her special gifts to the school.

Jan: Peer Coaching Progress Report: Implementing ITIP, discipline, writing

Jan: Tips to handle "End of the Semester Stress"

Feb: Motivating students for success: "What Works"—presentation by students

Feb: Progress report for scheduling/Electives by study group members

Mar: Teacher feature: Selected by parent advisory group to acknowledge special efforts by particular teachers.

Apr: Model cooperative learning with staff meeting agenda

May: Present plan for schedule & elective changes

May: Motivating students: Keeping them going through the end of the year

June: Celebrating our successes: Reflection and evaluation of our year

Indicators of Success

♦ Completion of the above-listed staff meetings, in-service programs, classes, and workshops.

♦ The level of staff participation

♦ Evaluations of each staff development in-service

♦ Feedback, both formal and informal, regarding staff development activities, and staff meetings

No Child Left Behind

The recent passage of the No Child Left Behind Act (NCLB) is requiring school and its leaders to operate differently. This law surely has some staff development components and implications for the principal. Some of the NCLB requirements of the teacher quality are:

♦ States must produce a plan that sets annual measurable goals for increasing their number of highly qualified teachers.

♦ Every public school teacher of a core academic subject must be highly qualified by the end of the 2005–06 school year.

♦ Core subjects are English, reading/language arts, math, science, foreign languages, civics and government, economics, art, history and geography.

♦ Highly qualified means that teachers must be licensed to teach in their state, must hold at least a bachelor's degree and must show mastery of the subjects they teach.

♦ States must publish a yearly report card, including the percentages of students not taught by highly qualified teachers. School districts that receive Title 1 money must do the same.

♦ Any school that receives Title 1 money must notify parents if their child has been taught for four or more consecutive weeks by a teacher who is not highly qualified.

Incentive Programs

Incentive programs in education can be divided into three major categories: (1) programs with monetary incentives for improved performance; (2) programs that provide extra pay/extra responsibility for extra work; and (3) programs that offer nonmonetary/recognition incentives. Because the monetary incentives for improved performance are not very prevalent and a discussion of them often generates more heat than light, the focus of this section will be on the other two categories and the relation of incentives to staff development. Although the thrust here is on the teaching staff, other school employees should be able to participate as well.

The case can be made that in a comprehensive staff development plan, as illustrated by Figure 8.1, incentives are a part of the staff development program of a district. Incentives can be thought of as anything that encourages teachers to grow professionally and to enhance their skills. Principals will want to do all that they can to encourage teachers in this growth and, therefore, must be knowledgeable about the role of incentives.

There are a wide variety of programs that fall into the extra pay/extra responsibility category. Some examples are: department or grade level chairs; curriculum coordinators; cocurricular assignments such as coaching, advising, and supervising; mentoring new teachers; extended contracts for curriculum development; teaching extra classes; teaching beyond the school day (drivers' education); and asking the teacher to serve as a consultant in the district or outside the district. These activities can be good for the teacher as well as the district. The pay for this category should be thought of as an investment rather than strictly as an expenditure. A caution here is for the principal to be alert that the extra responsibility does not take the place of the classroom instruction and that teaching the students does not become secondary to the extra assignment.

Recognition can be a strong incentive to grow professionally. Some examples are: recognition in the newspaper and/or with the school board; a letter or certificate of appreciation; the Golden Apple Award from the Parent-Teacher Association; release from duties to attend professional conferences; naming facilities after the staff member: Jones Field, Smith Auditorium; teacher of the year, new teacher (rookie) of the year, coach of the year. Other examples are: printed business cards, frames for teaching certificates, lapel pins for number of years of service, and printed note pads. Still others are: thank you notes sent to the home address for extra impact, audiotapes, and semimonthly breakfasts to hear a motivating speaker or discuss a book or article. There are innumerable opportunities for the alert principal to recognize members of the staff if time is taken to focus on it. This activity should not be thought of as an addition to the principal's job but a vital part of it. It is also important to be timely with the recognition so that the recognition is connected to a specific deed.

The recognition program can develop awards for completion of the wellness program of the district. This is the next topic to be discussed as a part of the staff development program.

Wellness Programs

Another staff development program that can pay dividends for all employees of the district is the wellness program. The wellness program is a series of health measures and activities designed to support the employees in meeting their personal wellness goals. It is a voluntary program and can make a difference in classroom instruction and in the work life of district employees. When employees feel good and are healthy they can be more effective employees and coworkers. The activities generally fall into two categories: *preventive checks* and *wellness activities*.

The *preventive check* category includes:

♦ physical examination

♦ cholesterol screening

♦ blood pressure screening

♦ body composition screening

♦ prostate screening

♦ colon screening

♦ mammogram/medical doctor breast examination

♦ PAP smear

♦ flu shot

♦ one-mile walk test

♦ annual dental check-up

♦ biannual vision check

♦ hearing check

♦ personal health history

♦ breast self-exam

♦ testicular self-exam

The *wellness activity* category includes:

♦ fitness/exercise program—3 times a week for 30 minutes.

♦ nutritional assessment—keep a nutrition diary, low-fat cooking classes, etc.

♦ develop one leisure/hobby activity

- regular meditation and reflection time
- recycling/composting
- healthy back workshops
- skin mapping
- seat belt use 100% of the time
- positive behavior change
- water consumption

Besides being good for the individual some of the activities can bring about a positive climate in the school. Aerobics classes and faculty/staff volleyball games are just two examples.

Use of Technology in Staff Development

The use of electronic portfolios (e-folios) is a recent innovation that holds some promise. Ziechner and Wray (2003) are currently following 14 students over their five semesters in the University of Wisconsin–Madison elementary education program and documenting how the construction and use of electronic portfolios influences their development as teachers. At Seattle Pacific University, Bjork and Bond are using electronic portfolios in a pilot program in the principal certification program. They report early technical problems but state that the e-folio process holds potential for use by principals. It will be informative to use these experiences to inform both principals and teachers in the use of e-folios.

- http://nsdc.org

  This is the key site for staff development which is sponsored by the National Staff Development Council.

- www.ccsd.net/jobs/PDE

  This site of the Clark County School District, NV has a comprehensive catalog of courses for all employees.

- www.eduation-world.com

  Click on professional development; on teacher lessons among other rich   resources.

- www.alpine.k12.ut.us.depts.accounting.profdev.pdf
- www.gateway.org

  A key one-stop access to educational resources on the internet.

- www.nbpts.org

  Sets standards for what accomplished teachers should know and be able to do.

- http://ncrl.msu.edu

  Center provides leadership in defining teacher learning. This site includes a variety of research publications regarding teacher learning.

- www.ncrel.org

  This site offers a variety of resources on pre-service and professional development.

- www.nwrel.org

  Presents research available to guide decisions regarding the selection, design, and implementation of effective staff development.

- www.mcrel.org

  Mid-continental Regional Educational Laboratory site, which currently sponsors high quality out of district staff development

- www.ascd@smartbriefs.com

  This is a daily site of newspaper articles sorted by relevance to education by the Association of Supervision and Curriculum Development. It is a great way for the principal to keep up on current issues across the United States.

Conclusion

Designed to make a significant difference in the teaching lives of the staff, and thus, make a similar difference in the learning lives of students, the staff development function will take on a greater role in the improvement of instruction and the achievement of students. The principal, likewise, will have greater responsibilities for the development of the staff. The principal is the key person in the staff development process, much like the teacher is for students. As district office staff members are eliminated, this is a responsibility that the principal should eagerly accept. If done correctly, staff development will not be seen as merely a collection of various in-service activities but rather a carefully planned, research-based, curriculum-oriented program.

Comprehensive Questions

1. Why would a site-based staff development model likely lead to educational improvement?
2. Why is staff development for "everyone?"
3. Why are long-range goals important when implementing staff development?

4. What can you do to build a learning community and a culture of improvement?

Extended Activities

1. Devise a plan for your own personal growth and development after you obtain your principal's certificate.

2. Read *The Journal of Staff Development* regularly.

3. A good book to read and have on your professional bookshelf is *Staff Development: Practices that Promote Leadership in Learning Communities* by Sally J. Zepeda. It is a comprehensive book on staff development.

4. Start a "book of the month" club with your staff. Make it voluntary and fun as well as educational.

References

Ankeny Community Schools (1989). *Staff development plan.* Ankeny, OH: Ankeny Community Schools.

Asayesh, G. (1994). Effective advocacy for staff development. *Journal for Staff Development, 15*(2).

Asayesh, G. (1993). Staff development for improving student outcomes. *Journal for Staff Development, 14*(3).

Bergeson, T., M. A. Heuschel, D. Billings, and S. Anderson (2003). *Washington state professional development planning guide,* Part One. Olympia, WA: Office of Superintendent of Public Instruction.

Bjork, L., and S. Bond. (2003). Pilot e-folio project for principals. Personal interview. Seattle, WA.

Burden, P. R., and D. Wallace (1983). Tailoring staff development to meet teacher needs. Paper presented at the Association of Teacher Educators meeting, Wichita, KS.

Cline, B. (1993). *Planning and implementing effective staff development programs.* (ERIC Document Reproduction Service No. 372538).

Corcoran, T. (1995). Helping teachers teach well: Transforming professional development. *Consortium for Policy Research in Education Policy Brief.*

DuFour, R., and T. Berkey. The principal, a staff developer. *Journal of Staff Development, 16*(4).

Ellis, S. S. (1994). Principals as staff developers. *Journal of Staff Development, 15*(2).

Floden, R. E., and G. W. McDiarmid (Directors). (1995). *Learning to walk the reform talk.* East Lansing, MI: National Center for Research on Teacher Learning, Michigan State University.

Gall, M. D., et al. (1985). *Effective staff development for teachers.* Eugene, OR: College of Education, University of Oregon (ERIC Clearinghouse on Educational Management).

Gersten, R., D. Carnine, and P. Williams (1982). Measuring implementation of a structured educational model in an urban school district: An observational approach. *Educational Evaluation and Policy Analysis*.

Goodlad, J. L. (1983). The school as workplace. In G. A Griffin (Ed.), *Staff Development*. Chicago: University of Chicago Press.

Guskey, T. R. (1997). Research needs to link professional development and student learning. *Journal of Staff Development, 18*(2).

Hall, G. E., and S. F. Loucks (1980). *Program definition and adaptation: Implications for in-service*. Austin, TX: Research and Development Center for Teacher Education, University of Texas.

Holly, M. L. (1982). Teachers' views on in-service training. *Phi Delta Kappan*, (63), 417–418.

Jakicic, C. (1994). Taking small steps to promote collaboration. *Journal of Staff Development, 15*(2).

Joyce, B. R., K. Howey, and S. Yarger (1976). *ISTE Report I*. Palo Alto, CA: Stanford Center for Research and Development in Teaching.

Kirkpatrick, D. L. (1975). *Evaluating training programs*. Alexandria, VA: American Society for Training and Development.

Lawrence, G., and D. Harrison (1980). *Policy implications of the research on the professional development of education personnel: An analysis of fifty-nine studies*. Washington, DC: Feistritzer Publications.

Loucks, S., and H. Pratt (1980). A concerns-based approach to curriculum change. *Educational Leadership*.

McBride, R. E., J. Reed, and J. Dollar (1994). Teacher attitudes toward staff development: A symbiotic relationship at best. *Journal of Staff Development, 15*(2).

McDiarmid, G. W. (1994). *Realizing new learning for all students: A framework for the professional development of Kentucky teachers*. National Center for Research on Teacher Learning, Michigan State University.

Mizell, H. (1997, November). Ineffective use of staff development. *Results*, p. 5.

Nolan, J. F., and T. Huber (1989). Nurturing the reflective practitioner through instructional supervision. *Journal of Curriculum and Supervision, 4*(2), 128.

Northwest Regional Educational Laboratory. (1994). High quality professional development. Portland, OR.

Orlich, D. C., A. L. Remaley, K. C. Racemyer, J. Logan, and Q. Cao (1993). Seeking the link between student achievement and staff development. *Journal of Staff Development, 14*(3).

Porter, A. (1981). Curriculum content influenced by many factors. *IRT Communication Quarterly*.

Rogers, C. R. (1983). *Freedom to learn for the 1980s*. Columbus, OH: Merrill Publishing Co.

Sadowski, L. L. (1993). Staff development 101 for administrators: Alternatives for thirteen management myths. *Journal of Staff Development, 14*(3).

Seyfarth, J. T. (1991). *Personnel management for effective schools*. Boston: Allyn and Bacon.

Sousa, D. A. (1992). Ten questions for rating your staff development program. *Journal of Staff Development, 13*(2).

Sparks, D., and S. Vaughn (1994) What every school board member should know about staff development. *Journal of Staff Development, 15*(2).

National Staff Development Council. (2001). *Standards for staff development*, Revised ed. Oxford, OH.

Stallings, J. (1985). *How effective is an analytic approach to staff development on teacher and student behavior?* Nashville, TN: Vanderbilt University, Peabody College.

Stallings, J., and E.M. Krasavage (1986). Program implementation and student achievement in a four-year Madeline Hunter follow-through project. *The Elementary School Journal.*

Sullivan, R. (1981, Jan. 26). City's teacher training program criticized in 1977–1978 state audit. *New York Times.*

Todnem, G., and M. P. Warner (1993). Using ROI to assess staff development efforts. *Journal of Staff Development, 14*(3).

U.S. Department of Education (1997). Office of Educational Research and Improvement.

Wenatchee Public Schools. *Staff Development.* Wenatchee, WA.

Williams, R. (1993). Initiatives for systemic change. *Journal of Staff Development, 14*(2).

Wood, F. H., and S. D. Caldwell (1991). Planning and training to implement site-based management. *Journal of Staff Development, 12*(3).

Wood, F. H., and F. McQuarrie Jr. (1999). On the job learning. *Journal of Staff Development, 20*(3).

Wood, F. H., and S. R. Thompson (1993). Assumptions about staff development based on research and best practice. *Journal of Staff Development, 14*(4).

Zeichner, K. and Wray, S. (2003). Portfolios as professional development tools. *WCER Research Highlights, 15*(1).

9

Collective Bargaining and Contract Management

Reasons for Studying Collective Bargaining and Contract Management

♦ Principals work with teachers. Teachers belong to groups that bargain. Therefore, it is important for principals to understand bargaining and contract management.

♦ An understanding of the art of negotiating will help principals in their daily tasks of managing and resolving conflict.

♦ Failure on the part of the principal to be knowledgeable about the bargained contract and process can lead to leadership difficulty.

♦ The principal's role on the district management team can provide a site-based emphasis to the bargaining process.

> *Principals and teachers in a conflict situation should come to see themselves as working cooperatively, attacking the problem not each other.*
>
> Fisher and Ury

ISLLC Standard Covered in this Chapter

Standard 6:

♦ A school administrator is an educational leader who promotes the success of all students by understanding, responding to, and influencing the larger political, social, legal, and cultural context.

Introduction

The National Education Association (NEA) was formed in 1857. However, it was formed as a professional association rather than a labor union. Its development into a labor union is recent and, in part, can be traced to the unilateral, authoritarian action by administrators. In fact, some states retain laws that prohibit collective bargaining by public school employees. In Washington State, a bill was introduced to the legislature that would severely limit the scope of collective bargaining. In the words of the Washington Education Association, it would "...drag education employees back into the pre-1965 'meet and confer' era when the balance of power in all employer-employee matters lay with the school boards." Even in the current conservative political climate, the bill is viewed as having little chance of being enacted. However, it serves as an illustration of a political reaction to the perceived power of the labor unions that represent school employees.

In the 1960s the NEA developed a bargaining agenda, which had met with initial success in some of the Great Lakes states such as Michigan and Wisconsin. This bargaining agenda was exported to other states. The state and local affiliates pressed for representation rights and, subsequently, for greater control over terms of employment and working conditions. More than 30 states had passed legislation approving bargaining in the public sector and thus collective bargaining between boards of education and employees was well established. What was not established was the approach to bargaining. Initially, the bargaining style that emerged, was positional and confrontational. It pitted a teacher agenda, which was often heavily influenced by the state and national organization, against that of the district. Districts had been accustomed to dictating terms and conditions to employees. Thus, the typical initial response to bargaining was for positions to be directed by school boards and the administrators of the district. The limited roles of principals on the bargaining team were to defend the prescribed district positions and to lend credibility to those positions by virtue of their position on the front lines with the teachers. Things in this arena are changing.

The trend toward revised governance structures in schools is having a profound influence on the bargaining process. As we are in the midst of this change, it is difficult to predict the long range effects. However, some changes are clear and easy to describe at present. These include an emerging consensus that the management of schools is not and should not be the exclusive province of the board, central office administrators, and principals. Rather, it is increasingly accepted that those closest to the educational process should have an increasing and perhaps dominant voice in decisions. Thus, teachers and principals are beginning to assume more influential roles. This is beginning to be felt in the area of collective bargaining. The principal now serves as much more than a source of credibility. The principal is a partner in the development of language that creates terms and conditions of employment, which facilitate new management-teacher relationships. We are beginning to see the emergence of a partnership designed to create the new educational structures needed to deliver services to our changing clientele. Principals no longer seem willing to serve as spokespersons for a board of directors that is detached from the educational process. Rather, they are stepping up to a lead position in collective bargaining, even in states that do not.

Principals sense the shift in the importance of their role in the bargaining process and they attribute that shift to changing governance structures. However, districts are slow to recognize this shift and continue to relegate principals to a secondary role in the bargaining process. This seems to support the contention that this is an emerging change.

Transition From Positional to Collaborative Bargaining

Bargaining between professional educators and boards of eduction is shifting from the positional bargaining that developed in the 1960s and 1970s to the collaborative bargaining model. A comparison of the models is set forth in Figure 9.1.

Figure 9.1 A Comparison of Bargaining Models

Positional Bargaining

- Follow rituals
- Stake out positions
- Vague and closed about interests
- Backward looking
- Content expert
- Emphasize potential for mutual gain

- Emphasize risks
- Leverage deadline to force movement
- Focus on quick fixes and closure
- Allocation of resources

Collaborative Bargaining

- Be flexible
- Focus on interests
- Open and direct about interests
- Forward looking
- Process expert
- Allocate time in relation to importance of issue

- Focus on lasting solutions
- Expansion of resources

Principal's Behaviors and the Collaborative Bargaining Model

Principals, whether or not in the collaborative bargaining arena, should develop a thorough understanding of the collaborative model and the behaviors that promote a climate of trust. Figure 9.2, outlines an integration of the four steps of collaborative bargaining and the appropriate behaviors that reinforce collaboration. When the collaborative model breaks down, principals would be wise to first consider their behavior and whether it was a contributing factor before looking at either the process or the other professionals involved in the conflict.

Figure 9.2 An Integration of the Stages of the Collaborative Bargaining Model with Appropriate Behaviors

- ◆ Stage 1—**Moderating Culture**
  - Control Emotional Expression
  - Avoid posturing, confrontation, and personal attacks and remain calm in the face of volatile or provocative behavior.
  - Promote Positive Group Climate
  - Develop ground rules for how labor/management committee meetings will be conducted and enforce constructive behavior in these meetings.
  - Suspend Judgment
  - Actively try to understand the other side's point of view by listening before joining arguments, by not taking rigid positions, and by exhibiting a willingness to collaborate.
  - Apply Interpersonal Skills

    Use verbal and nonverbal cues to help structure committee members' understanding of agendas, decisions, and action plans and give committee members supportive feedback to encourage active, balanced, and creative participation.
- ◆ Stage 2—**Building Relationships**
  - Acknowledge Systems

    Understand and respect relevant aspects of organization/work-site policies and procedures, union structure, and the bargaining agreement.
  - Accept the Bargaining Process

Respect the differences between labor and management and actively support the negotiations team as a legitimate forum.

- Project Commitment

  Exhibit confidence in own judgment. Take and change positions based upon an analysis of factual information, and stand up to negative or confrontational people.

- Maintain Credibility

  Demonstrate reliability by honoring agreements, avoiding surprises, sharing constraints, and communicating without hidden agendas.

◆ Stage 3—**Integrate Interests**

- Combine Systematic and Creative Thinking

  Define issues clearly, gather relevant information, explore alternative remedies, and strive for innovative/imaginative solutions.

- Integrate Formal and Informal Activities

  Use an appropriate balance of formal and informal meetings and settings to address issues, formulate solutions, and build support.

- Emphasize Mutual Benefits

  Formulate solutions that address the other side's underlying interests and concerns and that emphasize benefits to the other side when presenting solutions.

◆ Stage 4—**Agreements**

- Build and Protect Alliance

  Identify key players on both sides. Anticipate their positions and reactions and take steps to gain their support.

- Make Efficient Use of Resources

  Maximize committee effectiveness by using relevant subgroups and individuals inside and outside the committee to help define and resolve issues and problems.

- Press for Closure

  Focus on issues and problems that both sides want to resolve and do whatever it takes to assure that committee decisions and agreement are implemented.

- Use Feedback to Improve Results

  Evaluate committee process and outcomes regularly and initiate remedial actions needed to assure achievements of committee goals.

Collaborative Bargaining Principles and Assumptions

The principal needs to develop an operational model, which differs from positional bargaining in order to develop positive and trusting relationships with others. This is true not only when the principal is on the bargaining team but also when performing normal day-to-day leadership and management duties. Figure 9.3 lists key elements of the principles and assumptions.

Figure 9.3 Collaborative Bargaining Assumptions and Principles

Assumptions	Principles
♦ All can benefit	♦ Focus on issues or problems—not on people
♦ Relationships can be enhanced	♦ Focus on interests of each party—not on position
♦ Synergy is key—the whole is greater than the sum of its parts	♦ Focus on options or choices
♦ Feelings are facts	♦ Focus on fairness
♦ The process never ends—although there may be a pause	

Mukilteo School District: A Case Study of Collaborative Bargaining

What is the best way for school districts and associations to deal with their differences? After having the longest teacher strike in the history of the State of Washington at that time (about 33 days), the Mukilteo School District and the Mukilteo Education Association were able to work out a three-year contract by using *collaborative* bargaining. Negotiation is a fact of life. We do it every day of our lives in varying settings from deciding where to go to dinner with our spouse to setting a curfew for our children. Negotiation is a back and forth communication process designed to reach an agreement between two sides.

With the advent of site-based decision making, a trend has emerged where everyone wants to participate in decisions that affect them and fewer people are willing to accept decisions dictated by someone else. Standard strategies for negotiation often leave people dissatisfied and alienated. This was the situation that faced Mukilteo after the strike.

Standard strategy consists of two ways to negotiate: soft or hard. Soft negotiation tries to avoid conflict by willingly making concessions to reach an agreement with the other side. Soft negotiators often end up feeling exploited and bitter about the negotiations.

The second common strategy is hard negotiation. In this type of negotiation, the negotiator sees every situation as a contest of wills where the side that takes an extreme position and holds out the longest wins. Hard negotiators want to win, which will elicit a tough response from the other side that ends up harming the relationship between the two sides.

As the Mukilteo School District found, there is a better way. It is neither hard nor soft. It is based on deciding issues on their merits, not on what each side says what it is willing to do and not do. With this method, you look for mutual gains and, if there is a conflict of interests, the outcome is based on a fair standard independent of the will of either side. Collaborative bargaining is hard on problems but soft on people.

Using collaborative bargaining principles and assumptions together with the stark realization that positional bargaining did not work very effectively, the Mukilteo School District and Mukilteo Education Association built a more positive climate that led to a more trusting relationship and to the development of site-based school councils. The collaborative negotiation brought out an "us" attitude rather than the previous "we–they." This process took time, but as one of the participants summed up the feelings of all sides, "it was worth it." The students, teachers, parents, district, and community all benefited. Much work remains to be done to make these gains part of the culture, but there is a good start. Other school districts and education associations would be well advised to adopt this model. Principals can play a key role in the establishment of the collaborative model.

Steps to Success

Prior to any new approach to bargaining, members of both parties and other significant leaders should be involved in training sessions so that they understand the approach and develop new skills. Such training is best done by an outside facilitator agreed upon by both sides and should be done in a retreat setting of two days, followed by a one-day retreat immediately prior to the commencing of the process.

The following steps are key to *the process*, *the agreement*, and the *length of the agreement*:

♦ **Ground Rules**

   After the training and after the general assumptions and principles have been agreed upon, the Collaborative Bargaining Team members (both labor and management) must act on those agreements. One of the first places to do this is to develop the ground rules. Figure 9.4 presents a list of possible topics for ground rules. An example of the ground rules is shown in Figure 9.5. These ground rules were arrived at collaboratively.

Figure 9.4 Possible Topics for Ground Rules

Possible Topics for Ground Rules

1. Scope of agenda issues—scope of issues
2. Use of caucus
3. Participation by negotiating team
4. Alternates
5. Visitors
6. Interruptions/messages
7. Communication/connections to constituents/media
8. Targeted completion date
9. Frequency of meetings/length of meetings
10. Potential use of sub-committees
11. What to do if this process breaks down/stalls out (Notifying other party of concern, etc.)
12. All "agreements" tentative until final agreement reached
13. Tentative agreement must be ratified
14. Preparing language before/After reaching tentative agreement
15. Facilitator role; Sharing of role of facilitator
16. Adding issues; Jointly developing new issues
17. Note taking/Record keeping; Record maintenance
18. Meeting location
19. Adapting/Accommodating work schedules

Figure 9.5 Excellent School District Collaborative Bargaining Ground Rules

1. Meetings will be held on Thursdays from 5 to 7 pm beginning February 3, 1994, in the Excellent School District Board Room, unless otherwise agreed to.

2. Issues presented will represent the legitimate goals and purposes of each party. Each party will respect the legitimacy of the other party's issues.

3. Negotiating Team Members will:

   - Arrive at the meetings on time.

   - Keep the discussion focused on the issue being addressed.

   - Let one Team Member speak at a time with no interruptions.

   - Pay attention to whomever is speaking.

   - Make constructive comments and suggestions, avoid value judgments, and try to suggest alternatives.

   - Be open to new ideas and explore other Team Members' ideas.

   - Exercise patience with the process and the people involved.

4. Each Negotiating Team Member agrees to participate in the process, and no Team Member will dominate the discussions. There will be no chief spokesperson for either party, and there will be no alternates for absences.

5. A caucus may be held at any time. The Facilitator will assist if requested.

6. Visitors are welcome as observers and to attend caucuses; however, they will not participate in the Negotiating Team discussions. Visitors will be asked to contact the Association President or the District's Human Resources Manager before they attend a session.

7. Each Team Member will be mindful of the impacts of his or her public and private statements about the negotiations on the efforts of the Negotiating Team.

8. As issues are resolved, proposed language for the agreement will be written by a subcommittee of the Negotiating Team, the whole Negotiating Team, or a caucus of either party.

9. If new issues are generated as a result of developing options for original issues, they will be addressed at a time agreed upon by

the members, consistent with the issue topic as it relates to other issues.

10. The Human Resources Manager's Secretary will be the custodian for all tentative agreements.

11. Both parties agree that the role of the Facilitator is to keep the Negotiating Team Members on the process.

12. Each Team Member should feel free to remind other Team Members to follow these guidelines.

13. If the process breaks down, Negotiating Team Members agree to discuss the reasons why and attempt to resolve the problem and return to the process.

◆ Agree on the List of Issues

All team members should meet with the groups they represent to develop the issues important to the members of the group and to inform them of the process to be used during collaborative bargaining. After the team members come together and establish the ground rules, the issues should be listed on easel paper and taped around the room. Make sure that each member has one chance to speak before any member has the second chance. Repeat this process around the room allowing members to pass if they have no more issues or if their issue has already been mentioned. The list can then be refined by combining like issues, and adding or deleting others. When deleting, always obtain absolute concurrence from the entire group and anyone who suggested that issue.

◆ Prepare and Present Interest Statements

An interest statement is one party's concern about an issue. These interest statements are best developed during caucus or between meetings. It is helpful to enlist other members of your party in this process so they also develop an understanding.

All interest statements should be presented, then paraphrased by the nonpresented parties to ensure good communication.

◆ Develop Options

An option is one of several solutions that can satisfy an interest or an issue. It is important here to attempt to develop many options to satisfy the interest. This should be done by each party separately, then jointly. An example of issues, interest, and options is given in Figure 9.6.

- **Test Options Against Standards**

  After the many options have been developed, they should be tested against objective standards. Standards could be legal, mission-driven, good for students, and financially responsible, among others.

- **Choose the Best Solution**

  This is the final step to the success of the contract language. From among the many options the team chooses the best possible solution that meets the standards at the current time. The best approach to the choosing is a consensus approach. Consensus means that all members can honestly say:

  - I believe that you understand my point of view and that I understand yours.

  - Whether or not I prefer this option, I support it because it was reached fairly and openly, and it is the best solution for us at this time.

Figure 9.6. An Example of Issues, Interest, and Options

Issue

Seniority

Interest

We are interested in a system where length of service with the organization shall be considered a criter

ion for promotion.

Options

- Strict Seniority
- Experience
- Qualifications
- Trial Period
- Performance Evaluations
- Length of Service in Other Positions

Communication Skills

Communication is often the key problem in negotiations. Without communication, there is no negotiation. Communication in negotiations has three major problems to overcome.

First, negotiators may not be *talking to each other in a way that can be understood*. If hostile and suspicious feelings are being harbored on one or both sides, you should expect that the other side will almost always hear something different than what you said. Frequently, when distributive win/lose bargaining is taking place, both sides are not attempting any serious communication; instead they are just talking to impress their own association or district. This leads to the **second** problem—*listening*. Even when you are talking directly to them, they don't hear you because they are so busy thinking about how they are going to reply. This is referred to as the "shoot and reload" syndrome.

The **third** problem is *misunderstanding*. Negotiations can be compared to sending smoke signals in a high wind: What is said is often misinterpreted by the other side. To solve these communication problems, you need to become an active listener. Standard techniques are to pay close attention, to ask the other party to spell out what they mean in a clear and careful way, and to request that the other party to repeat their ideas if there is any ambiguity for you. The other side will feel comforted by your questions because they will know that they are being heard and understood.

Another factor to consider in communicating when participating in collaborative negotiations is perception. It is all right to discuss each other's perceptions. Make the perceptions explicit and discuss them with others in an honest manner without blaming another for the problem. A discussion like this can go a long way toward clarifying perceptions between associations and school districts. If people are not involved in the process, they are not likely to approve of the outcome, so give them a stake in the outcome by making sure that they can participate in the process. Figure 9.7 lists some communication skills that need to be part of the training and used in bargaining as well as daily management of a school.

Listening is critical to the collaborative bargaining process as well as to school leadership. If you are good at listening, you are a good communicator who takes time to acknowledge other people's ideas and feelings.

Some people, especially those in authority positions, tend to be better at talking than listening because they are used to being "listened to." Other factors such as mood and timing can undermine our ability to listen to and hear what someone else is saying. Figure 9.8 presents techniques for developing listening skills.

Productive Group Behaviors

The quality of a group's relationship can frequently be directly linked to the quality of the communications. There are identifiable communication behaviors, which can be shown to have either a positive or negative influence on the interactions of the groups. Individual group members can have a positive impact on the group's function by monitoring the nature of the contributions, including their own, and working to ensure that interactions contribute to, rather than inhibit, successful outcomes.

The following framework of communication behaviors is adapted from the work of Schein (1969), who summarized the work of Gordon, Rogers, Ginott, and others. The "Roadblock" behaviors are those that impede the accomplishment of group goals. "Productive" behaviors are those that must occur consistently for satisfactory progress to be made (see Figure 9.9).

Figure 9.7 Techniques for Developing Communication Skills

♦ Use "I" not "You" Messages

Ex: "I am upset that I can't schedule a meeting in the next week" versus "You never are available to meet with me."

♦ Ask Questions for Clarification First

Ex: "I need clarification on how you understand the assignment of overtime in this department" versus "Isn't overtime always given to the same people in this department?"

♦ Paraphrase

• For Accuracy

Ex: "I hear you saying that in calculating overtime if the employee works four (4) hours and 22 minutes that will be considered as four and one-half (4 1/2) hours of overtime."

• For Understanding

Ex: "Are you saying that sick leave can be used for bereavement for five (5) days guaranteed and more could be granted if needed?"

♦ Check Assumptions/Perception

Ex: "Are you concerned that people will use bereavement leave for a family member they barely know?" versus "You always assume that people will use any excuse to get out of work."

Figure 9.8 Techniques for Developing Listening Skills

♦ Focus on the ideas being presented, on the speaker, and on the delivery.

♦ Get the meaning behind the words. Ask questions to clarify.

♦ Resist the urge to respond immediately. Even though you may want to express something, it's better to listen first.

♦ Don't rush or interrupt the speaker. And don't change the subject until the speaker is finished.

♦ Don't plan a response while the speaker is talking. You'll be thinking and not listening.

♦ Acknowledge that the speaker has been heard before responding.

♦ Avoid getting provoked by strong words. Hear the speaker out.

♦ Connect feelings and emotions to the words. They are part of the message.

♦ Work at listening. It requires energy and attention.

♦ Watch body language. It often tells more than the words.

Figure 9.9 Group Communication Behaviors

Productive Behaviors	Roadblock Behaviors
→	←
+ Initiating	– Avoiding
+ Information Giving	– Personal Attacks
+ Active Listening	– Poor Listening
+ Maintenance	– Directing
+ Proposing Closure	– Judging

Caveat:

Some effective behaviors can be dysfunctional if not balanced with other effective behaviors.

Examples:

Over-Defining the Problem

"Hyperactive" Listening

Opinion Overload

Excess Maintenance Behavior (process over substance)

- ◆ **Roadblock Behaviors**
  - *Avoiding*: Diverting the topic, bird walking and "stonewalling"
  - *Personal Attacks*: Put-downs, "sharp" humor, false humor, and name calling
  - *Poor Listening*: Planning ahead, daydreaming, and assuming
  - *Directing*: Use of positional power and authority through ordering, threatening, paternalistic advising, and monopolizing time
  - *Judging*: Unsolicited diagnosing and criticizing before the appropriate time for evaluation
- ◆ **Productive Behaviors**
  - *Initiating*: Identifying issues and defining the problem
  - *Information Giving*: Offering facts, data, ideas, opinions, perceptions, or feedback
  - *Active Listening*: Seeking first to understand by soliciting opinions and information, clarifying, summarizing, and remaining open to feedback
  - *Maintenance*: Process checking, harmonizing, management of the environment, encouraging, "gate keeping," and time keeping
  - *Proposing Closure*: Using techniques for closure, including: evaluation against interests, "straw" designs, testing for consensus, and intuitive summaries

Conflict

Whatever the skill, training, or intent of the team members, conflict in schools is inevitable. Jandt and Gillette (1985) make the following assumptions about conflict:

- ◆ Conflict is inevitable and not necessarily harmful.
- ◆ Some kinds of conflict can contribute immeasurably to the health and well-being of the organization—for example, by stimulating productive competition.
- ◆ No matter what the conflict, it can be managed in such a way that losses are minimized and gains maximized.

It is beneficial for the principal to think of *managing* rather than *resolving* conflict. Some conflicts can be solved; others need to be managed because the resources of time and money to resolve them plainly are not worth it.

It is also helpful to think of satisfying the conflict along three dimensions: **procedural**, **substantive**, and **psychological**. To satisfy the parties to the conflict the principal must attend to the *process*, the *content* of the agreement, and to how the parties *feel* about the "solution" to the conflict (see Figure 9.10).

Figure 9.10 Elements of Conflict Management /Resolution

Substantive
(Contract)

Procedural
(Process)

Satisfaction
of Conflict

Psychological
(Feelings)

Key Idea	
Feelings are facts.	

A comprehensive list comparing the elements of a relationship that may promote conflict and collaboration is detailed in Figure 9.11. The principal and others can check their behaviors against these contrasting elements.

Figure 9.11 Elements of the Labor Relationship that May Promote Conflict or Promote Collaboration

Promote Conflict	*Promote Collaboration*
Attitudes	
1. Managing is done "around the contract."	1. Managing is done "through the contract."
2. "Distributive" bargaining of separate interests with compromise.	2. "Collaborative" bargaining of mutual interests.
3. Mediation takes place only after impasse is formally declared.	3. Informal mediation processes are built in so they happen continuously.
4. The other side is viewed as a problem in an involuntary relationship.	4. The other side is accepted as a necessary part of a bilateral process.
Financial Structures	
5. Budgetary information is restricted by the district.	5. Open budget processes and/or financial formula are used.
Bargaining Processes	
6. Bargaining is done from positions.	6. Bargaining is done from problem statements.
7. One person talks for each side, or communication is restricted.	7. Open communication with everyone encouraged to talk.
8. Caucuses are frequent, and the purpose and outcome is kept secret.	8. Caucuses are held less frequently, with each side openly explaining the reason for the caucus and the outcome.
9. Bargaining chips are used frequently.	9. Both sides strive for consensus and the elimination of bargaining chips.
10. Bargaining consists of a "package" of small tentative agreements into which each side is fixed.	10. Bargaining involves conceptualizing the "bigger picture."
11. Bargaining planning involves the selection of positions.	11. Process planning tools are utilized to analyze interests, options, and parameters.
12. Each side sits directly across the table from the other.	12. Participants are arranged in a circle around a mutual focal point such as a flip chart.

13. Communications to the constituencies and general public are frequently conflicting and divisive.	13. Communications with constituencies and the general public are developed together.

Working Relationships

14. The labor-management relationship evolves as a by-product of the collective bargaining process.	14. The two sides work together to plan and develop a relationship which supports the achievement of mutual goals.
15. Relationship issues and substantive issues are mixed and traded off for one another.	15. Relationship issues and substantive issues are addressed separately and independently.
16. Field representatives and consultants are perceived as outsiders.	16. Field representatives and consultants are perceived as insiders, or as bringing unique mediation and dispute resolution skills.
17. Formal bargaining is the only problem-solving mechanism.	17. Mechanisms for solving problems are developed, including communications and issue-focused committees and brainstorming strategies.
18. The superintendent and board are insulated from the labor relations process.	18. The superintendent and board are involved in the labor relations processes, although not at the table.
19. There is a positional approach to work-site problems.	19. There is a "consensus" approach to work-site problems.
20. There is a reliance on format grievance procedures, unfair hearings, and concerted job actions for resolving conflict.	20. There is a reliance on problem-solving techniques for resolving conflict.

Shared Decision Making

21. Bargaining is narrowly confined to scope.	21. Discussions and decisions address all aspects of the mutual relationship (even beyond scope).
22. Employee groups feel excluded from decision making.	22. Employee groups feel included in relevant decisions.

Compensation

The principal's role in compensation programs is minimal. This is an area for centralization with the district office staff. Centralization provides standardization and equity as well as accurate information in a sensitive and critical area. Nevertheless, the principal should have a general understanding of the salary schedule and the benefits program in order to provide assistance, which must be confirmed by the district office staff.

In addition, the principal must also provide information to the superintendent when the salary and benefits for teachers do not allow the school to compete for outstanding teachers. Membership of the principal on the collaborative collective bargaining team can be beneficial to both teachers and the district personnel. The principal can often view potential conflict from another position and thus, improve communication among all participants.

Grievances

A grievance is a complaint usually filed by a teacher or group of teachers alleging a violation of the collective bargained contract between the teachers' union and the district. To solve the grievance the teacher is bound by the procedures in the contract. The grievance procedure must be seen by the principal as a reasonable way to resolve a problem rather than a threat to the principal's ability to lead. The teacher and principal are bound by the procedure and by the outcome. Each contract has its own grievance procedure and the principal needs to know the procedure and the timelines that relate to the effective handling of the grievance. Timelines are very critical since missing a date without agreement of the other party usually sends the grievance to the next level or step. A general grievance procedure is found in Figure 9.12.

Figure 9.12 General Grievance Procedure

Step 1—Informal   The grievant meets with the principal/supervisor informally to state the problem relating to a contract violation.

If solved, the process stops; if not, move to Step 1—Formal within three working days.

Step 1—Formal   The grievant files a written statement (usually on the form provided by the union) to the principal/supervisor stating the problem and requesting remedy.

If solved, the process stops; if not, move to Step 2 within three working days.

Step 2   The grievant files the written statement with the superintendent or superintendent's designee. Usually a conference is held to discuss the grievance with the grievant and often the teacher's union.

If solved, the process stops; if not, move to Step 3 within three working days. In many districts, especially the larger districts, Step 3 is replaced with mediation prior to Step 4.

Step 3   The grievant files the written statement with the Board of Directors. Usually a conference is held to discuss the grievance with the grievant and often the teacher's union.

If solved, the process stops; if not, move to Step 4 within three working days.

Step 4   The grievant files the written statement with an arbitrator, if law permits, or the courts, seeking resolution.

Marysville (WA) School District Case Study

The Marysville School District developed the six, 10-year goals through the collaborative process as shown in Figure 9.13. In addition, the district and the association developed their respective roles in the achievement of those goals, as shown in Figure 9.14. This is an excellent example of the collaborative bargaining process. To understand that a school district and its teachers need to constantly care for each other as well as the collective bargaining agreement consider that the Marysville Education Association struck against the Marysville School District in 2003 and had the longest (46 days), most contentious strike in the history of the state of Washington. Shortly after the strike, three incumbent school board members were soundly defeated.

Questions for the principal regarding collective bargaining:

♦ Based on the information presented here could you have anticipated a strike?

♦ What is your role in the collective bargaining process during a strike?

♦ What is your role after the strike has ended?

♦ Who would you use as a support group during a strike?

Figure 9.13 Marysville School District—Ten-Year Goals

♦ Financial security

♦ Quality facilities

♦ Culture of collaboration and cooperation within the educational community (trust, respect, honesty, and caring)

♦ Plan to address rapidly changing student needs

♦ Recruit, retain, and develop a quality, culturally diverse staff

♦ Ongoing flexible strategic planning process

- Technology
- Shared decision making
- Performance-based education

Figure 9.14 Marysville School District—
District and Association Roles in Ten-Year Goals

Goal 1: Financial Security

District Role	*Association Role*
◆ Ensure that resources support district priorities ◆ Ensure communications and involvement in fiscal planning and management ◆ Assemble budget ◆ Provide leadership for levies	◆ Seek ongoing sharing of financial information by the district ◆ Review information from Association's perspective ◆ Make members aware of the financial realities that exist ◆ Become partners with the District in planning and prioritizing the budget ◆ Active involvement in levy campaigns ◆ Actively participate in legislative lobbying efforts ◆ Participate in grant writing

Goal 2: Quality Facilities

District Role	*Association Role*
◆ Develop long-range facilities plans through collaborative process ◆ Maintain and update existing facilities	◆ Keep district informed of facility needs ◆ Help plan healthy facilities and see them through ◆ When costs meet needs, we get to help decide what to give up

Goal 3: Trust, Respect, Honesty, and Caring

District Role	*Association Role*
◆ Build trust ◆ Create a climate that values trust, respect, honesty ◆ Adhere to operating principles and model these qualities	◆ We commit to you that we will be honest with the district and to our members ◆ Be ambassadors out in the community with the public ◆ Active participation information of District committees

Goal 4: Develop a Plan to Address Rapidly Changing Student Needs

District Role

- Stay abreast of current research and proven models/programs/strategies
- Provide continuous staff development

Association Role

- Identify needs of teachers for coping effectively with changing needs of students
- Provide resources for staff development to meet those needs
- Design a staff development plan cooperatively with the District
- Be proactive, not obstructionist

Goal 5: Recruit, Retain, and Develop Quality, Culturally Diverse Staff

District Role

- Implement community developed recruitment and training plan that ensures a quality, diverse staff
- Model lifelong learning

Association Role

- Provide resources and help plan for staff development
- Be role models for students and peers with regard to racial and gender issues
- Encourage minority students to pursue careers in education

Goal 6: Strategic Planning

District Role

- Participate with staff and community in the goals and process
- Provide information and support
- Base decisions on priorities of the strategic plan

Association Role

- Be participants on implementation committees
- Analyze and inform the district of anything that would potentially impact the contract

Uses of Technology in Collective Bargaining

- www.mackinac.org

  This site systematically analyzes hundreds of collective bargaining agreements for every school district in the state of Michigan.

- http://ideas.repec.org

  This site discusses the efficiency of collective bargaining in public schools.

Conclusion

The role of the principal in collaborative bargaining can be critically important—directly to the success of the process, and indirectly to the school and district. The principal's understanding of the collaborative process and the roles that the elements of trust, communication skills, and conflict management play in the process can help both the teachers' association and the district management team fashion an agreement that will serve everyone well. Further, in learning and refining these skills, the principal becomes more skillful in the day-to-day leadership of the school.

One of the best ways for the principal to become knowledgeable about the contract and its significance at the building level is to be a member of the collaborative bargaining team. It is in this role that the principal can assist other members of the team realize the impact that the contract has on students and teachers, as well as on principals and parents.

Comprehensive Questions

1. What is the difference between conflict resolution and conflict management? What are the advantages and disadvantages of each?

2. The principal must attend to three dimensions when dealing with conflict. What are they and what do they mean?

3. Why is it important for the principal to be represented on collaborative bargaining teams?

Extended Activities

1. Practice conflict mediation with a group of high school students.

2. Practice your listening skills by rephrasing, summarizing, and asking for feedback on a regular basis.

3. Participate as an observer in a collective bargaining session.

References

Adams, J. L. (1974). *Conceptual blockbusting: A guide to better ideas*. San Francisco: W.H. Freeman.

Attea, W. J. (1993). From conventional to strategic bargaining: One superintendent's experience. *The School Administrator*, 16–19.

Bluestone, B., and I. Bluestone (1992). *Negotiating the future: A labor perspective*. New York: Basic Books.

Conley, D. (1993). *Roadmap to restructuring: Policies, practices, and the emerging visions of schooling*. Eugene, OR: ERIC Clearinghouse on Educational Management.

Covey, S. R. (1991). *Principle-centered leadership*. New York: Summit.

Covey, S. R. (1989). *The seven habits of highly effective people*. New York: Simon and Schuster.

Decker, R. H. (1991). Helping the board of education and negotiating team understand their roles in collective bargaining. *School Business Affairs*, 6–10.

Fisher, R., and S. Brown (1989). *Getting together*. New York: Penguin Books.

Fisher, R., and W. Ury (1981). *Getting to yes*. Boston: Houghton Mifflin.

Jandt, F. E., and P. Gillette (1985). *Win-win negotiation: Turning conflict into agreement*. New York: Wiley.

Janes, L., and N. B. Lovell (1982). A systematic labor-relations model: Returning the principal to the driver's seat. *NASSP Bulletin, 66*(451), 73–78.

Kerchner, C. T. (1988). Professional negotiations: The critical role of administrators. *Thrust*, 10–14.

Kerchner, C. T. (1993). Building the airplane as it rolls down the runway: Administrators discover labor relations as the linchpin to school change. *The School Administrator*, 10–14.

Malito, R. T. (1992). A new era in negotiations. *The Clearinghouse*, 51–52.

Peters, T. J. (1987). *Thriving on chaos*. New York: Knopf.

Schein, E. H. (1969). *Process consultation*. Reading, MA: Addison Wesley.

Sharp, W. L. (1993). *Collective bargaining in the public schools*. Madison, WI: WCB Brown and Benchmark.

Smith, S. C., D. Ball, and D. Liontos (1991). *Working together: The collaborative style of bargaining*. Eugene, OR: ERIC Clearinghouse on Educational Management.

Weisbord, M. R. (1987). *Productive workplaces: Organizing and managing for dignity, meaning, and community*. San Francisco: Jossey-Bass.

10
Continuity
and Legal Issues

Reasons for Studying Continuity and Legal Issues

- Our contemporary society is a very litigious one. Staying out of legal troubles is critical to your success as a principal.

- Your teachers, staff, students, and parents will, from time to time, ask you about the legality of certain actions. You will want to know the legal basics.

- The failure to follow certain statutes on your part is *prima facie* evidence to revoke your certificate as principal.

- One element of treating people fairly is to treat them legally.

> As school districts move to more decentralized decision making, the principal becomes more vulnerable in the legal arena.

ISLLC Standards Covered in this Chapter
Standard 6

- A school administrator is an educational leader who promoted the success of all students by understanding, responding to, and influencing the larger political, social, legal, and cultural context.

Legal Issues in
School Human Resources Administration

Introduction

This chapter provides a reference guide to legal issues concerning human resources administration. Following an outline of legal sources, this chapter includes six major sections that address specific areas of concern in human resources administration: recruiting and hiring, contracting, working with staff, dealing with conflict, employee discipline, and dismissal. Each section includes three subsections: a list of the most common problem situations, guidelines for preventing legal problems, and a reference list of applicable legal references. Omitted from this chapter are the state statutes that apply to human resources administration. These must be examined to have a more complete understanding of the legal issues. Since these statutes vary from state to state, no effort has been made to include them here. However, the building handbook outline, which can be found in Figure 10.2 will provide guidance that principals will find helpful.

Legal Sources Documents

The purpose of this section is to orient the reader to the sources of legal requirements and to highlight those of most concern in human resources administration. The major sources of law, and other legally related requirements, include constitution, statutory, and administrative rule.

Figure 10.1 Sources of Law

	Constitution	*Statutory Law*	*Administrative Rules*
United States	Constitution	Federal Statutes	Federal Agencies
State	Constitution	State Statutes	State Agencies
Local District		Board Policy Contracts	Administrative Regulations & Procedures
Building		Governance Council	Building Handbooks

Additionally, case law, arbitration decisions, and attorney general opinions give guidance on which personnel actions are acceptable and which are not. To avoid conflict, each level is subject to the laws at all higher levels. Principals must follow their own school rules plus their district rules, state laws, and federal laws. Within a given level, administrative rules are subject to statutes that in turn, are subject to the constitution.

The United States Government

Federal laws include the U.S. Constitution, federal statutes enacted by the Congress, and administrative law put into place by federal agencies.

Constitutions, both federal and state, limit the powers of the legislative, the judicial, and the executive branches of government. The U.S. Constitution is the supreme law of the land. Any rules or laws found to conflict with the U.S. Constitution would be declared unconstitutional and, therefore, not legal. Although the U.S. Constitution does not address education directly, several of its provisions affect school human resources administration:

♦ *Article 1, Section 10*: Contracts with employees or bargaining units, once agreed to by the board, must be honored.

♦ *First Amendment*: Personal freedoms of religion, speech, and assembly are protected.

♦ *Fifth and Fourteenth Amendments*: Employee contracts are considered to be contract rights that cannot be taken away without following due process requirements that include, at a minimum, the right to: know the charges being brought against you, confront your accuser, tell your side of the story, and have representation present.

♦ *Fourteenth Amendment—Equal Protection Clause*: Discrimination on the basis of race, sex, and handicap is prohibited.

Statutes are those laws passed by legislative bodies like Congress or the state legislature. Examples of statutes passed by Congress include:

♦ The Occupational Safety and Health Act (OSHA) requires employers, including schools, to provide a safe working environment.

♦ The Civil Rights Act (CRA) requires employers, including schools, to ensure fair treatment of those in "protected classes" based on race, gender, age, disability, and veteran status.

The concept of "states' rights" limits Congress' ability to impose federal statutes on the states, therefore, Congress often makes receipt of federal funding contingent on following the statutes enacted by Congress. Examples of these are found in the exhibits at the end of the chapter.

Administrative law comes from federal or state agencies with authority to regulate public functions. Federal agencies most concerned with education include: the U.S. Department of Education (USOE) and the National Institute of Education (NIE). Other agencies that impact laws related to school personnel administration include: the Department of Labor, which administers the Occupational Safety and Health Act (OSHA), the Office of Civil Rights (OCR), and the Equal Employment Opportunity Commission (EEOC). Examples of these are found in the exhibits at the end of the chapter.

The State

The State Constitution limits state laws in the same way that the U.S. Constitution limits Federal laws. The most important parts of a state constitution from a personnel perspective relate to equity. Two examples are:

◆ Schools must make ample provision for the education of all children residing within its borders, without regard to race, creed, religion, or sex.

◆ Schools must remain forever free of sectarian control or influence.

Most statutory laws affecting school personnel administration come from state legislatures. Each principal should develop a good working knowledge of those laws.

Administrative laws are rules and regulations adopted by state agencies with the power to regulate public schools. In most states, administrative laws are adopted by the State Board of Education and by the Office of the Superintendent of Public Instruction.

School Districts

Schools and school boards, although administered locally, have been consistently found by the courts to be under the authority of the state. State governments delegate to school boards specific authority for operation of the schools. Boards are given the authority to pass *policies* to implement those laws that they have been charged with implementing. School boards, in turn, sometimes delegate to the superintendent the responsibility of writing *administrative regulations and procedures,* which give further direction for carrying out board policies. Policies enacted by local school boards have the weight of law for that specific school district and it is the responsibility of district employees to act in ways consistent with adopted policies and procedures.

In addition to adopting policies and procedures, school boards regularly approve at least two kinds of *contracts,* which have a direct bearing on the role of the principal. School boards bargain with and subsequently enter into formal negotiated agreements, or contracts, with formally recognized bargaining units. By approving these contracts, the board pledges itself and its employees to abide by these agreements. The second type of contract that the board approves is the individual employment contract. These contracts, made with each certificated employee (and some supervisory classified employees), set forth the terms and conditions of employment, which usually include the salary and the term and length of the contract. The U.S. Constitution and other laws require that, once agreed to, the terms of the contract be adhered to by the district and by the administrative representatives of the district.

Local School Buildings

Individual school buildings may also set forth a variety of administrative rules. *Handbooks* may outline rights and responsibilities for staff and/or students. Schools with local decision-making councils may adopt *bylaws* or other self-governance rules. Once adopted, schools may be expected legally to abide by those rules. School rules that conflict with district procedures, board policy, administrative law, statutory laws, or state and federal constitutions will be overturned. A lilst of topics to be included in a school building handbook is shown in Figure 10.2. Pay close attention to the "acknowledgment of employee handbook" at the end of the table. This is a critical document.

Figure 10.2 Guidelines for School Building Handbook

■ Federal/State Posting Requirements

There is a long list of Federal and State Posting Requirements that need to be posted in: (1) Hiring location—a conspicuous place, usually the place where applicants are first received; (2) Work location—where the notice can be readily observed by the employees in the course of their activities, i.e., faculty lounge, or department location. Contact state officials for the requirements of your state.

■ Personnel Records

These files are confidential to school district employees authorized by the Superintendent to access them. Any other persons or agencies may not see these files without the written consent of the staff member, or when subpoenaed by a court of law. These files are kept at the district office under supervision.

■ Professional Organizations

Do your staff members have to belong to the union? Some districts have this negotiated into the contract. Are there any other restrictions on other professional organizations that they might join?

■ Professional Research and Publishing

Most districts encourage research and publications on the part of staff members. But make sure it is clear that a situation doesn't occur where proprietary rights to materials are in doubt because the employee worked on them during school hours.

■ Reduction-in-Force

Know the district's policy on how a RIF is processed in the district.

■ School Calendar

Make sure your staff is aware of the school calendar and copies are always available in the school office. This is usually a negotiated item with the union.

■ School Day

Know the contracted school day that is set down in negotiations, or if flex time or any other adjustments to the school day can be made for individual staff members.

- **Sexual Harassment**

  Make sure your staff knows what does and does not constitute sexual harassment and what the complaint procedure is if needed. Remember, it can be verbal, sex-oriented "kidding" or insults, or at the other end of the spectrum, demands for sexual favors. No matter how innocent it seems, make sure your staff knows it will not be tolerated at any level.

- **Staff Complaints and Grievances**

  Discover and practice effective means to resolve differences that may arise among your staff. Maintaining open communication and reducing potential areas of complaint are important, and resolving issues in a timely fashion helps staff members focus on their teaching. Make sure you know your district's grievance command channel.

- **Staff Conduct**

  Most school districts have a policy that requires all staff members to conduct themselves in a manner that not only reflects credit to the school system, but that also sets forth a model worthy of emulation by students.

- **Staff Conflict of Interest**

  This could deal with the hiring of "immediate family" within the same building, or a conflict of interest in the hiring of outside contractors or consultants.

- **Staff Development**

  Know what staff development is available, and whether it is a required or optional part of your staffs needs.

- **Staff Code of Ethics**

  You and your staff should be knowledgeable of any requirements that the Board has set as policy. This deals with transactions in school business, making sure the staff uses the proper channels, etc. The Code of Ethics or code of conduct should be given and discussed with all staff at least once per year.

- **Staff Evaluations**

  Know the dates of completion that your district requires of all staff observations and evaluations.

  First-year teachers:

  　　1st Observation by _____

  　　2nd Observation by _____

Returning teachers: Evaluations due by _____

■ Staff Extra Duty

Know if any part of the staff's day is considered extra duty. Is it contracted? Is it extra pay?

■ Staff Health and Safety

Make sure Appendix C is posted, and beyond that, make sure your staff is aware of any programs offered to them in the form of assistance in any personal difficulties, such as Employee Assistance Programs (EAP).

■ Staff Hiring

Know that you are always looking to attract, secure and hold the most highly qualified personnel for all professional positions and that the selection process should be based on an alertness to candidates who will devote themselves to the education and welfare of the children attending your school. Know your EEOC requirements, and that federal law prohibits discrimination against protected classes of people. The protected status categories are: age (40 years and above), sex, race, color or national origin, religion, disabled, Vietnam veteran, citizenship, pregnancy or related medical conditions. Many states also prohibit discrimination on the basis of other categories including: sexual orientation, marital status, appearance, and medical conditions such as AIDS. See Figure 10.3 for acceptable preemployment inquiries under EEOC guidelines.

■ Staff Leaves and Absences

Know the district policy on leaves and absences. This includes sick leave, bereavement leave, emergency leave, personal leave, district business, etc. Know if a precedence has already been established in the district as to how some of these leaves can and cannot be used.

■ Staff Meetings

Make sure your staff knows your expectations for staff meetings, and whether or not they are required to attend.

■ Staff Non-school Employment

Does your district have a policy on outside employment for full-time certificated staff members?

- **Staff Participation in Community Activities**

  Some districts encourage staff to participate in community activities. If yours does, are they representatives of the school system or are they on their own?

- **Staff Participation in Political Activities**

  Individual and personal rights and freedoms cannot be dictated by school districts, but some school districts do have policies whereby a staff member's political activity must not compromise his or her professional integrity. The academic process must not be influenced in the interests of the staff's own political ambitions or those of a political group.

- **Staff Protection**

  School districts are now posting "Gun Free and Drug Free Zone" signs, and every precaution must be taken to protect all employees from physical and/or psychological abuse.

- **Staff Status**

  Know the status of all of your staff members, whether they are on a probationary or continuing contract, etc. Know the date (usually in April) when termination letters need to be delivered.

- **Staff Visitations and Conferences**

  Because most school districts want their staffs to stay abreast of current trends, does the district budget allow for staff visitations and conference attendance?

- **Staff Work Load**

  Whether it be number of preps or class size, know the contract language regarding both. Make timely adjustments when these are not in compliance.

- **Staff-Student Relations**

  Know the district's policy on the professionalism of staff in regard to their relationship with their students.

- **Suspension and Dismissal of Staff Members**

  Make sure you know the steps required in the suspension or dismissal of one of your staff. Make sure there is complete documentation, and that there is just and reasonable cause. Know the time line for written reports, and response times allowed by law.

- Transfers

  Know how your district feels about transfers within the district. How does the transfer process go?

Acknowledgment of Employee Handbook

I understand that the information in the North Thurston Employee Handbook represents guidelines only and that the District reserves the right to modify this handbook or amend or terminate any policies, procedures, or employee benefit program whether or not described in this handbook at any time, or to require and/or increase contributions toward these benefit programs.

I understand that I am responsible for reading the handbook, familiarizing myself with its contents, and adhering to all of the policies and procedures of the North Thurston School District, whether set forth in this handbook or elsewhere.

I understand that this handbook is not a contract of employment, express or implied, between me and the North Thurston School District and that I should not view it as such or as a guarantee of employment for any specific duration. However, I do agree to abide by the terms of the handbook relating to arbitration of employment disputes.

_____   _____
(Print name of Employee)   Employee's Signature

Date _____

Please review, sign and return to Human Resources.

Other Rules

The laws and rules listed above create an array of rules to follow. Although they may not be readily available to the principal, each of the above laws and rules may be found in written form in standard reference works. In addition to the foregoing sources, there are at least four other sources of laws and guidelines, which may regulate the actions of the well-informed school principal.

What each of the four sources has in common is that, although they can be found in writing, they are not easily found in standard reference guides. Knowing about these sources of information is therefore more difficult, but sometimes necessary, to the well-informed principal. The four sources are:

Case Law

Case law (also called *common law*) comes from the court decisions made over decades and centuries in a given area. *Due process* and *just cause* are two examples in the personnel area. The U.S. Constitution guarantees due process in the fifth and fourteenth amendments. No definition is provided in the Constitution. Hundreds of court cases have since helped define what is meant by due process. Other cases have helped define just cause. These two terms will not be defined in any statute, but case law—the collection of previous cases in this area—will define what principals can and cannot do in disciplining or dismissing employees.

Administrative Rules

In addition to rules adopted by agencies that directly control schools, the U.S. Department of Education, and the State Board of Education for example, there are many other agencies concerned with public health, safety, and welfare. These agencies write rules regarding fire drills, food preparation, use of pesticides, and other activities which go on in schools.

Arbitration Decisions

When an employee files a grievance under the terms of the negotiated agreement, that grievance may eventually be decided by an arbitrator. The arbitrator's decision then reinterprets the negotiated agreement in the same way that case law defines terms found in statutory or constitutional law. Once decided, the arbitrator's ruling becomes a precedent, meaning that the district and the association must abide by that ruling in future cases.

Attorney General's Opinions

Occasionally a district or a state agency will ask the attorney general to offer an opinion about laws that are hard to interpret clearly. An attorney general's opinion (AGO) is just that, an opinion. It does not have the weight of law, however, it does serve as a useful guideline for how that law can best be interpreted.

Recruiting and Hiring

Recruiting consists of all activities designed to attract potential employees to the school or district. Activities may include brochures, job announcements, advertisements, and initial interviews.

Potential Problems

Any exclusionary or discriminatory recruitment practices or failure to safeguard against such practices present the greatest potential problems in recruiting. The administrator must make special efforts to avoid discrimination against individuals in a protected class: females, minorities, disabled, those over age 40, and/or veterans.

How to Prevent Problems

The following information provides a practical guide for preventing potential legal problems in the recruiting process and comes largely from information by Shoop and Dunklee (1992).

- ◆ *Position Analysis*: When a position becomes available:
  - Perform a job analysis to determine the critical work behaviors to be used as criteria for measuring employee performance. Include supplemental needs such as coaching and supervising.
  - Develop a job description—see Recruitment in Chapter 4, for examples.
    - Make sure the job standards allow for a beginner in the job.
    - Every job standard specified must be verifiable as a valid requirement for the job.
    - For nonteaching positions, every job specification should include levels of skills or abilities necessary for progressively higher-level positions in the same job family.
  - Evaluate the qualifications for all positions to ensure that there are no excessive or unnecessary requirements that might have the effect of disqualifying a disproportionate number of minorities, women, or others in a protected classification.
- ◆ *Recruitment*: Include as many possible sources of qualified applicants as possible when recruiting.
  - Use representatives of both protected and nonprotected classifications of employees as part of the overall recruitment team.
  - Add colleges and universities with predominately minority and female populations to contact lists of sources of qualified applicants.
  - Maintain records of recruitment methods for the dual purposes of evaluating effectiveness and documenting practices.
- ◆ Initial Applications and Screening:
  - Make sure not to ask preemployment questions that may lead to a charge of discrimination.

- All required information, whether asked on the employment application or in an interview, must be related to the job and the applicant's qualifications for the job.
- All applicants must be asked the same questions. Follow-up questions may differ, however, if the intent is to seek clarification or expansion.
- If the applicant volunteers information that is illegal to ask, do not reject the applicant based on that information. Liability exists for discrimination whether or not the information was volunteered.
- If the applicant volunteers information regarding a handicapping condition that directly relates to the job requirements, the employer may be obligated to investigate whether the applicant can be reasonably accommodated to perform the job.

- Be sure that notes or summaries of interview with job applicants:
  - Refer only to job-related aspects of the position.
  - Are stated in neutral, objective terms.
  - Have no negative inferences.
  - Do not include coded information.

- Interviews:
  - Be careful with "ice-breaking" small talk and comments. Case law has demonstrated that these aspects of the interviewing are the most susceptible to legal problems. Only job-related and legally allowable questions may be asked in the interview. Consequently, the principal who is completely familiar with the job being filled should lead the interview.

  - Document the interview including the date of the interview, the interviewer's name, and the results (e.g., "eliminate" or "application processed further").

  - The most important principle in interviewing, at any stage, is to ask only questions which are related to job requirements.

  - Questions better left alone deal with:
  - Health
  - Income
  - Marital status or lifestyle
  - Race, religion, or politics
  - Age, date of birth, height, weight, gender

- Nonwork-related issues
- Children and family plans
- Preemployment Testing:
  - Preemployment tests must not limit any protected class from consideration for employment unless the employer can prove that the test is job-related and properly validated.
  - Physical testing may only be used for jobs clearly requiring physical standards. All applicants for such a position must be given the same test.
    - Drug testing law remains an unclear legal area.
    - Employers may not test prospective employees for HIV, ARC, or AIDS.
- Reference Checking:
  - Any personal characteristics known to be important for job performance should be included in the listed qualifications for the job. Typical characteristics include honesty, dependability, and ability to work with others.
  - All questions asked in a reference check must be related to the applicant's past performance.
    - Make sure to obtain all information from someone knowledgeable about the applicant's work performance.
    - Have all applicants sign a form authorizing release of the information requested from references to protect against potential defamation suits.
    - Gather the same information from references for all applicants and use the information consistently.
- Hiring Decisions:
  - Make all decisions without regard to race, color, national origin, sex, or religion. An exception here is private church-related schools.
  - Evaluate all aspects of recruiting and hiring to detect biases that might adversely impact protected groups.
  - Any restrictions related to race, color, national origin, sex, religion, or protected groups must be based on a bona fide occupational qualification necessary to job performance.
  - Document each stage of the selection process for purposes of evaluation.

Legal References for the Principal

- Title VII of the Civil Rights Act of 1964
- The Equal Pay Act of 1963
- The Age Discrimination in Employment Act (ADEA)
- The Rehabilitation Act of 1973
- The Americans with Disabilities ACT of 1990 (ADA)
- The Veterans' Reemployment Act
- The Immigration Reform and Control Act of 1986 (IRCA)
- Title IX of the Education Amendments of 1972

Contracting

Contracting consists of ensuring that the employee meets all hiring criteria, clarifying all terms and conditions of the contract, obtaining school board approval, and adhering to the terms of the contract.

Potential Problems

Employee Qualifications

In addition to the job-related requirements listed in the previous section, there may be several additional checks designed to ensure against the hiring of noncitizens, pedophiles, or those with criminal records. Several checks may need to be carried out either before the contract is signed or with the clear written understanding that the successful completion of these checks will be required to fully enact the contract.

All employees are now required to provide proof of citizenship (Form I-9) or other documentation showing entitlement to be employed in the United States. Fingerprinting may be required by your district as a basis for running a criminal background check to ensure against the hiring of those convicted of child molestation or other crimes. Checking certificate numbers against those recorded at the state level may be required to ensure that certificates are current and have not been revoked. Each state maintains computer links to other states for lists of certificates that have been revoked. In addition, a call to the state office can often tell whether there is a current investigation of the teacher in question. Checking driving records may be required in the case of hiring bus drivers.

Certification

Schools make a distinction between two categories of employees: certificated and classified. Certificated employees are those who hold state certificates as requirement of the position they hold. All other employees, who are not required by their position to hold certificates, are usually referred to as classified employees.

Teachers must be certificated and, depending on the state, have an endorsement for each area in which they teach. This creates two potential problems. The first is that the teacher must have a certificate. Schools are also required to make sure that classrooms are under the supervision of a certificated employee. Teachers who have not yet been granted a certificate or those whose certificates have expired cannot continue to teach.

The second potential problem may come from hiring teachers who lack the proper endorsement. Failure to check for the proper endorsements may mean that the district is obligated to employ individuals but may not be able to assign them to teach the courses for which they were hired. This is a recurring problem in smaller high schools where teachers are expected to teach a variety of subjects. Care must be exercised in checking for valid certificates and the necessary endorsements for the position being filled.

Written Contracts

Employment contracts must be written, define an offer by the school board and acceptance by the employee, and involve consideration (a legal term denoting an exchange of value, in the case of employment contracts, services for money). Principals and human resource administrators must be aware that any written correspondence, statements on application forms, job descriptions, position posting, advertisements, or personnel manuals may be construed as contractual. Care must exercised in all written documents. Care must also be exercised in all discussions, being careful not to offer or appear to offer anything more than is explicitly stated in the contract.

Only school boards have the authority to enter contracts. School principals and human resource administrators are cautioned to condition all offers of employment upon approval of the school board.

Supplementary Contracts

A supplementary contract is a contract for work being done above and beyond the regular school day. A coaching contract, for example, could be included in a supplementary contract. Supplementary contracts are similar to regular full-time teaching contracts in that both must be fully adhered to during the term of the contract. Supplementary contracts differ from regular full-time contracts in one important aspect—there is no guarantee of continued employment for supplemental duties after the expiration of the current contract. Regular contracts carry an implied right to continued employment, after the teacher has been tenured, from year to year (more details on continuing contracts are included in the next section). Supplementary contracts may not imply any right to continued employment from year to year.

How to Prevent Problems

Openness and quality communication prevent legal problems arising from contracts. To prevent problems in the area of contracting:

♦ Make sure that employees know *all* terms and conditions of employment, including such conditions as citizenship and criminal checks.

♦ Exercise care in hiring and assigning teachers only in the areas for which they have the proper certificates and endorsements.

♦ Exercise care in all written communication. Make sure to include conditions of employment in writing. Take care to avoid putting into writing or stating verbally any implied promises that you cannot guarantee as a part of the contract. Avoid, for example, implying that a supplemental coaching contract will be extended later. Condition any offer of employment on formal approval by the board of directors.

♦ Clarify for the benefit of employees that any supplemental contracts are extended only for the term of the current year and that the district may choose to renew or not renew the supplemental contract for the following year.

Legal References for the Principal

♦ Certification Laws
♦ Contract Law
♦ Theory of Contracts
♦ Any offer or claim may be construed as a contract

Working with the Staff

Courts recognize the need and the desirability for order and control to be maintained in the school environment. The principal is the state's representative in the school building. This section on *working with the staff* includes an overview on board policy and areas about which the school staff need to be well informed.

Potential Problems

School Board Policy and Responsibility

The School Board (and its superintendent) is a most important entity in an administrator's life. School Boards are officials of the state, and are given powers expressed and implied in the state statutes. The school district is formed under the policies of the Board. Boards establish rules, regulations, and school district policies whose only limitation is that they cannot be contrary to state and federal laws.

In personnel matters the Board is considered to do the actual hiring, transfer, and termination of employees. It is responsible for Equal Opportunity Employment, Affirmative Action, union contracts, and many other activities that impact the terms and conditions of employment. Boards that have objective, current, written policies covering these actions and follow them will have the fewest problems.

Policies, regulations, and procedures, once in writing, can then be studied with an eye toward assuring that federal and state laws, rules, and regulations are satisfied. Compliance with procedures will thus reduce the majority of complaints and legal actions to a minimum. Inevitably, there are situations where the conditions of the case are not clearly answered by current policies and laws. In those situations, administrators are often called on to make decisions, handle problems, and make recommendations to the Board. In the current climate there is always some danger that legal action will result if a decision is not favorable to all concerned.

Therefore, it is very important that principals be aware of the basics of educational law. District insurance generally protects administrators from personal liability as long as they act in good faith. Administrators can be found to be personally liable when they neglect their duties by ignoring violations that they should have known about, or if they cause harm through deliberate violations of law. The administration must be conversant with the law.

The importance of all this is that the principal is a representative of the School Board and therefore, the state. The majority of the actions performed by the principal for the school district reflect the School Board policies set out by the Board. While the Board has ready access to legal counsel, the administrator will more frequently have to rely on their own immediate understanding of educational law. The principal must know the law well enough to follow the basics and well enough to know when the district administration and/or the district attorney need to be consulted.

Handbooks and Training

As the representative of the board and therefore the state, the principal has a duty, not just to be informed, but also to inform others who work under their supervision. This is best done through putting rules into writing in the form of a building handbook, which can provide one single source of the legal information needed by the majority of staff. This information can then become the basis of further training, emphasis in the daily bulletin as needed, or personal follow up in the course of the administrator's daily supervision of the staff.

The section that follows is a practical, hands-on checklist that building principals can use to make sure that their building staff is aware of the laws and policies of the district in which they are employed. The handbook becomes a useful guide when making decisions regarding the building personnel. In addition, the personnel administrator must have access to the full and current board policy manual, the laws of the state, and a copy of the negotiated agreement. These will provide direction for the school administrator.

School administrators may find that it has been some time since a particular section of the board policy has been changed. If the policy is out-of-date, or nonexistent, then it needs to be brought to the attention of the Superintendent. And when board policies are being reviewed and revised, the school administrator needs to be involved in helping to shape policies that are legal and that will aid in the administration of the schools. Likewise, staff, parents, and students should be involved in shaping the content of district policies.

The section that follows is intended to be an outline for your building handbook (Figure 10.2). Many entries come from state and federal law and should be a part of every handbook. Other entries must be customized for your particular district. Figure 10.3, which begins on page 318, presents acceptable preemployment inquiries under EEOC guidelines.

In addition to general board policies and the more specific collective bargaining agreement, if any, the implied obligations of a teacher are considered to be: duties related to subject matter, duties inherent in contracts with all teachers, appropriate dress, behavior, and speech, moral obligations, cooperation with administrators when given reasonable requests, and helping to maintain discipline and order when special circumstances occur in a school. School staff are also responsible for promoting civic virtues and understanding in their classes. These are areas that you may wish to add to your building handbook to ensure good, clear communication of expectations.

Figure 10.3 Acceptable Preemployment Inquiries Under EEOC Guidelines

Subject Area	Acceptable	Unacceptable
Name	For access purposes, whether applicant's work records are under another name	To ask if a woman is a Miss, Mrs., or Ms., or to ask for maiden name
Residence	• Place and length of current and previous address • Applicant's phone number or how applicant can be reached	None
Age	After hiring, proof of age by birth certificate	• Age or age group of applicant • Birth certificate or baptismal record before hiring
National Origin	None	• Birthplace of applicant, parents, grandparents, or spouse • Any other inquiry into national origin
Race	Race for affirmative action plan statistics, after hiring	Any inquiry that would indicate race or color
Sex	Inquiry for affirmative action plan statistics, after hiring	Inquiry which would indicate race sex unless job related
Religion or Creed	None	• Birthplace of applicant, parents, grandparents, or spouse • Recommendations or references from church officials
Citizenship	• If U.S. residence is legal • Required proof of citizenship, after hiring	• If native-born or naturalized • Proof of citizenship before hiring • Whether parents or spouse native-born or naturalized • Date of citizenship

Subject Area	Acceptable	Unacceptable
Marital Status	• Status (only married or single) after hiring for insurance and tax purposes • Number and ages of dependents and age of spouse after hiring for insurance and tax purposes	• Status before hiring • Number and age of children, who cares for them, and if applicant plans to have children
Military Service	• Service in the U.S. Armed Forces, including branch and rank attained • Any job-related experience • Require military discharge certification after hiring	• Military service records • Military service for any country other than United States • Type of discharge
Education	• Academic, professional, or vocational schools attended • Language skills, such as reading and writing foreign language	• Nationality, racial or religious affiliation of schools attended • How foreign language ability was acquired
Criminal Record	Listing of convictions other than misdemeanors	Arrest record
References	General and work references not relating to race, color, religion, sex, national origin, or ancestry	References typically from clergy or any other person who might reflect race, color, religion, sex, national origin, or ancestry.
Organizations	• Organizational membership—professional, social, etc., so long as affiliation is not used to discriminate on the basis of race, sex, national origin, or ancestry • Offices held, if any	Listing of all clubs to which applicant belongs or has belonged to
Photographs	May be required after hiring for identification purposes	• Request photograph before hiring. • To take pictures of applicants during interview
Work Schedule	• Willingness to work the required work schedule • Whether applicant has military reservist obligations	Willingness to work any particular religious holidays.

Subject Area	Acceptable	Unacceptable
Physical Data	♦ To require applicant to prove ability to do manual labor, lifting and other physical requirements of the job, if any ♦ Require a physical examination after a job offer is made	To ask height and weight, impairment, or other non-specified job-related physical data
Disability	If the applicant can perform the essential functions of the job with or without reasonable accommodation	To exclude disabled applicants as a class on the basis of their disability. Each case must be determined individually.
Other Qualifications	Any area that has a direct reflection of the job applied for	Any non-job-related inquiry that may present unlawful discrimination.

Source: Civil Rights Act of 1964, Title VII as amended; Equal Employment Opportunity Act of 1972; Education Amendment of 1972, Title IX; Age Discrimination in Employment Act of 1967; Equal Employment Opportunity Guidelines, 1978 and revisions.

How to Prevent Problems

To prevent problems in the area of working with staff:

♦ Take your role as representative of the Board and state seriously; remain well-informed on changes in district policy and state law; take an active role in influencing Board policy.

♦ When in doubt, ask. Don't be afraid to ask for legal advice from district administrators or from the district attorney.

♦ Put it in writing. Create and constantly update a building handbook that will serve as a summary of the responsibilities of staff. Keep your calendar current and record notes, which may serve you better. Besides a subject file for letters and memos, create a chronological file for each year that contains all correspondence for one school year.

♦ Reinforce key expectations through formal training, daily bulletin, faculty meetings, and daily one-on-one supervision.

Legal References for the Principal

- State School Law Manual
- School District Policy Manual
- Master Agreement with the Teachers' Association
- Other negotiated agreements
- Department of Labor and Industries
- Human Rights Commission
- Occupational Safety and Health Act of 1970 (U.S.)
- Family and Medical Leave Act of 1993 (U.S.)
- Civil Rights Act of 1964, Title VII as amended
- Equal Opportunity Act of 1972
- Education Amendment of 1972, Title IX
- Age Discrimination in Employment Act of 1967
- Equal Employment Opportunity Guidelines, 1978 and revisions.

Dealing with Conflict

Hiring the right staff and clearly communicating rules and expectations go a long way toward the effective operation of schools for students. Conflicts over differing opinions and interpretations are a reality of life and resolving those conflicts is one of the duties of the principal. This section on dealing with conflict addresses: balancing demands, avoiding lawsuits, and dealing with employee grievances.

Potential Problems

Balancing Demands

The principal is responsible for virtually everything that occurs in and around the school building and grounds. Every aspect of the public school system is regulated in one form or another by some federal or state law. The principal is expected to do his or her best to comply with each and every law. It behooves the principal to devote adequate time to evaluating decisions and balancing competing demands of government, board policy, politics, parents, students, staff, and union. Throughout any given day the principal is likely to encounter any or all of these demands. They influence every decision, and every course of action taken.

The interaction of these demands necessitates constant compromise as competing forces push to influence decisions and actions in their favor. Ultimately, the principal is responsible for running the school efficiently and effectively for the achievement of students. This is a responsibility carried out in the public's interest. To that end it is imperative that as many of the basic policies and procedures of the school be in writing as possible. This is to ensure consistency.

Lawsuits

Schools can be sued in civil court to collect damages that result in injury received as a result of the action or inaction of the district. Technically, a lawsuit brought by a parent or patron is known as a tort. Torts are also known as private wrongs. They do not involve contracts. To be successful in this type of suit, there must be: (1) a duty on the part of the district, (2) failure to exercise reasonable care, and (3) injury. If the school has no duty to provide care, as in a fight between two students on the way to school, there is likely to be no school liability. If there is a duty to provide care and the district did in fact exercise proper care, as in an accident on a properly supervised play field, there is likely to be no liability. And if no injury occurred, physical or emotional, there is no liability.

The biggest pitfall in this area is failure to supervise students properly. All student activities must be supervised. The nature of the activity and number of students involved influence the number of staff required. Staff needs to be informed of the importance of providing proper supervision. The state holds that teachers have a definite legal duty to the students and that duty is the protection of the students from reasonably foreseeable risks. The school may be liable if evidence indicated that there was sufficient time for the teacher to know what was going on, or should have known, or was inattentive.

Another major pitfall in this area is proper maintenance of facilities. Playground equipment, athletic equipment, shop, and science laboratory classes are potential targets for this type of action. If the school or the principal creates a hazardous environment that presents unusual dangers to students, they can be found liable. The risk of liability goes up sharply when the principal knew of the danger and did not correct it in a timely fashion. Each principal should develop a safety committee and see that it meets regularly.

One additional area that involves risk comes from teachers physically harming students by intervening in a fight, forcibly restraining students, or striking students in anger. Increasingly, teachers are also bringing suits against students for physical injuries caused by student violence.

Principals can reduce liability by training new teachers and staff for their assignments. Staff needs to be trained in the importance of proper supervision, the best ways to reduce the risk of injury to students, and the dangers of using physical force on students. Staff, in turn, may need to provide special training for students who will be using science, shop, or P.E. equipment that increases the risk of injury. Failure to follow stated policies and guidelines increases the risk of harm and therefore the charges of negligence and/or malpractice.

The defense of principals or teachers, as public officials and at public expense, depends on whether or not it can be shown that they were performing their duty in good faith and in the furtherance of their responsibilities. School staff do not enjoy total immunity from lawsuits. There is the potential that staff may be held personally liable for damages if they acted knowingly to endanger students.

Collective Bargaining and Grievances

In addition to the individual contract between an employee and the district, there often is another master contract between recognized bargaining units and the district. Traditionally, the areas that are subject to the collective bargaining process are: salaries, fringe benefits, hours of work, and working conditions. The district has a continuing duty to bargain with a union over these subjects before any rules or rule changes can be made.

Because no contract can specifically address all the details regarding rights and obligations of the parties, there is always room for different interpretations. The principal, therefore, as the representative of the Board, will often have to decide on the meaning of key parts of the negotiated agreement. To monitor the interpretation of the contract, most collective bargaining agreements include a grievance procedure whereby employees who are "aggrieved" by actions of the district can file a complaint. Contracts usually specify a standard grievance procedure and state whether grievances apply to only the master contract or whether grievances can also be filed over Board policy, administrative rules, and past practices. Unions usually favor broad definitions while Boards tend to favor narrow definitions of what can be grieved. If not defined as grievable in the current contract, then it is not grievable.

Because of the stigma attached to grievances and the time they consume, even the master contract in which they are found encourage resolution through informal processes. When informal processes prove to be insufficient, knowing and following the formal procedures become essential. Your district's process may vary, but most grievances include the following steps:

- *Step One—Informal:* An informal meeting and discussion takes place between the teacher and the principal in an attempt to solve the alleged problem. If unsuccessful, then the teacher (aggrieved) moves to Step One—Formal.

- *Step One—Formal:* A grievance form (usually found in the master contract) is completed by the aggrieved and submitted to the principal. The principal has a set amount of time in which to respond to the grievance. If no response is given before the deadline, or if the grievance is not resolved to the satisfaction of the aggrieved, the grievance proceeds to the next step.

♦ *Step Two:* At this level the grievance is appealed to the school district superintendent or a designated representative at the district level. The district has a set number of days in which to respond. Again, if no response is given or the grievance is not resolved, it goes to the next step.

♦ *Step Three:* Some contracts call for Step Three to be heard by the school board. Others call for an outside arbitrator. Some call for final and binding arbitration while others leave open recourse to the courts.

Failure of either side of the disputed grievance to follow the negotiated procedures is classed as an unfair labor practice and is subject to legal action. While the procedures for handling grievances vary widely, many grievances are best resolved at the administrative level through sincere efforts to find resolution. Most grievances seek to clarify contract language, procedures, and potential safety issues and expectations.

How to Prevent Problems

To prevent problems when dealing with conflict:

♦ Seek first to understand the needs of the parties involved and then the nature of legal requirements that apply.

♦ Know that you can't always please everyone; take care to provide first for the safety and welfare of the student.

♦ Reduce the risk of law suits by providing for proper supervision at all times, by inspecting and repairing hazardous equipment and by providing adequate staff training.

♦ Seek to resolve grievances informally if possible; take care to follow the procedural requirements when formal grievances are filed.

♦ Follow the advice of Walter Baer, *Do's and Don'ts in Handling Grievances* (Figure 10.4).

Figure 10.4 Adapted from Dos and Don'ts in Handling Grievances

by Walter E. Baer

In most school districts, the building principal or program supervisor is given responsibility and authority to deal with the problems and grievances of employees—and to resolve them by application of the proper remedy.

In most cases, the principal or supervisor had no hand in negotiating the contract nor did he or she share in drafting its provisions. Nevertheless, the principal is the one who deals most frequently with employees and with the association—and must be equipped to represent the district's interests and preserve the district's rights, or they will quickly go down the drain.

The following checklist pinpoints the major practices and pitfalls that the principal or supervisor should be familiar with in handling the grievance machinery. Naturally, all these points are not applicable in every case, but if the principal or supervisor is familiar with all of them—and observes them in handling the grievances—he or she will be prepared for almost any kind of case that may arise.

DO

- ◆ Do investigate and handle every case as though it will eventually result in an arbitration hearing.
- ◆ Do talk with the employee about his or her grievance. Give the employee a good and full hearing.
- ◆ Do require the grievant to identify the specific contractual provision allegedly violated. Determine whether the matter can properly be constituted a grievance—as deemed by the agreement.
- ◆ Do determine whether the grievance was filed, appealed, and processed from step to step.
- ◆ Do examine the contract negotiations record for new or changed contract provisions on the grieved matter. If there is a *new* provision, which party proposed the language, and for what reason? Which party's language was eventually adopted? What do the negotiation minutes reveal regarding discussions on the provision in dispute—whether it is new, changed, or unchanged? Who was present during discussions on the relevant provision?

- Do record all results of your investigation.
- Do determine whether there is a political connotation to the grievance. Is the grievant a deposed union official, or is he or she now aspiring to a union office? What is the grievant's relationship with current union officials? If unfriendly, why?
- Do control your emotions—control your remarks—control your behavior.
- Do pass along to your district's personnel supervisor your experience with any troublesome contract clauses.
- Do remember your case may result in an arbitration hearing. Fully inform your supervisor of all discussions about the grievance.

DON'T

- Don't discuss the case with the association representative alone—if the (grievant) employee is at work and can be present during the discussion.
- Don't argue with the association representative in the presence of employees. Hold your discussion privately.
- Don't admit to the binding effect of a past practice—for settlement of the grievance—until you have first discussed it with your district's personnel supervisor.
- Don't forget that the association is a political institution—it must sometimes attempt to justify itself. Some grievances are irreconcilable.
- Don't assume a judicial role. Hear the association's case, then be an advocate. Represent management's interests.
- Don't argue the merits of the grievances first, if grievance was untimely raised or filed. If untimely:
- Present your arguments on that issue first—give reasons for considering it untimely.
- Be very clear—you are denying it first on that basis.
- Do not excuse or waive the timeliness issue on untimely filed grievances (unless you have caused employee or union delay).
- Don't withhold any relevant facts—if they reveal weaknesses in your case, prepare logical and persuasive defenses.
- Don't make settlements that obligate the district to prior approval, mutual consent, or joint consultation with the association before management can act.

- Don't ask favors of the association. They won't forget—they will someday expect a reciprocal concession.
- Don't give lengthy written answers on grievance forms when denying a grievance. If the grievance should be legitimately denied—after exhausting all persuasive efforts to resolve it—give the simple written answer, "No contract violation. Grievance denied."
- Don't make any settlement "outside" the terms of the agreement—unless you have first discussed it with your district's personnel supervisor.
- Don't hold back a remedy if the district is wrong. Make correction in the amount you calculate to be proper—even if it is less than the relief sought by the association.
- Don't settle grievances on the basis of what is "fair"—the contract determines what is fair.
- Don't pay the grievant if the grievant was the improper employee to file the grievance—even if an actual contract violation has occurred. Instead, determine the employee who was wronged by the contract violation and apply the remedy to that employee, even if such action does not resolve the original grievance.
- Don't count on the association to assume authority for resolving your problems; exercise authority and dispose of issues.
- Don't interrupt or stop the educational program to convenience an association representative demanding instant handling of a grievance—but don't postpone or delay grievance handling beyond the time when such procedure will no longer interfere with the educational program.
- Don't, by action or inaction, cause the employee or association to default on their compliance with any time limits. If you do, don't later deny the grievance for reason of their noncompliance with such time limits.
- Don't settle the grievance—if in doubt. Discuss the case with your district's personnel supervisor.

Legal References for the Principal

- State School Law Manual
- Master Contract(s)
- Grievance Procedures
- Torts
- Liability
- Negligence

Employee Discipline

Staff members have the right to be treated with respect and they have a right to be informed of the duties that are expected of them. Principals have a duty to provide proper training, informal correction and, if needed, formal discipline when rules or duties are not performed properly. This section on employee discipline addresses the concept of progressive discipline, due process procedures, and just cause requirements followed by a section on sexual harassment and abuse.

Potential Problems

Progressive Discipline

Discipline of staff may come from documented negligence, inadequate supervision, assault and battery, failure to perform specific duties, insubordination, abuse of sick leave, failure to maintain proper discipline, inappropriate dress or language, chronic lateness, or violation of any other known rule. Incompetent performance is usually dealt with through evaluation and probation (addressed in the next section) rather than discipline.

Discipline procedures are designed to protect the employee from arbitrary or unfair action by management. Following proper procedures is also important to the district in that it reduces the risk of loss to the district. Most districts have adopted a series of discipline steps that are progressive. That is, the steps progress from mild corrective actions to more severe actions, which could result in dismissal:

- *Oral Warning*—a clear verbal statement of the rule, the expectation that the rule be followed, and the consequences that can occur if the rule is not followed in the future. The time, date, and substance of the warning should be noted in your daily calendar or some other informal written record (*not* the personnel file).
- *Written Warning*—a clear written statement similar to the above delivered personally to the employee. Technically, these two

steps are not discipline. Rather they are warnings that give notice to the employee as to the existence of the rule and expectation that it be followed.

♦ *Reprimand*—This is a formal discipline step (see Figure 10.5). A reprimand cannot occur unless there has been:

- Notice—ensuring that the employee knew of the rule and the charges;

- Investigation—to determine if, in fact, the rule was broken; and

- hearing—to ensure that you hear the employee's side before deciding. If justified, a reprimand giving the above details is put in writing, delivered in person to the employee, and placed in the employee's personnel file at the district office. Figure 10.6 is an example of a reprimand.

Figure 10.5 The Requirements of an Official Written Reprimand

1. The reprimand must be individually written stating specific material facts such as date, time, place, witnesses to, and actions of the individual(s) involved.

2. The reprimand must include a quotation of the rule or regulation violated or breached, or the misconduct if not in the written rules.

3. The reprimand should outline all previous oral warnings. These should be usually limited to the current school year, or immediate past year.

4. It must be explicit and to the point. Avoid using hearsay evidence or assumptions or conclusions of third parties. Tell what you saw, heard or investigated, and found to be true. Findings of fact are the usual way these are presented.

5. It should state that the staff member is being given another opportunity to improve his/her conduct and express the hope that he/she does so.

6. It should state that if the staff member is found guilty of repeated misconduct he/she will be subject to further disciplinary action. This is a critical point, but the principal must remain flexible by not stating what the exact further action will be.

7. The staff member must be given a copy of this letter; do *not* mail it.

8. Forward a copy of the letter to the central administration office to be included in the employee's official personnel file.

**Figure 10.6 Sample Letter of Reprimand—
Neglect of Job During Working Hours**

Date _____

Mr./Ms. _____

_____

_____

Dear Mr./Ms. _____:

I am giving you this written reprimand as disciplinary action for your improper conduct and failure to fulfill the duties and responsibilities required of you and your teaching assignment. Our Evergreen School rule on page 11 of the manual states that "students are not to be left unattended."

On December 15, 200_, at 10:35 a.m., I came to Room 102, your assigned room, and found you not in your room. Your students were making an excessive amount of noise and creating a disturbance for surrounding classrooms. Two of your students, Anthony Able and Joe Benson, were leaning out of the windows in your room. Gertrude Cable and Myrtle Denson were pulling each other's hair. I found you in the teachers' lounge, reading the newspaper, unaware that your students had returned from their physical education class in the multipurpose room at 10:30 a.m. as scheduled. I stated to you my concern for the safety and well-being of your students if they were left unattended. You indicated you shared that concern and that in the future you would meet your students at the multipurpose room and return to your classroom with them. You were given a verbal warning by me at 10:45 a.m., December 15, 200_. I stated that unless you were able to be at your assigned classroom when your students returned from their class with Ms. Everhart, the Physical Education Teacher, you would be subject to further disciplinary action. On January 3, 200_, only two weeks after the verbal warning given to you on December 15, I went to your room following the afternoon recess at 2:15 p.m. Once again your students were in your room unattended. The door to your classroom was open and the noise being made by your students was disturbing nearby classroom teachers. I found you at 2:20 p.m. in the boiler room with the building engineer. You informed me that you were requesting the engineer to repair the dripping drinking fountain. This excuse as a reason for leaving your students is not acceptable to me as this matter could be taken care of at a time other than when your presence in your classroom to teach your students was essential to their safety and to the instructional program in this school.

It appears from your improper conduct that you have not corrected your actions and remain negligent in meeting the responsibilities of your teaching assignment. By this written reprimand, I am giving you an opportunity to correct your improper conduct and perform the duties and responsibilities required of you and your teaching assignment. Unless you correct your conduct and perform your duties and responsibilities equally with other teachers in this building, you will subject yourself to further disciplinary action.

Very truly yours,

(Administrator)

cc: Central Administration Office
Personnel files

- *Suspension*—Suspension with pay is often a nondisciplinary step that provides time for an investigation to determine if discipline is justified. Suspension with pay can also accompany a second reprimand to emphasize the seriousness of the infraction. Suspension without pay can be used with salaried employees but is not easily used with contracted employees. Contracts are considered a property right. The U.S. Constitution states that we cannot be deprived of property without due process of law (see next section).
- *Termination*—Employees who have not responded to the discipline steps above may eventually be terminated. For contracted employees termination may be made effective at the end of the contract (for the reasons outlined above) with the employee placed on administrative leave with pay until the end of the contract term. Courts generally demand more exact procedures and extensive documentation the closer an action gets to depriving an individual of income or the right to continue in the job.

In all of the previously mentioned steps, the burden of proof lies with the school district to demonstrate that the actions taken are warranted. For less severe kinds of misbehavior, or for a long-time employee, the district may have to go through the above steps more slowly, more frequently, or more thoroughly. For more severe kinds of misbehavior, such as criminal activities or immoral behavior, the process may begin and end with the termination step.

Due Process

The fifth and fourteenth amendments to the U.S. Constitution state that no one is to be deprived of life, liberty, or property without due process of law. As stated above, a contract is considered to be property. Therefore, school districts cannot take any action that may have an adverse effect on an employee's contract without providing due process. Based on case law from hundreds of previous court cases, due process includes:

- *Charges*—The employee must know what he or she is accused of doing or not doing. This is best done through a written memo delivered directly to the employee stating the nature of the charges, the time, date, and location of a meeting with the principal, and (recommended but not required) the right of the employee to bring a representative to the meeting.

- *Time to Prepare*—There must be some reasonable time period between the date of the notice and the time of the meeting. The notification of charges also needs to be specific enough for the employee to prepare a defense.

- *Hearing*—The employee must have the opportunity to hear the specific charges, confront the accuser(s), and give his or her side of the story.

Following the previously mentioned steps, the principal may choose to render a decision at the meeting, take the time to write out a decision and hand-deliver it to the employee, choose to investigate further, or decide that discipline is not justified in this case. If formal discipline is being given, the decision must be put into writing, delivered personally to the employee (could be certified mail with return receipt requested), and filed in the employee's personnel file.

The definition of due process is flexible depending on how likely it is that the action will adversely affect the employee's contract. Lower levels of discipline, known as predetermination hearings, require steps similar to those listed. In a termination hearing, all facts and evidence applicable to the action must be presented so that the person can respond to them. This includes documentation of the warning steps, subsequent discipline steps that reiterated the deficiency in performance, and the events leading up to termination proceedings. This means that the principal must have documented evidence over a long period of time including names, dates, occurrences, and any other data. The staff member has the right to confront the principal bringing the charges and make a defense of his or her actions. The staff member has the right to appeal the action taken to terminate his or her employment. The master contract may specify that the appeal is to a hearing officer, to an arbitrator, or may give to the employee an "election of remedy"—the employee's choice of hearing officer or arbitrator.

The school district has several options that fall short of termination. The position can be modified to allow the strengths of the staff member to be capitalized on. The employee can be retained and provided with additional training. The position or assignment may be changed; however, any reduction in pay requires due process to justify the change or adjustments. Transfers may be an option if the system is large enough. Here it is best if the staff member volunteers for the transfer rather than being forced into the move, again because due process procedure is required.

Just Cause

Just cause, like due process, means far more than is meant by any literal definition. Like due process, just cause has been defined by many court cases. Again the definition is flexible depending on how severe the punishment. Generally, the following steps are required to ensure that there was just or good cause for the discipline being meted out (Figure 10.7).

Figure 10.7 Tests for Determining "Just Cause" for Disciplinary Actions

A basic principle underlying most disciplinary procedures is that management must have "just cause" for imposing the discipline. This standard often is written into negotiated labor-management agreements or read into them by arbitrators. Even in the absence of a negotiated agreement, it sums up the test used by employees in judging whether management acted fairly in enforcing company rules.

While the definition of "just cause" necessarily varies from case to case, one arbitrator has listed these tests for determining whether a company had just cause for disciplining an employee.

1. Was the employee adequately warned of the consequences of his conduct? The warning may be given orally or in printed form. An exception may be made for certain conduct, such as insubordination, coming to work drunk, drinking on the job, or stealing company property, that is so serious that the employee is expected to know it will be punishable.

2. Was the company's rule or order reasonably related to efficient and safe operation?

3. Did management investigate before administering the discipline? The investigation normally should be made before the decision to discipline is made. Where immediate action is required, however, the best course is to suspend the employee pending investigation with the understanding that he will be restored to his job and paid for time lost if he is found not guilty.

4. Was the investigation fair and objective?

5. Did the investigation produce substantial evidence or proof of guilt? It is not required that the evidence be preponderant, conclusive, or "beyond reasonable doubt" except where the alleged misconduct is of such a criminal or reprehensible nature as to stigmatize the employee seriously and impair his chances for future employment.

6. Were the rules, orders, and penalties applied evenhandedly and without discrimination? If enforcement has been lax in the past. management can't suddenly reverse its course and begin to crack down without first warning employees of its intent.

7. Was the penalty reasonably related to the seriousness of the offense and the past record? If employee A's past record is significantly better than that of employee B, the company properly may give A a lighter punishment than B for the same offense.

How to Prevent Problems

To prevent problems when dealing with employee discipline:

- *Notice*—Make sure that employees know what is expected of them.
- *Investigate*—Make sure that an infraction has occurred; never discipline without an investigation.
- *Due Process*—Always have a hearing before disciplining employees; let the employees know in advance what the charges are, invite them to bring a representative with them, give them an opportunity to confront their accuser and give their side of the story.
- *Progressive Discipline*—Give lower-level discipline for first time offenses and more severe discipline for repeated infractions or more severe misbehavior.
- *Just Cause*—Make sure that the employee knew the rule, verify that a violation occurred, be even-handed in administering discipline, and make sure that the punishment fits the crime.

Sexual Harassment

There are two types of sexual harassment: quid pro quo (this for that) and the hostile environment. Sexual harassment is a form of unlawful discrimination based on sex. Because of this, two factors must be present for a behavior to be considered sex discrimination:

- The complaining person must be a member of a protected class; and
- The complaining person must be treated differently because she/he belongs to a protected class.

Both males and females are considered members of protected classes. This means that sex discrimination laws protect both women and men, as well as girls and boys. It is possible for men or boys to sexually harass other men or boys, for women or girls to sexually harass other women or girls, for men or boys to sexually harass women or girls, and for women or girls to sexually harass men or boys.

McGrath (2003) has developed a five-point criteria that outlines what must be present before a finding of unlawful sexual harassment in employment or education may be made under Title VII of the 1964 Civil Rights Act or under Title IX of the 1972 Education Amendments:

- Is the behavior sexual in nature?

- Is it unwelcome or unwanted?
- Is it severe, persistent, or pervasive?
- Does the behavior unreasonable interfere with work or study?
- Does it meet subjective/objective tests or standards to its level of interference with work or study?

The principal must proactively arrange for sexual harassment training of the staff/self, and must have definitions and procedures to follow listed in the faculty and staff handbooks. Additionally, the principal must be professionally vigilant regarding the possibilities of sexual harassment. Figure 10.8 is an example of a form to use to document harassment.

Figure 10.8 Harassment Complaint Form
Highline School District No. 401

By providing the information requested below, the complainant has obligated the district to investigate the allegations made and to take appropriate corrective or disciplinary actions.

To: _____
(Name and Title of School Official)

From: _____
(Name of Complainant)

1. State the specific nature of your complaint and other relevant facts and circumstances. (Explain in narrative form and furnish sufficient background so as to identify the person(s) and/or omission(s) that led to the allegation). Attach additional pages as necessary.

   Include in your narrative the following:

   A. On what date(s) did the alleged harassment occur? Where?

   _____

   B. Who did what (be specific)?

   _____

   C. What specific verbal remarks were made by whom?

   _____

   D. What, if any, physical contact was made?

   _____

2. Names of any witnesses present: _____
3. Names of any individuals you told of the incident: _____
4. What did you do in immediate response to the alleged sexual harassment incident?
5. What efforts, if any, have you taken so far to stop the harassment? _____
6. What remedy are you seeking from the district? _____

Signature: _____ Date: _____

For Office Use Only

Date received: _____

Received by: _____

Investigation Completed (Date): _____

A special case of sexual harassment is teacher/staff member harassment or abuse of students. Sexual harassment and abuse in school is serious business both in terms of emotional and financial impact. Too often school administrators say, "But how was I to know?" McGrath (2003) asserts that early detection of both sexual harassment and abuse is possible if we know what to look for and how to respond to what we are seeing. She gives six early signs to such behavior:

- Profile of a Winner—Often the teacher is an outstandingly popular and effective educator. The highest percentages of violators are coaches, drama, music, and special education teachers and others who have opportunities to isolate certain students.

- Brutality not Sensuality—Essentially harassment and abuse in school are acts of violence and domination, not sensuality and flirtation.

- Trolling for a Target—These are preliminary tactics to engage the victim in minor boundary violations to judge the reaction of the targeted person.

- Boundary Violations are the Clue—The perpetrator will look for someone whose boundaries are not in tact and who will tolerate a violation without signaling back.

- Think Subtle not Grand—These are interactions that are almost imperceptible unless your know what to look for. The teacher who frequently leans too close, or a staff member who talks too long and too personally are examples of the commencement of boundary violations, which if intercepted can be cut off before escalation.

- Grooming is Part of the Problem—This interaction may start with the compliments and attention that feels friendly and warm. Then escalate to lulling the victim closer and closer through behaviors that are in the arena of special attention, assistance, or counseling.

The principal can be held liable if a student can prove the following:

- The principal received notice of a pattern of improper acts committed by a teacher or employee.

- The principal demonstrated deliberate indifference to or tacit authorization of the offensive acts.

- The principal failed to take sufficient remedial action, and

- Such failure proximately caused injury to the student. (McGrath, 1993).

How to Prevent Problems

- Know the early warning signs
- Take every complaint very seriously
- Take appropriate and timely action and document carefully
- Hold staff training on the topic of harassment and abuse
- Attend training for principal on the topic
- Cover the topic of harassment in your handbook
- Intervene sooner than later

Legal References for the Principal

- Due Process
- Just Cause
- Title VII of the 1964 Civil Rights Act
- Title IX of the 1972 Education Amendments
- The Fourteenth Amendment of the U.S. Constitution

Employee Evaluation and Dismissal

The previous section on employee discipline dealt with misbehavior by the staff. This section deals with employee performance, or nonperformance, in the classroom. Ensuring staff competence is one of the most important and most difficult roles of the principal. This section addresses employee contract status, employee evaluation, probation, and dismissal.

Potential Problems

Evaluation

One of the most important duties of a school principal is the evaluation of staff. Board policy and the union contract may provide other requirements as to when and how evaluations are to be conducted. In some states, failure to ensure that evaluations are performed is *prima facie* evidence for the dismissal of the principal.

Status

Several teachers teaching side by side in the same building may have different contractual status and therefore be entitled to different levels of evaluation and supervision. In Washington state, teachers fall into one of the following categories (other states may have similar categories):

- *Noncontinuing*—A noncontinuing contract can be issued only when the teacher hired is replacing a teacher who is on leave of absence. The contract is good only for the one year and states that it expires at the end of the year.

- *Provisional* (nontenured but tenured track)—During the first two or three years, a new teacher is said to be "provisional." The new employee must be evaluated during the first 90 days of employment. Your master contract may require that provisional employees be placed on probation if found to be unsatisfactory. In some states the power is vested almost entirely in the school district. The district may choose to give reasons for its decision or it may choose not to give reasons. The employee may be entitled to a hearing before the Board but may not appeal the decision.

- *Continuing Contracts* (tenured)—Contracts given to employees during the third or fourth year are said to be "continuing" or "tenure" contracts. The employee has the reasonable expectation that the contract will be continued from year to year unless there is good cause.

- Probation—If there are problems with competence in the classroom, the administrator must evaluate the employee, identify areas to be improved, and send a recommendation for probation to the superintendent. The superintendent reviews the recommendation and notifies the employee. During the probation period, the employee must be observed every two weeks, be given oral and written feedback, and assisted in the improvement process. If adequate progress has not been made, the district may notify the employee that the contract will not be renewed for the following year. The employee is entitled to a hearing and may appeal the decision.

Dismissal Steps

Care must be exercised in giving fair consideration to all employees. Although this section is titled "dismissal steps," the principal must remain open to improvement up to the final step when improvement has failed. Failure on the part of the administrator to keep an open mind may provide the employee with evidence of prejudice and denial of due process.

- *Observation*—All contractual steps regarding evaluations must be completed and completed on time. Union contracts may call for prenotification of the employee prior to observing the classroom. They may call for 30 minute observation. Care must be taken to do the evaluations exactly as required. The follow-up conferences also need to be held on time and provided in writing. If performance is of continued concern, additional observations may be required in order to document deficiencies.

- *Deficiencies*—Due process requires that the employee be given detailed information on deficiencies along with the opportunity for improvement. For continuing contract employees in Washington State, the principal will need to prepare detailed evidence of deficiencies for the probation when sending the recommendation to the superintendent.

- *Probation*—The evidence is reviewed by the superintendent and a decision is made regarding probation. The employee being placed on probation receives a detailed letter outlining the deficiencies, notifying him or her of their probationary status and what assistance will be provided, and that failure to improve by a certain date may result in nonrenewal of the contract.

- *Observations*—During the probation period, the school principal must observe the employee every two weeks, meet subsequently with the employee for a postobservation conference, and put observation evaluations in writing. The employee has the right to have a union representative present during the postobservation meetings. Completing these steps represents a major commitment in time and energy for the principal.

- *Assistance*—Additional assistance toward improvement is required. This might take the form of visits to other classrooms, demonstration units in the teacher's classroom, and/or provision of a support team consisting of master teachers and union representatives.

- *Recommendation*—At the end of the probationary period, the principal must carefully review the documentation of the last several months, comparing the observations to the deficiencies stated in the letter of probation. If deficiencies continue to exist, they must be documented as observed on specific occasions and dates in the classroom. Efforts for assistance also need to be documented. All of this is included in a letter and sent to the superintendent. A copy should be shared personally with the employee and his or her representative.

- *Pretermination Hearing*—The superintendent may elect to hold a pretermination hearing (or may consider that the principal has already done this at the building level). The employee would have already received a copy of the recommendation outlining the continued deficiencies. The employee and his or her representative would be invited to meet with the superintendent to present any evidence that argues against dismissal. They would have the right to question the principal recommending dismissal.

- *Dismissal Notice*—Prior to the legal and/or contractual date the superintendent must notify the employee that the contract will not be renewed for the following year. The letter would include similar details as were included in the building administrator's letter of recommendation for dismissal.

- *Appeal*—The employee has 10 days in which to appeal the decision of the superintendent to the school board. If requested, the Board will have a hearing (open or closed at the choice of the employee) in which both sides present arguments and have an opportunity for rebuttal. To preserve the fairness of the process, the superintendent must not have previously discussed the case with the Board. The Board has a limited time in which to make its decision.

- *Remedy of Election*—Following the Board's decision, the employee again has 10 days in which to appeal the decision. Depending on the terms of the contract, the employee may elect to have a hearing before a hearing officer (someone licensed to practice law; often a retired judge) or an arbitrator. Generally, decisions by the hearing officer are appealable in the courts while arbitration decisions are final.

The process previously described applies to "nonrenewal" of a continuing contract. Terminating a contract in mid-year would require much more evidence because it would be depriving an employee of a property right in an unexpired contract. Even when employees are removed from a classroom mid-year, they are usually paid for the remainder of the year to avoid meeting the higher standards required for mid-year termination.

Uncommon Terminations

There are a few unusual forms of termination that do not fit the preceding issues.

- *Voluntary Resignation*—An employee may, in the midst of probation or other stages of dismissal, volunteer to resign or retire at the end of the year. If a resignation is indeed provided, this may allow any dismissal proceedings to be concluded. Caution is advised here. A resignation is complete only when indicated in writing, signed, *and* accepted by formal action of the Board. Suspension of any dismissal proceedings prior to that time may cause a due process flaw in the dismissal case.

- *Counseling Out*—Although some principals do this well, caution is advised. Due process requires an open mind on the part of the supervisor. Encouraging an employee to resign gives evidence that you do not think that the employee can improve. If you later begin probation or dismissal proceedings the employee may be able to prove that you were biased against him or her.

- *Disability*—If the employee is no longer capable of performing his or her duties due to reasons of impaired health, the employee may qualify for disability or a disability retirement. The principal should coordinate with district policies and state requirements and be sensitive to the feelings of the employee.

- *Negotiated Settlement*—Administrators may not pressure an employee into resigning. However, after dismissal notice has been given, the two sides may enter into negotiations that would conclude the dismissal without lengthy (and costly) appeals. This is also a way in which assistance can be provided in outplacement, counseling, or continuation of benefits.

- *Death*—The other form of termination is that brought on by the death of a staff member. The administration will be expected to represent the school to the family, assisting them in meetings with the district and the retirement system regarding salary and benefits. Other school employees will have to be notified as will students. Care must be taken, depending on the circumstances around the death. Counseling for students and staff may be needed.

How to Prevent Problems

To prevent problems when dealing with evaluations and dismissals:

- *Evaluations*—Make sure that all employees are evaluated in a timely fashion according to provisions of state law, Board policy, and master contract.

- *Deadlines*—Due process requires that all timelines be met. Key timelines are evaluation of first-year employees within the first 90 days, recommendation for probation by January 20th, and notification of nonrenewal by May 15th.

- *Documentation*—Dismissal proceedings place a heavy burden of proof on the district. The school administrator must document time, date, and location for deficiencies.

- *Open Mind*—The administrator must keep an open mind about the employee's ability to improve. Failure to do so may cause the case to be lost.

Legal References for the Principal

- State Law
- Negotiated Contract

Record Retention

Maintaining records efficiently can be difficult. The first step is to know the requirements of the law. Figure 10.9 lists legally mandated requirements for personnel document retention periods, as specified by federal law.

Figure 10.9 Federally Mandated
Retention Periods for Personnel Records

Law	Records	Retention
ADEA	Payroll records	3 years
	Personnel records used in hiring, termination, and promotion. Results from employment tests. Job advertisements and training records.	1 year from date of personnel action
	Employee benefit plans, writtenseniority systems, and written merit plans.	1 year longer than duration of plan
	Personnel records for temporary position	90 days after personnel action
Equal Pay Act	Records regarding the work week definition, the number of hours each employee works, pay rates, total wages, and total deductions.	3 years
	Collective bargaining agreements.	3 years
	Timecards/sheets, merit system and seniority system records, wage rate tables.	2 years
Title VII	Personnel records (résumés, applications, records on promotions, demotions, transfers, layoffs, and compensation information).	1 year
	All information pertaining to discrimination charge.	Until charge is resolved
	Apprenticeship records including: applicant names and addresses, dates of application, applicant sex, minority group i.d., test scores.	2 years or duration of apprenticeship program, whichever is longer.
Executive Order 11246 (Affirmative Action)	Test records and results, job group analysis, affirmative action program evaluations.	(Law applies to certain government contractors) Law specifies no retention period. Recommended: 7 years
	Written Affirmative Action program.	Recommended retention: 7 years
OSHA	OSHA Form 200 and OSHA Form 101.	5 years
	Records of medical exams used to monitor exposure to hazardous materials.	Duration of employment plus 30 years.

Uses of Technology
in the Legal and Continuity Issues

The internet is a great source of information. Unfortunately, it can be a source of serious problems. The wise principal will want to make good use of the technology as well as being cautious of possible staff member abuses of e-mail and unauthorized and inappropriate uses of the system. Good policies, regulations, and handbook references to the use and abuse of school owned computers and systems are critical.

- www.mcgrathinc.com

  An excellent site for information written by a law firm.

- www.hrms.com

  This site publishes a legal newsletter.

- www.law.cornell.edu/uscode/

  This site is an excellent site, especially for U.S. Supreme Court cases.

- www.access.gpo.gov/su_docs/ac es/aces140.html

  U.S. Federal Regulations Code

- www.supremecourts.gov/opinions/opinion.html

  Opinions of the U.S. Supreme Court

- www.ca9.uscourts.gov/ca9/newopinions.nsf/

  Opinions of the Ninth Circuit of Appeals

Conclusion

There are many aspects of school law that have implications for the principal. Knowledge and awareness of legal requirements are assets in running a well-managed building. To assist the principal, terminology commonly used in personnel law is listed and defined in Figure 10.10 that follows. In this chapter we have reviewed ways in which the principal can use knowledge of the law in recruiting and hiring staff, contracting with staff, notifying staff of expectations, dealing with conflict, disciplining employees, and evaluating and dismissing employees.

The potential problems, legal guidelines, and strategies reviewed tend to be specific to certain portions of the human resources process. There are many principles, however, which are more generic, applying to many aspects of the process and provide a suitable summary.

- Principle 1: *Be Compassionate*—Hope. Trust. Work toward improvement. Go the second mile. Believe in people. People don't care how much you know (or how right you are) nearly as much as they want to know that you care.

- Principle 2: **Be a Good Steward**—Do the right thing. The right decision may not always be the easy one. It may be unpopular to support the employee, but still be the right thing to do. Or it may be necessary to remove a popular employee. Do the right thing. Act for the greatest good, the safety and well-being of all.

- Principle 3: **Be Fair**—Listen to both sides. Seek out the truth. Investigate. Follow due process. Be consistent. Be even-handed.

- Principle 4: **Be a Good Example**—People follow what you do, not what you say. Treat people the way you would want to be treated.

- Principle 5: **Look for Win-Win Solutions**—There are *always, always, always* options. Too many issues go to court because of stubborn people. Think about what is most needed, consider the pros and cons of your best two options, and make a decision that will be best for all concerned.

- Principle 6: **Give Clear Notice of Expectations**—Most people want to do the right thing—and will if they know what it is. Be clear on expectations. Involve staff in setting expectations. Review expectations frequently. Enforce expectations fairly.

- Principle 7: **Be Proactive**—He who hesitates is lost. If negative evidence is accumulating, do something about it. Begin an investigation, seek counsel, talk to the employee. Don't assume that it will get better on its own.

- Principle 8: **Keep an Open Mind**—Truth is often stranger than fiction. Give the employee the benefit of the doubt but be open to information that may prove otherwise. And as evidence accumulates, be open to the need to act, but remain open to the possibility of improvement.

- Principle 9: **Get the Best Advice Possible**—Build a personal support team. Seek out those who have been there. When in doubt, ask. Listen. Hire the best experts available.

- Principle 10: **Seek First to Understand**—Investigate. Listen to both sides. Be fair. Ask tough questions.

- Principle 11: **Don't Use a Sledge Hammer When a Fly Swatter Will Do**—Punishment causes resistance and resentment. Look for a better way. Use small doses. Use greater force only when other options have been exhausted.

- Principle 12: *Be Prepared*—Time is of the essence. Better early than late. Use your calendar. Document everything. Do your homework. Stay informed.

- Principle 13: *Hope for the Best, Plan for the Worst*—Everything will become public. People will turn against you. Morale will plummet. Things will go wrong at the worst possible moment. Prepare for the worst case scenario. Always have a fall-back position.

- Principle 14: *Give the Benefit of the Doubt to Those Who Like Kids and Want to Improve*—Those who don't like kids or don't want to improve are hard to change.

- Principle 15: *Check Your Support Levels Daily*— Stay in constant communication with your superiors. Say it four times. No surprises. Ask for needed support. Don't assume anything. Communicate more—not less—when the going gets tough.

- Principle 16: *Trade Short-Term Cost for Long-Term Benefit*—Pay now or pay (usually more) later. Why is there never enough time to do it right the first time but always enough time to fix it later? Invest time up front. Cut your losses. Don't double up on your bets or go for broke.

- Principle 17: *Pick Your Battles*—What you stand for and what you fall for are both important. Know when you can make a difference and have the courage to do so. Know when you have to cut your losses and have the courage to do so. Pick the ones that are most necessary and the most doable.

- Principle 18: *Don't Take it Personally*—People will attack you personally. Stay out of the kitchen if you can't take the heat.

- Principle 19: *Aim for Joint Decision*—Make time your ally. Meet often. Take small, steady, consistent steps. Telegraph your thinking. Say it four times. Find a way to get the message across. Be honest. Give the employee time to see the true situation.

- Principle 20: *Show Respect*—Let people disagree with what you did but not how you did it. Treat everyone with respect.

- Principle 21: *Count the Cost*—Know in advance what you stand for, what you will bleed and die for. There are things that are worth fighting for. And others that are not.

Two concepts run through this list. There is forever dynamic tension between knowing when to bend and when to stand. Kenny Rogers put it brashly in *Know When to Hold 'em and Know When to Fold 'em.*

The Serenity Prayer may say it aptly:

God grant me…The courage to change that which I can change, The humility to accept that which I cannot change, and The wisdom to know the difference.

Figure 10.10 Terminology Commonly Used in Personnel Law

Administrative Remedy—Nonjudicial remedy provided by an agency, board, commission, or the like. In most instances, all administrative remedies must have been exhausted before a court will take jurisdiction of a case. For example, U.S. District Courts will not consider a claim of employment discrimination arising under Title VII unless all remedies before the Equal Employment Opportunity Commission (EEOC) have been exhausted. Collective bargaining agreements typically contain an administrative remedy in the form of procedures for the resolution of grievances. For this reason, employers operating with labor contracts have reduced exposure to lawsuits filed by employees in civil court.

Adverse Impact—A term used to describe a substantially different rate of selection in hiring, promotion, transfer, training, or other employment decision that works to the disadvantage of members of a protected class. If such rate is less than 80% of the selection rate of the race, sex, or ethnic group with the highest rate of selection, it is generally regarded as evidence of adverse impact. (This "80% rule" is also referred to as the "4/5ths" rule.)

Affirmative Action Plan (AAP)—Written employment programs or plans required by federal statutes and regulations. Such plans are designed to eliminate discrimination or the effects of past discrimination, and to create systems and procedures to prevent further discrimination. They apply to hiring, training, and promotion that consider race, color, sex, creed, national origin, and handicap. AAPs are required for employers holding over $50,000 in federal government contracts and who have 50 or more employees. Employers holding over $10,000 in federal government contracts must develop and implement AAPs for disabled veterans and Vietnam-era veterans.

At-Will Employment—A traditional American rule in private sector employment stating that the employer is free to fire an employee for any reason—or for no reason at all—and the employee is free to leave employment for any reason or for no reason at all. In the past, there have been only four types of exceptions to "at-will" terminations:

♦ Employees covered by a union agreement.

♦ Employees with individual employment contracts.

- Members of a "protected class" under antidiscrimination laws.
- Public sector employees, generally considered to have constitutionally protected "property" interest in their jobs and due process rights.

While these exceptions continue to apply, new limitations on the employers right to discharge have emerged over the last few years, including:

- Discharge in violation of public policy.
- Discharge in breach of an implied contract.
- Discharge breaching an implied duty of good faith and fair dealing.

Bona Fide Occupational Qualification (BFOQ)—"Bona Fide" means genuine, honestly or in good faith. The employer who regards sex, age, religion, or another protected characteristic as a bona fide qualification for a job must be able to demonstrate business necessity. For example, sex is a BFOQ for modeling dresses or work in a men's locker room. Sex is not a BFOQ, however, for heavy physical work because some women are physically strong. Customer or employer preference may not be considered in determining BFOQ. There is no race BFOQ.

Business Necessity—Policies or practices essential for the safety or efficiency of an organization. If an employer's practices or policies tend to result in a disparate impact affecting members of a protected class, then the employer must be able to demonstrate that these practices or policies are a compelling (i.e., essential for safety or efficiency) business necessity. The employer may be required to show that no alternative, nondiscriminatory practice with a lesser impact can achieve the same required business results.

Civil Case or Civil Action—A lawsuit brought by private parties to enforce or protect private rights (such as medical malpractice, divorce, or breach of employment contract). A criminal case is one involving a charge by a state or federal government against a defendant alleging a public wrong, such as murder.

Class Action—A lawsuit where one or more persons are suing as representatives of a class in a pertinent matter. Every member of the class need not be named. It is brought on behalf of, or names as defendants, others in similar circumstances. Members of the class must be so numerous that it is impracticable to bring them individually before the court. Named representatives must fairly and adequately represent the members of the class.

Common Law—The body of principles and rules of action relating to the government and security of persons and property, which come solely from traditional usage and custom. This "unwritten law" is recognized, affirmed, and enforced by court decisions. Common law in the United States was inherited from England and enlarged and changed by our courts. The rule, "one is presumed innocent unless proven guilty beyond a reasonable doubt," is from the common law, as is "employment-at-will."

Constructive Discharge—An end of employment caused by actions of an employer, or employer's representative, which make an employee's job so unbearable or onerous that the employee, acting prudently, has no other reasonable choice but to quit. Some jurisdictions have ruled that a demotion involving a substantial reduction in compensation and status is a constructive discharge.

Contract—An agreement between two or more persons or entities that creates an obligation to do or not to do a particular thing. Contracts are the body of law governing the agreement process in business. Some kinds of contracts are:

- *Implied Contract*—An agreement, which is implied by the acts or conduct of the parties and not evidenced by express agreement. The circumstances surrounding the transaction imply that the parties understood that a contract or agreement existed. In some states, courts have held that a long period of employment combined with the absence of employer criticism of employee behavior or performance gives rise to an implied contract of continued employment.

- *Oral Contract*—A contract that depends on spoken words, all or in part. It can be a written contract that was later orally changed. Offer and acceptance of employment in an interview is an example of an oral contact for which the employer can be held responsible. Similarly, representations by a manager contradicting the employee handbook may amount to an oral modification of a written contract.

- *Written Contract*—A contract that has all terms and conditions set down in writing, for example, a collective bargaining agreement between a union and an employer. In many states, an employee handbook is considered a written contract.

Defamation—Holding out a person to ridicule, scorn, or contempt in the community; that which tends to injure the reputation. Defamation is a civil wrong and includes both libel and slander.

- *Libel*—Defamation by means of print, writing, pictures, or signs; publication that is injurious to the reputation of another.
- *Slander*—The speaking of false, malicious, and defamatory words harming the reputation, trade, business, or means of livelihood of another.

Discrimination—In personnel law, discrimination refers to the adverse treatment of an employee or group of employees, whether intentional or unintentional, based, for example, on race, color, national origin, religion, sex, disability, age, or veteran status. The term also includes the failure to remedy the effects of past discrimination.

Disparate Impact—The result of an employer's action or policy, which is not unlawful on its face, but affects one or more classes of employees differently than other classes of employees. In antidiscrimination law, concern with disparate impact deals with unequal treatment received by members of a protected class or classes. For example, a policy requiring that all applicants for employment possess no greater than 2-years experience, while not unlawful on its face, could have a disparate impact on persons over age 40.

Disparate Treatment—Different treatment of employees or applicants based directly an race, religion, sex, national origin, deity, age, or veteran's status.

Equal Employment Opportunity Commission (EEOC)—A federal enforcement agency created by Title VII of the Civil Rights Act of 1964. The purposes of the Commission are to end discrimination based on race, color, religion, age, sex, or national origin in hiring, promotion, firing, wages, testing, training, apprenticeships, and all other conditions of employment, and to promote voluntary action programs by employers, unions, and community organizations to put equal employment opportunity into actual operation.

EEOC Guidelines—Positions expressed by the EEOC that don't have the force of law when issued, but tend to be supported by the courts and hence become law. These positions are outlined in various EEOC publications such as "Discrimination Because of Sex," and "Discrimination Because of Religion."

EEO-I Report—The Equal Employment Opportunity Information Report is an annual report filed with the Joint Reporting Committee (composed of the OFCCP [Office of Federal Contract Compliance Programs] and the EEOC) by employers subject to Executive Order 11246 or to Title VII of the Civil Rights Act of 1964. The EEO-I report details the race, sex, and ethnic composition of an employer's work force by job category.

Exempt—A term used to describe the status of employees whose positions meet specific tests established by Fair Labor Standards Act (FLSA). Employees who meet certain standards are not subject to (i.e., are exempt from) overtime pay requests.

Good Faith and Fair Dealing—A concept employers use that has no technical or statutory definition. Basically, it means acting on the basis of honest intentions and beliefs. Employers who are thought to act in bad faith may have a lawsuit brought against them. In such a case, the court looks to see whether the employer acted out of malice toward the employee, and whether there was an attempt to defraud or seek an unconscionable advantage over the employee. The courts in a few states, including California, have accepted good faith and fair dealing as a theory on which to base an exception to "employment-at-will."

Handicapped Individual—Under federal law, any individual who (1) has a physical or mental impairment that substantially limits one or more of his or her major life activities; (2) has a record of such impairment; or (3) is regarded as having such an impairment. A handicap is substantially limiting if it is likely to cause difficulty in securing, retaining, or advancing in employment. The term Qualified Handicapped Individual refers to a handicapped individual who is capable of performing the essential functions of a particular job with reasonable accommodation to his or her handicap.

Just Cause—Labor arbitrators have long applied a definition of "just cause." A definition useful in personnel law is: "Good and sufficient reason related to the needs of business operations and supported by demonstrable fact."

Nonexempt—A term used to describe employees whose positions do not meet Fair Labor Standards Act (FLSA) exemption tests, and who must be paid 1½ times their regular rate of pay for hours worked in excess of 40 per week computed at an hourly rate.

Protected Class—Any group (or member of that group) specified in, and therefore protected by, antidiscrimination laws.

Public Policy—Generally, this term refers to standards for behavior that the court believes are necessary to support the common good and maintain the fabric of our society in its critical dimensions. Public policy is reflected in a statute, a constitution, or, less clearly, in commonly-accepted values. Perhaps the most vague and unpredictable standard in personnel law today, is the definition of public policy change as society changes.

Punitive Damages—Punitive damages are sums of money awarded by a court to punish a party because of that party's acts of violence, oppression, malice, fraud, or wanton and wicked conduct. They are intended to provide solace to the wronged party for mental anguish and exacerbation of the wrong. Unlike compensatory or actual out-of-pocket damages, punitive damages are based on a different public policy consideration—that of punishing a particular defendant or of setting an example for others. Punitive damages are awarded in addition to compensatory or actual damages, and punitive damages are not covered by insurance policies.

Reasonable Accommodation—Alterations, adjustments, or changes in the job, the workplace, and/or terms or conditions of employment that will enable an otherwise qualified disabled individual to perform a particular job successfully, as determined on a case-by-case basis.

Systemic Discrimination—Employment policies or practices, which, though often neutral on their face, serve to differentiate in terms or conditions of employment between applicants or employees because of their race, color, religion, sex, national origin, age, disability, or veteran's status. Systemic discrimination relates to a recurring practice rather than to an isolated act. Intent to discriminate may or may not be involved.

Torts—The law of private wrongs, other than breach of contract, governing the behavior of persons and setting out their obligations to each other. The courts provide a remedy for these wrongs in the form of an action for damages. Assault is an example of a tort, as are intentional infliction of emotional distress and personal injury. Civil suits can be filed for such wrongs.

Validation—The study of an employer's tests or selection standards, which proves that those who score high turn out to be successful on a specified job and those who score low turn out to be unsuccessful. The study requires a large sample of applicants and must include representatives of protected groups in the employer's labor market.

Comprehensive Questions

1. If information is volunteered and the information is illegal to ask about, what procedure should the principal follow?

2. Which part of the hiring process seems to be the most susceptible to legal problems?

3. What is the difference between a regular full-time contract and a supplemental contract? How should the principal approach these differences?

4. If a teacher is arrested and charged of crimes against students, would you advocate putting the teacher "on-leave with pay" or "on-leave without pay" pending the outcome of judicial proceedings? Why or why not?

Extended Activities

1. Attend board meetings regularly in your district to ascertain board policy making in action.
2. Research specific violations made by administrators to become more aware of necessary process and procedure.
3. Review your staff handbook to edit and revise policies that no longer apply or may be contradictory to state or federal laws.

References

Castetter, W. B. (1992). *The personnel function in education administration*. New York: Macmillan.

Contract administration: Understanding limitations on management rights. (n.d.). Eugene, OR: Center for Educational Policy and Management, College of Education, University of Oregon.

Drake, T. L., and W. H. Roe (1994). *The principalship*, 4th ed. New York: Macmillan.

Huges, L. W. (1994). *The principal as leader*. New York: Macmillan.

Hunt, J. W. (1984). *The law of the workplace*. Washington, DC: BNA Books. (Available from BNA Books, BNA Inc., 2550 M St. NW, Westbridge, Suite 699, Washington, DC 20037).

Jackson, G. E. (1986). *Labor and employment law desk book*. Englewood Cliffs, NJ: Prentice-Hall.

McGrath, M. J. (1993). *Sexual harassment: Minimizing the risk*. Santa Barbara, CA: McGrath Systems, Inc.

Ramesey, R. D. (1984). *Management techniques for solving school problems*. West Nyack, NY: Parker Publishing.

Reutter, E. E., Jr. (1985). *The law of public education*, 3rd ed. Mineola, NY: The Foundation Press.

Schoop, R. J., and D. R. Dunklee (1992). *School law for the principal: Section II*. Boston: Allyn and Bacon.

Smith, S. C., and P. K. Piele (Eds.) (1989). *School leadership: Handbook for excellence*, 2nd ed. Eugene, OR: College of Education, University of Oregon (ERIC Clearinghouse on Educational Management).

The school personnel management system. (n.d.). Alexandria, VA: National School Board Association. (Available from National School Board Association, 1680 Duke St., Alexandria, VA. 22314.)

Understanding personnel law. (1994). Council on Educational Management: Borgman Associates.

Webb, D. L., A. Metha, and K. F. Jordan (1991). *Foundations of American education*. New York: Merrill, Chap. 11.

11

A Glance into the Future of Human Resources

Reasons for Studying the Future of Human Resources

- To be able to anticipate the future will allow us to prepare for it.
- A major element of human resources management is planning. It is critical in planning to know not only where you are, but also the direction you are heading.
- Things change. Those human resources elements that work well now may be only minimally effective in the future.

> *Tomorrow's problems will be the results of today's solutions.*

ISLLC Standards Covered in this Chapter

Standard 4:

- A school administrator is an educational leader who promotes the success of all students by collaborating with families and community members, responding to diverse community interests and needs, and mobilizing community resources.

Standard 6:

- A school administrator is an education leader who promotes the success of all students by understanding, responding to, and influencing the larger political, social, legal, and cultural context.

Introduction

This chapter points toward the future by identifying trends, which may influence the human resources activity as well as the people who are involved in it. The trends generally pertain to the topics discussed in the chapters of the book and are influenced by the discussion in each chapter. However, forecasting the future is difficult if not impossible, so each of these trends ought to be monitored for future viability.

Trend 1: School-Based Leadership

School-based leadership is one trend that will be gaining prominence. There will be adjustments as to which activities belong with the central office and which ones belong with the school site. The human resources function will continue to gain importance for the building principal. The principal and the site council committee will be making major decisions in this area. Figure 11.1 below illustrates the topics contained in this text and the respective human resource roles of the principal and the central office.

Figure 11.1 Text Topics and Roles

Elements	Principal	Central Office
Planning	Major	Secondary
Recruitment	Major	Secondary
Selection	Major	Secondary
Supervision/Evaluation	Major	Secondary
Assisting the Marginal Teacher	Major	Secondary
Staff Development	Major	Secondary
Collective Bargaining/ Compensation	Secondary	Major
Continuity and Legal Issues	Secondary	Major
Technology	Major	Secondary

Trend 2: Proactive Leadership by the Principal

The principal will need to be more proactive in the anticipation of the entire human resources function. An example will indicate the need for being proactive. The central office business department often plays a major role in predicting the enrollment and thus, staffing needs for the next year. Often, to maintain a safe budget position, the enrollment estimates are ultraconservative. "We will wait until we see the whites of their eyes," is often a business office approach. However, when more students arrive on the first day of school than predicted, there are not enough teachers or staff to instruct them.

Quickly, the principal begins the search for staff only to find that the number and quality of available candidates is below the spring or early summer level. The principal, under pressure to hire staff, will often make a decision only to regret it later. The point is that the principal must be proactive and persuasive regarding the estimate of enrollment and staffing needs. The district may need to be conservative, but not ultraconservative.

Trend 3: Human Resources Development Exceeds Curriculum Development

Curriculum development is very important and has been for many decades. However, staff development will take on a much greater importance than it has and will surpass the development of curriculum in terms of budget allocation, time, and importance. The birthright of every child will be to have a competent, caring teacher who is well trained.

Trend 4: Pressure on the Principal to Eliminate Poor Performing Teachers

There will be more and more pressure on the principal to eliminate poor performing teachers. There will be efforts to improve the teachers performance or exit them from the system. Parents and community members will be demanding this action. It will be very important for the principal to have well-developed evaluation and supervision skills first, to be able to assist teacher improvement, and then the courage to use those skills to eliminate teachers who are significantly below standard. This is a critical component of the role of the principal in the focus on student learning and accountability.

Trend 5: Induction Will Be More Than Orientation

Induction will play a significant role beyond that of two or three days of orientation. The process will be well-planned and year-long in duration. Feedback from beginning teachers and other staff members will be used to revise and modify the induction program. Mentor teachers will also need to be trained specifically to assist the beginning teacher.

Trend 6: Diversity of the Workforce Will Be Important for Schools

Although there will be modifications to the affirmative action goals/quotas from a legal standpoint, schools will continue to recruit and select a diverse work force to provide role models for students. The current strong economy presents the entire work force with increased options for those positions that will pay more than education. The principal must be proactive in the role of recruiting minorities.

Trend 7: Collaboration
Between K–12 and Universities

There will be more collaboration between public school and university schools of education to provide a longer and more intense "student teaching." Principals and other administrators will become more active as guest lecturers or adjunct professors in leadership classes. Conversely, as the demands for results of reform continue to escalate, university professors will be sought for guidance in the research process or third-party evaluation of reform efforts. An example of this is the Tahoma School District (WA), which, through a Bill and Melinda Gates Grant was able to hire a professor-in-residence. This professor works 80% of the time in the school district and 20% in the university. The preliminary reports suggest a very positive collaboration, which meets the needs of the school district and also informs the university.

Trend 8: Childcare Programs
for Children of Staff Members

Schools will provide more benefits for the teaching staff in terms of childcare programs. This will encourage teachers to stay in the work force and raise a family rather than choose between the two roles. Elizabeth Church reports that The Ford Motor Co. of Canada Ltd. has such an on-site daycare at its plant in Oakville, Ontario. This is, as the headline of the article states, "On-Site Daycare a Rare Boon." Nevertheless, the article points out that childcare options are at the top of the parents wish list. This need is far too common and must be addressed proactively.

Trend 9: Tuition to Be Paid
by School District

Schools will direct and thus pay for the continuing education development of the staff. Tuition will also be paid for at public universities as long as the education relates directly to improving the teacher's competency level and improving the instructional program.

Trend 10: The Use of Technology Will Significantly Increase in the Human Resources Function

Technology will play an increasing role in the human resources function. Résumés, letters, and placement files will be scanned by the computer and produce a profile of the teacher. This profile will be matched against the needs of the school and district. Interviews will still play a major role in the selection process but some interviews will be done over two-way video-audio computers for those candidates who are far from the school. Additionally, application forms, where used, will be completed on computer and sent to the district electronically. Abuses of technology and e-mail will also increase.

Trend 11: Employee Assistance (EAP) and Wellness Programs Will Increase

The school year/day will be extended, thus providing opportunities for teachers to earn substantial pay increases. With this, however, will come increased stress and pressure to provide more extensive employee assistance and wellness programs.

Trend 12: Legal Complaints in Human Resources Will Escalate

Legal complaints in the human resources arena will mount: sexual harassment for both employee-to-employee and employee-to-student, equal employment/affirmative action challenges, dismissal confrontations, as well as others. The Equal Employment Opportunity Commission (EEOC) does not keep a record of how many cases end up in litigation since many are settled out-of-court. Nevertheless, the legal costs for school districts will be substantial.

Trend 13: Accommodations for the Disabled

The Americans with Disabilities Act will have a significant impact in schools. Schools must be proactive in accommodating coworkers with disabilities. The building modifications are minor compared to the negative attitudes that some administrators hold.

Trend 14: Differential Pay

School districts will be more aggressive in recruiting hard-to-fill positions such as special education, mathematics, science, specialized vocational programs, and technology. Further, teachers who are bilingual in English and Spanish are in demand. Some school districts are paying "bonuses" to sign top candidates in hard to fill positions. This is a trend that will escalate.

Trend 15: Benefits and Domestic Partners

More and more companies, including school districts, will provide benefits to the employee's domestic partners. Currently one in ten employers gives benefits to gay or heterosexual partners.

Trend 16: The Principal as Leader

Historically the role of the principal has evolved from the head teacher, to the principal-teacher, to the manager, to, most recently, the instructional leader. This role is near the end of its thrust. In the future the principal will need to be seen as a leader who empowers others to become instructional leaders. An indicator of this is the growth in the role of teacher leaders, or Teachers on Special Assignment (TOSA).

Conclusion

The pace of change is escalating and never is it more true than in human resources in education. The trends listed above could come about very soon. Regardless of the pace, it is anticipated that the principal in a site-based leadership role will have to deal with them and deal with them successfully. Teachers, students, parents, communities, and the central office personnel are counting on the principal to be successful in this endeavor.

Comprehensive Questions

1. Read the trends and prioritize them as high, medium, or low concern for your school.
2. How could a principal begin the planning process for employee childcare at his school?
3. What trends seem to be happening in human resources at an accelerated rate?

Extended Activities

1. Research a specific trend in human resources and devise a plan to meet the changing need.

2. Devise a long-range plan that will address trends in a proactive manner for your school and district.

3. Devise a year plan that will address staff development needs in regard to upcoming trends.

References

Bensimon, H. F. (1994, Jan.). Violence in the workplace. *Training and Development*, 26–32.

Berry, W. E. (1993, Autumn). HRIS can improve performance, empower and motivate "knowledge workers." *Employee Relations Today*, 297–303.

Church, E. (2000). *On-site daycare a rare boon.* (August 17). As reported on http://Workopolis.com

Forehand, P. (1993, Dec.). What cures job stress? *Training*, 32–36.

Hall, F. S. and E. I. Hall (1994). The ADA: Going beyond the law. *The Executive*, 8(1), 17–34.

Kutscher, R. E. (1992). Outlook 1990–2005: Major trends and issues. *Occupational Outlook Quarterly*, 2–5.

Monford, J. (1993). HIV/AIDS education and the workplace. *SIECUS Report*, 21(6), 13–16.

Index